Prayer and Prophecy

Prayer and Prophecy

The Essential Kenneth Leech

EDITED BY DAVID BUNCH AND ANGUS RITCHIE

Seabury Books

NEW YORK

Phototypeset by Kerrypress Ltd, Luton, Bedfordshire

Library of Congress Cataloging-in-Publication Data

A catalog record for this book is available from the Library of Congress.

First published in the UK 2006 by
Darton, Longman and Todd Ltd
1 Spencer Court
140 – 142 Wandsworth High Street
London SW18 3EU

First published in North America 2009 by
Seabury Books
445 Fifth Avenue
New York, New York 10016

www.seaburybooks.com

An imprint of Church Publishing Incorporated

Printed and bound in Great Britain by Athenaeum Press, Gateshead, Tyne & Wear

Contents

To Kenneth Leech – for his seventieth birthday on 15 June 2009.

The prophetic voice and the spirit of inner prayer are not two alternative ways of Christian witness: they are inseparable in a healthy Christian life, and history shows that where they are not held together, both decay.

KENNETH LEECH
sermon preached at Canterbury Cathedral, 7 July 1973[1]

Preface

This selection of writings by Ken Leech has been produced by the Contextual Theology Centre (CTC). The intention was to bring together in one volume a representative sample of Ken's writings in order to illustrate how theology can inform prayer and action in a local context and to highlight wider themes – including the impact of religious commitment on public life in a multi-faith context. Subsidiary aims were to draw on material from both Britain and North America and to encompass various modes of communication associated with his work, including articles, books, essays, letters, reviews, sermons, and work not hitherto in the wider public domain.

The Project Researcher, David Bunch, worked in collaboration with a Steering Group convened by CTC Director Angus Ritchie with Ann Morisy (like Ken, a Fellow of the Centre) and Terry Drummond (one of Ken's closest friends and colleagues).

A fivefold structure has been used for the work. Part One looks at some underlying principles of Ken's work, illustrating how his revolutionary political convictions align with Trinitarian orthodoxy. Part Two explores his views about the Church in 'the public square', focusing on his Anglican denomination, and on reaction and renewal of the Catholic tradition there and elsewhere. Part Three highlights Ken's work in various aspects of ministry, especially with respect to anti-racism, drugs, homelessness, and young people. Part Four contains his reflections about prayer and worship, noting particularly the indivisibility of spirituality and social justice. The concluding Part is more biographical, looking at people and places that have influenced Ken in his lifetime's work. It also includes early examples of his writing and personal reflections about discipleship and ministry.

In selecting material, key criteria were continuing relevance, popular appeal, and readability. The process was assisted by comments from Ken's past or present colleagues, advice from the steering group, as well as feedback from some of his readers (obtained through publicising the project, including via email and information sheet attachment). Among emails and letters received, from men and women on both sides of the Atlantic, there were appreciative comments about the project: 'Ken's work deserves a wider audience and is certainly worthy of historical record'; 'it is so nice that Ken is being written up in his lifetime'; and 'I'm very glad you're doing this work. It needs doing.' Various respondents requested the selection of specific extracts or subjects and wherever practicable these requests were accommodated.

Some people referred to his personal impact: 'I owe so much to *True Prayer* and am everlastingly grateful to, and glad of, Kenneth Leech'; 'the Americans have always been hugely appreciative of him'; and another emailed to say that he and his wife 'have known Ken for 35 years and hold him in the highest esteem'. An acquaintance from Ken's Oxford University days in the early 1960s recalled his 'devout presence at chapel services every day in term-time', side by side with his political activism. Others focused on his writing: 'what I most value is his ability to draw together terse and apposite quotations from a wide variety of authorities'; and 'I have always valued the raw honesty of Kenneth Leech's writing'. Some correspondents dealt with both: 'Ken as a teenage youth was the then youngest member of Anglican Pacifist Fellowship, and I recall an article of his ... citing Daniel 2:44 on God's Kingdom supplanting all others.' Another pointed out how Ken's public support for the Lesbian and Gay Christian Movement, when they were evicted in 1988 from their then London church base, 'meant an enormous amount to us'.

The production of this anthology benefited from association with allied activities, particularly the cataloguing and digitalisation of resources in the Kenneth Leech Archive at the Royal Foundation of St Katharine; ongoing doctoral research at King's College, University of London, into Ken's contribution to theology and ministry; and planning for a celebratory 2009 event to mark Ken's East End ministry. The work is also the first published fruits of a developing partnership between the Contextual Theology Centre, the University of Notre Dame and Magdalen College, Oxford, on 'Just Communities: The witness of faith in a pluralist society'. There could be no better place to start such reflection than with the theology Ken has written and lived.

Many people helped, directly or indirectly in these ventures, including by facilitating selection and reproduction of documents, providing information and/or material, sharing memories, and/or suggesting contacts. Particular thanks are due to Jonathan Reiber for suggesting the project, and to Brendan Walsh and Cynthia Shattuck for supporting it; to Ann Morisy and Terry Drummond for serving on the Steering Group; to the Court of the Royal Foundation of St Katharine, and its Masters Ronald Swan and more recently David Paton (who granted us access to the archives), to the trustees of the Contextual Theology Centre, John Deacon, David Staples and Ralph Walker, and to other staff at St Katharine's and CTC including Pat Wright, David Driscoll and Maureen Toms. The diligence and good will of Margaret J. Shaw, sometime Librarian of St Katharine's, ensured that we found the archives in very good order. In England, especial thanks are also due to Aidan Mayoss, Alain Kahan, Andy Delmege, Angela Cunningham, Antony Grant, Brendan Walsh, Brian Lee, Chris Eames, Christopher Lloyd, Clemens Sedmak, Clive Barrett, Elaine Graham, Elspeth Millar, Eric Simmons, Frank McManus, Greg Smith, Harry Fancy, Helen Tandy, Hilary Stiles, Ian Tomlinson, James Wheeler, Janice Price, Jason Eames, Jenny Monds, John D. Davies, John Desmond, John Pridmore, Kate O'Brien, Leslie Houlden, Lottie Clark, Luke Bretherton, Malcolm Barr-Hamilton, Margaret Fancy, Maria Exall, Michael Ainsworth, Michael Champneys, Michael Futers, Mike Weaver, Paul D. Butler, Peter McGeary, Philip Nicol, Richard Kirker, Richard Wheeler, Ros Kane, Rosemary Irvine, Sally Jacobs, Sara Maitland, Sarah Farrimond, Savi Hensman, Steve Latham, Steven Saxby, and Thomas Seville. In Canada and the United States, particular thanks go to Ben King, Emmett Jarrett, Jonathan P. Gosser, John Kevern, John Orens, Linda Corman, Margaret R. Rose, Sara Fischer, Sam Portaro, and Vincent B. Rougeau.

During the project, Ken Leech made useful comments, gave, and encouraged others to give, information and material additional to that which he had previously lodged in archives, either at the Royal Foundation of St Katharine in London or the Working Class Movement Library in Salford, both of which were consulted in the preparation of this volume. The Jubilee Group papers in the Christian Socialism archive at Sarum College, Salisbury was also rich in relevant resources. Among numerous other collections consulted, particular reference was made to the Archives of the Episcopal Church in the United States; the British Library Sound Archive; St Botolph's Church, Aldgate, East London; and Tower Hamlets Local History Library and Archives, also in East London. Further assistance was given by the Church Socialist Network email group; Community of Resurrection Library at Mirfield; Information and Library Services at King's College, University of London; Retreat Library in St Mary's Abbey, West Malling; Tanimara Printing and Office Services at Harthill, South Yorkshire; and Trinity College Library, Toronto.

The Contextual Theology Centre is grateful for financial support from MB Reckitt Trust for this project. Ken's more recent years of work as a community theologian were made possible by the generosity of this trust, and CTC thanks the Jerusalem Trust for funding its continuing work in the same communities. It is also grateful for the collaboration of the University of Notre Dame and Magdalen College, Oxford in the wider Just Communities project. It is hoped that this will be the first of many publications which emerge from the ongoing engagement between prayer, study and action.

Abridgement and editing has been kept to a minimum and mainly confined to eliminating dated and/or gratuitous sentences, omitting original footnotes, and establishing a uniform style, including, where practical and consistent with textual integrity, inclusive language. Acknowledgements are made to Ken Leech and the publishers of material cited in the endnotes for permission to reproduce copyrighted material in this form. Grateful thanks are also given to Alasdair MacIntyre for providing an overall Foreword to the collection and to Margaret R. Rose for contributing a ministerial perspective from New York.

David Bunch & Angus Ritchie,
The Contextual Theology Centre, East London, Advent 2008

Foreword

Professor Alasdair MacIntyre

It is a great pleasure to write this Foreword, and this for several reasons. First, I have known Father Kenneth Leech for over 50 years. When I was teaching at Manchester University in the early and mid 1950s, I lived on Werneth Low, above the village of Gee Cross just outside the town of Hyde, where Ken Leech was a student at the Grammar School. His excellent classics teacher, Charles Berry, invited me to speak at a Student Christian Movement meeting at the school and I came to know Ken Leech not only as admirably articulate and thoughtful, but also as liable to do the unexpected: playing a part, for example, in student protests against local attempts to preserve the morals of the young by banning the movie, *Rock Around the Clock*.

When we first met, our trajectories were taking us in apparently opposite directions. He was preparing to go to King's College, London, on the road towards the Anglican priesthood. I was increasingly aware of the incompatibility of my belief in God with a set of philosophical presuppositions that I could find no good reason to discard, so that during the first 15 years of his ministry – a period when we were not in touch – my view of what he was thinking and doing was from outside the Church. I was, even so, increasingly impressed.

What was I impressed by? The answer to this question provides a second reason for being glad to write this Foreword. Ken Leech has an unusual ability to identify what is going on in the world and to respond to it. In contemporary societies gross and urgent human need takes a remarkable number of different forms: homelessness, hunger, unemployment, victimisation and self-victimisation by drugs

and by debt, chronic and epidemic illness, most notably HIV, depri-
vations that arise from racism, from the plight of migrant workers,
and from exploitation by those who profit from badly paid labour,
from prostitution, and from renting out inadequate housing. It
matters, however, not only to engage with each of these types of need,
but also to respond to the local particularities of the situations of
individuals, families and groups in need, and at the same time to
understand how every one of these types of need is a symptom of
something amiss or wanting in the larger social order.

It has been one of the marks of Ken Leech's ministry that he has
recurrently involved himself deeply in local situations – I think, for
example, of the experiences that resulted in his 1970 book on *Pastoral
Care and the Drug Scene*[1] – so that his commitments to particular
needy individuals, families or groups have never been in doubt, yet he
has always kept in view the larger social contexts within which those
particular needs have arisen and by reference to which they have to be
understood. Too often in our culture responsiveness to the particular
needy is treated as one thing – 'philanthropy' – while action framed in
larger and more general terms is treated as another – 'politics'. Ken
Leech in his pastoral ministry has done as much as anyone to show
how these have to be integrated into a single mode of activity, rather
than treated as at best complementary. But he has been able to do this
only because of other more fundamental aspects of his work.

Very few guides to the life of Christian prayer are also and simultaneously guides to the life of action with regard to the needy. And few
such guides are able to make any claim to originality. For they cannot
but draw upon the extraordinary range of resources provided by their
predecessors, by the Desert Fathers, by Benedictines and Cistercians,
by Ignatius and John of the Cross and Teresa of Avila, as indeed Ken
Leech also does. But in his ability to relate contemplation to action
directed towards the needy and by his insistence on the need for such
action to be an expression of an inner turning towards God, Ken
Leech has taken the tradition of Catholic spiritual writing one stage
further, posing often neglected questions about the spiritual dimensions of radical action.

The theology presupposed by this path-breaking work was spelled
out in *True God*.[2] I hope that one effect on readers of the excerpts
from Ken Leech's books presented here is to send them to the books
themselves and perhaps especially to *True God*. It is a book that

demands unusually careful and thoughtful attention. On nearly every page there are almost too many thoughts. And it is a provocative book that needs to be read, discussed, and questioned argumentatively in the company of others. But there are few other books that state in so comprehensive a fashion what is at stake in believing or not believing in the God of Catholic Christianity. It draws on an astonishing range of authors: Saul Bellow and Leon Trotsky, C. G. Jung and Leon Bachofen, as well as on classical and contemporary theologians from all the major Christian traditions. It is above all grounded in Scripture. And it sets questions about the relationships of contemplation to action with which Ken Leech has engaged elsewhere in their proper theological context.

Finally, in expressing my debts to Ken Leech I am also, as a Roman Catholic, able to acknowledge the large debt that I and many other Catholic Christians owe to the Church of England and to that tradition of Anglican thought, devotion, and action which Ken Leech represents. The decades since he was ordained have not been easy ones for the Church of England. That in these hard times it has still provided us with teachers such as Ken Leech is cause for a quite unusual kind of gratitude.

Alasdair MacIntyre,
Center for Ethics and Culture, University of Notre Dame,
August 2008

Introduction –
from London

Revd Angus Ritchie

My first encounter with Kenneth Leech came when I received *The Eye of the Storm* as a Confirmation gift. I was immediately taken by his words:

> Our spiritual pilgrimage is not within an artificial religious world, but within the real world in which coal is mined and lemon meringue pie is made, the world in which companies are taken over and homeless people die in the streets, the world in which wars are declared and millions long for peace and for justice.[1]

This quote is typical of Ken. As I read on, I realised I had been introduced to an author who combined a breadth of scholarship with a striking lack of pretentiousness. Here was someone mercifully free from the theologian's professional temptation – that of writing in language which intimidates and obscures. Here, too, was someone who challenged the values of the dominant culture without falling into a simplistic dogmatism.

In the years which have followed, I have come to know Ken as a pastor as well as a writer. It is impossible to separate his ideas from his priestly ministry. Ken is fond of quoting Evagrius' maxim that 'the true theologian is one who prays.' Theology is necessarily a product of an encounter with the living God, of discipleship in dialogue with Scripture and Tradition. Prayer and prophecy must go together, and 'the Ken Leech who writes on social action' cannot be separated from 'the Ken Leech who writes on spirituality' – or from the pastor who knew and greeted each homeless guest at St Botolph's Crypt by name.

What does it mean to call Ken a 'contextual theologian'? From the Book of Genesis onwards, Christian theology is *necessarily* contextual. The authors of the Bible tell of specific encounters with God, and write letters to particular people wrestling with particular challenges and questions. To call one's theology 'contextual' is to acknowledge the very straightforward point that (in Ken's words) 'what you see depends on where you are standing.' The vast majority of Scripture is written by the poor and those who stand with them. While 'contextual theology' has sometimes been seen as unsound and relativistic, Ken's work is utterly orthodox in its subversiveness. It teaches us what it means to take the Bible's genre and perspective seriously.

Ken warns the readers of *Through Our Long Exile*[2] that if they jump past the first half (the description of East London and its history) and move straight to the more 'doctrinal' sections they will miss the point. Ken's ministry and his theology display an essential unity. In both he treasures the particular – the world of lemon meringue pie and coal, the names of each guest and the quirks of human character – as the place where God is encountered and salvation is wrought.

My Confirmation came as I was discovering the riches of the Anglo-Catholic tradition. Ken was a particularly sane companion for that journey. Amidst my initial enthusiasm, his work seemed perplexing. He engaged with the tradition passionately and prayerfully, yet wrote with genuine detachment about its future and its flaws. How could this be? Ken helped me to discover the glories of Anglo-Catholicism – its full-blooded engagement with the material world and actual (rather than idealised) communities and institutions as the place where God's word takes flesh. He also helped me recognise its less glorious tendencies. Among these is the way its orthodoxy can harden into sectarianism: the claim that God is *here* and nowhere else, and if *this* tradition is not renewed God's work cannot go on. I found in Ken an orthodoxy that was at once subversive and generous, willing to recognise God's word becoming flesh in an extraordinary range of places and to approach the future with openness and confidence rather than narrowness and trepidation.

Ken's writings and practice remind us that the Christian journey is one made in company, not always of our choosing and not always travelling at our preferred speed. To give up on the 'institutional Church' is in the end to give up on the possibility of sustained and faithful Christian communities. Religious debate can end up trapped in the unhappy alternatives of dogmatic conformity and a rather adolescent emphasis on personal choice and fulfilment. Ken's critical engagement with the Anglo-Catholic tradition suggests a more creative way forward.

It is fitting that many of Ken's records are now at the Royal Foundation of St Katharine – the home of the Contextual Theology Centre. The Centre seeks to embody that same combination of prayer, theological reflection and social action, and we are honoured that Ken agreed to be the first member of our Fellowship and to work with us to publish this collection. St Katharine's history and its location make it an excellent home for both the Centre and the Kenneth Leech Archive.

In terms of location, St Katharine's is fitting also because nearby Cable Street was the site of Ken's first home in East London. The majority of his ministry has been conducted within a mile or two of this spot. In terms of St Katharine's history, the ministry of social care and prophetic action exercised over centuries embodies the same tensions we see in Ken's ministry. The story of the Royal Foundation of St Katharine exemplifies the Church's compromises with privilege and status, yet it also speaks of its capacity to challenge earthly dominions on behalf of the Kingdom of God. Ken's life and writings show a patient commitment to live with those tensions, and a refusal either to 'sell out' or to indulge in self-righteous posturing. We need such prayerful and prophetic witnesses, now more than ever.

Angus Ritchie,
The Contextual Theology Centre, East London,
Feast of Christ the King, 2008

Introduction – from New York

Revd Margaret R. Rose

I do not pretend to encompass the relevance of Ken's theology in the American Church today. I can, however, attempt to give some over-view of how his theology and the lived convictions of his life have influenced the work and context in which I have served – the Episcopal Dioceses of Massachusetts, Atlanta, Georgia and now as Director of the Mission Leadership Center on the staff of the Presid-ing Bishop in New York City.

Ordained in 1981, in what might be called the second generation of ordained women in the Episcopal church, I first met Ken when he preached at the Anglo-Catholic parish where I was a young 'low church' trained curate. Immediately, the connection between liturgy and justice which I was already learning in this Oxford Movement parish on the down side of Boston's Beacon Hill, began to claim theological, institutional and personal relevance. Over the years, memories include visiting Ken in England in the parish where the church-run pub next door was the venue for parishioners to gather for fellowship after church so that the sacramental space of the church could be transformed into what one might also call the sacramental space of a theatre.

In the years of Ken's regular visits to the US on the 'lecture' circuit, he led a number of clergy retreats in the Diocese of Atlanta, as well as Schools of Prayer in successive Lenten and Easter seasons in parishes of the Diocese, including the one where I was rector. He keynoted the Episcopal Urban Caucus gathering when I was a board member and was a mentor in the attempt to nurture a fledgling Jubilee group in the Diocese of Atlanta, helping us think through what that might look like in the context of the American South. Without a deeply held political and historical understanding of Christian socialism, how-ever, that group was consistently small and struggling. Something about it just wasn't in American blood. Yet the conversations and the faithful few who gathered found the depths of Ken's theology at the heart of our work.

Not long before his retirement, my family and I visited Ken at St Botolph's in London's East End where the stories about the Bengali neighbourhood where he lived came to life. My two teenaged daughters' memory of that visit is punctuated by our dinner at a Bengali restaurant where we made room to do Morris dancing out the door and into the street. I was grateful to visit Ken in Manchester, not long after his 'retirement', when I was participating in a conference on the Ordination of Women in International Perspective hosted by the Lincoln Theological Institute. Ken had begun to reflect on the years in London and imagine what the work in this new context would be.

These initial reflections might seem to skirt the theological thought which undergirds an understanding of the relevance of Ken Leech's theology for today, but the lived experience was central to Ken's practice of Christianity and a conviction which he shared. Hence the journey into memory: long hours of story-telling in our living-room which interwove feminist theology with current events; a rousing verse of 'On Ilkla Moor Baht'at' or 'Geordie's Lost His Penker Doon the Koondy' and many other folksongs of the Cecil Sharpe vintage; Morris dancing; and stories of turtles. There were gifts of a cuddly sheep back-pack from Wallace and Gromit which became the overnight case of one child, and an erudite book on the English Parliament which served as research material for the other.

I tell these stories because they are not unique to my family. They were played out in the places he visited and in homes where delighted listeners heard a language that created and allowed connections (politics, religion, dance, suffering, music, abundance) when none seemed possible before. Ken, who I suspect has never forgotten anything he has ever read or done in his life, was able to see across boundaries and envision the new. And time spent with him made it seem possible for us too.

While Ken claims to have slowed down in retirement, the evidence is to the contrary. A recent book and a busy travel schedule suggest that he continues to offer us – Church and society – both the text of his life and the text of his theological work. All the better. As we look to the future of the Church and to those we hope will be engaged in it, Ken's work and thought remain vital.

Why? Because Ken refuses to divide. Over and over he speaks of the false polarising of spirituality and the social struggle, the inseparability of holiness and ministry, of justice and piety.

Recently I was at an Episcopal Church gathering of its Executive Council, leaders elected from the diversity of the Church in the United States, charged with governance in the years between its triennial convention. A lay member of the Council adamantly described the current rifts within the Anglican Communion and the Episcopal Church as a conflict between social justice and personal piety. There was no convincing him otherwise. He himself claimed to live by the 'personal piety' side of the argument. Yet, a quick inventory of his everyday life revealed a commitment to seeking justice for workers and a particularly activist care for children. He could not see, as Ken would suggest, that it was in fact his personal piety which propelled him to act for justice in what he would call the secular world.

In parish contexts, a similar divide continues to be raised in the insistence that the 'pastoral care' or 'inreach' committee is about caring for 'our own' and the outreach committee seeks justice for the less fortunate 'out there'. Ken Leech's theology would suggest that a pastoral outreach committee could do it all. There is really no out there/in here in the scheme of creation. Ken has no room in his theology for such dual loyalties. From *Soul Friend*[1] to *The Eye of the Storm*[2] and beyond, Ken's refusal to divide allows the authentic core of Anglican theology: a deep life of the Spirit informing and energising action toward a just social order.

It is not, however, only those who are already deeply engaged in the institutional work of the Church for whom Ken has a relevant message. It is also those young adults both within and outside the Church, who though they may not name it, echo Ken's words. Polls show, for example, that the resounding vote for Barack Obama by young people was less about democratic ideals or even addressing race issues than it was about the unifying language he used. His refusal to vilify opposing ideas or his opponent, and in the transition to choose leaders who are not identified as ideologues, continues that early commitment. Whether this can play itself out in the years of the Obama presidency is another question. But the inspiration for younger voters was about the refusal to capitulate to labels or to litmus tests of party affiliation. A refusal to divide. In what has been called an increasingly secular society, Ken's theology crosses boundaries and sees the sacred inextricably bound in the life of the city, in politics and in the joys and challenges of the everyday. For Ken, both heaven and earth are God's dwelling place. That is the place where these young voters also live.

Election night 2008, I was travelling home on a Manhattan bus, jubilant myself over the election of the first African American President of the United States. Others on the bus had similar leanings. But what struck me most was the phone conversation I overheard of an African American woman next to me. Exclaiming to the voice on the other end, 'Now we will really mean it when we tell our children they could be president one day.' She went on to recount her experience of voting that morning. 'I said my prayers in that booth when I voted. And I left them all over everything in there.' It was as if her prayer had encompassed the space of the voting booth, covered the levers, filled the room with Holy Spirit. Ken would love this, I thought, because this woman gets it. It isn't only that she was praying that her candidate would win (and I have no doubt she was), she was also filling the space with the Spirit of God. The earth space – ensuring God's dwelling there. Elizabeth Barrett Browning said it poetically: 'Earth's crammed with heaven; and every common bush afire with God'. No division.

Ken's early engagement in feminist theologies is another example. I remember well his insistence, along with many feminist theologians, that unity in the Anglican tradition does not and must not mean conformity. That clear message as we reflect on the experiences of women and the Church today is no less true now than it was in the early 1970s. We need not all agree to stay together. An example from my own experience as Director of Women's Ministries in the Episcopal Church is illustrative. During the past five years the Office of Women's Ministries brought women from around the Anglican Communion to participate as delegates to the United Nations Commission on the Status of Women. In addition to the work at the UN, however, the women came together to work toward the achievement of the UN Goals of alleviating poverty in their own Anglican communities. While those in power seemed to posit divisive arguments over issues of faith and order, the women shared best practices on how to educate and feed children, seek equal protection under the law, or adequate health care. Conversations among the women did not avoid those issues which divided the Anglican Communion – notably questions of sexuality – but they were clear that there was much more which bound them together. They said so publicly in a statement to the Primates of the Communion in 2007. For the women, who came from every Province of the Communion, it was from this point of unity, not conformity, that conversation among those who differed could get on with the work of the Gospel. Ken's deep commitment to open dialogue and his inclusivity might well be offered in the current work of the Communion today.

In the changing cultural context of the twenty-first century, Ken long ago understood that the Church is not bound by the walls of a building. Amid the rise of what is called the Emergent Church as well as among spiritual communities of young people, Ken's commitment to contextual theology is a key to understanding these multicultural, multireligious gatherings. He has long been open to claiming community and Church in the places where people gather to worship, share suffering, and seek healing for all God's people. Ken's work among marginalised peoples, which goes back decades, would have found resonance in a recent Easter service I attended. Organised by young adults, it was the story of the resurrection as experienced by sex-trade workers and former prostitutes.

Young adults, it is said, while less interested in denominational identity, are, however, deeply engaged in the work of the Gospel. Such work is at the centre of Ken's incarnational theology, grounded in the political world of today and in the abundance of possibility in newly formed communities. This is especially true as the United States moves from the assumption of Protestantism to an appreciation of an increasingly multicultural, multireligious social context.

I am reminded of one experience with Ken when he named that context at a baptism. It was a traditional Anglican service of baptism on the Eve of Easter. The water was duly blessed, and the baby was baptised in Trinitarian formula. Just as the congregation was awaiting the presentation of the child, Ken scooped the water in the four directions – a Native American tradition – and proclaimed God's blessing on the earth and sky and those from the north, south, east, and west. All around were splashed with the waters of baptism. The people were made new, the earth was blessed and recognised and so were we.

Margaret R. Rose,
Director, Mission Leadership Center, New York City,
Advent 2008

Part One

First Principles

I

The Trinity

*That is the meaning of the symbol of the Trinity:
that in God there is social life, community,
sharing. To share in God is to share in that life.*[1]

The Name of God[2]

The holiness and justice of God, his unique relationship with
Israel and his exclusive demand for allegiance, receive their most
powerful symbolic expression in the name of God: Yahweh, the great
I Am. In Hebrew thought, power resides in the name. To give a name
is to possess power over the named one. To know a name is to enter
into the mystery of the person's being. The greatest significance
therefore must be attached to the name of God as revealed, first, to
Moses. The name is a mark of identity to such an extent that to be
without a name is virtually to be without existence. Names were
essential to the being of gods as well as humans. Thus the Babylonian
creation epic began:

> When on high the heaven had not been named,
> Firm ground below had not been called by name ...
> When no gods whatever had been brought into being,
> Uncalled by name, their destinies undetermined –
> Then it was the gods were formed within them [i.e. the
>   primeval waters]
> Lahmu and Lahuma were brought forth, by name they were
>   called.

Genesis too associates creation with naming (1:5, 8, 10; 2:19). To
know someone's name is to have power over them, and so to withhold
one's name is to prevent the acquiring of such power. However,
nowhere does the Old Testament give the name of Abraham's God.
He himself did not know it, nor did Jacob discover it (Gen. 32:39).
He is therefore identified simply as 'the God of Abraham', for a

relationship with a nameless God raised problems. (On one occasion, Abraham's God speaks of himself as 'the God of Bethel' [Gen. 31:13], but this was to connect himself with an earlier revelation. Bethel never became a permanent seat.) The possession of a name was thus of great importance, and when Moses was to return to Egypt he knew that the first question he would be asked about his encounter with God was 'What is his name?' (Exod. 3:13). In fact, the question 'What is his name?' became a form of denial of existence (cf. Prov. 30:4).

In the Book of Exodus we are told that it was only in the time of Moses that God revealed himself by the name Yahweh. The Lord who appeared to Abraham, Isaac, and Jacob as God Almighty had not been known in those days by his name Yahweh (Exod. 6:2). There are several passages in Genesis where the name Yahweh is used, and one tradition assumes that its use goes back to the beginning of history. Thus, in relation to the time of Adam, we are told that it was then that people began to invoke Yahweh by name (Gen. 4:26). But in other passages the name is avoided in the pre-Mosaic period. In its place we find the name El, the name of one of the two principal deities of Canaan.

Originally El designated any god, but it also occurs as a proper name for specific deities. Some hold the view that El was a high god who was worshipped all over the West Semitic world under a variety of names. In the Old Testament, El occurs some 217 times, usually in conjunction with another name. Thus Abraham worships El Elyon (God Most High) at Salem (Gen. 14:17–21), El Shaddai (God Almighty) at Hebron (17:1) and El Olam (God Everlasting) at Beersheba (21:33). Isaac worships El Roi (God of Seeing) at Beer-lahai-roi (16:14; 24:62). Jacob worships El Bethel (God of Bethel; 35:6–7) and erects an altar to El at Shechem (33:20). It seems that El was a common name for the senior deity of the Canaanite divine hierarchy. In the patriarchal period there is a merging of the worship of ancestral gods with the worship of the Canaanite god El. The Ras Shamra texts show a society of gods with no clear antecedent for the later monotheistic world-view of Yahwism.

However, while the Elohim (plural of El) were absorbed into the faith of Yahweh, the same was not true of the Baal cult, an equally important part of Canaanite religion. There is some slight evidence of attempts to identify Yahweh with Baal (2 Sam. 5:20; 2:10; 9:6). In the early days of the monarchy, Yahweh may have been addressed as Baal;

but its association with the Canaanite cults led to the banning of the name. So Hosea insists that God will no longer be referred to as 'my Baal' and the very names of the Baalim will be wiped out (2:16).

Yahweh is the name under which Israel's God is to be known. The name of Yahweh occurs over 6,000 times in the Old Testament. According to Exodus 3—4, it was to Moses that God revealed himself first under this name. But this God was not a different God from the God of the patriarchs. Yahweh is the God of all the earth (Isa. 54—55). While the name was unknown to the patriarchs (Exod. 3:13f; 6:2) it would seem that various earlier gods were merged into Yahwism. Abraham is said to have instructed his descendants to observe the way of Yahweh (Gen. 18:19), but the revelation at Sinai initiated a new era in the history of Israel. So Yahweh became Israel's banner (Exod. 17:15) and individuals were called by names based on Yahweh (1 Kings 11:29; 14:1). The name was to be revered and not blasphemed, hence the prohibition of its use in curses and in magic.

The use of the plural form Elohim as a name for God was common in Israel, but it had the disadvantage that it was also applied to the false gods of Canaan. Thus 'Thou shalt have no other *elohim* but me' (Exod. 20:3). So, from the time of Amos and Hosea, the alternative usage of *Yahweh Tsebaoth* (Lord of Hosts) enters the vocabulary, and is adopted by Jeremiah and the post-exilic prophets. Yahweh and Elohim were not mutually exclusive. Yahweh Tsebaoth was the Elohim of the armies of Israel (1 Sam. 17:45). The 'hosts' were not only Israel's armies, for Yahweh was Lord of the stars and of the angels. So the visitor who met Joshua at Gilgal announced himself as captain of the hosts of Yahweh (Josh. 5:14). In Isaiah 6 the hosts appear, distinct from Yahweh, yet giving glory to him, and praise is seen as their central role (Ps. 148:2).

What then is the meaning of the revelation to Moses of the name of Yahweh? The name is usually rendered into English as 'I am that I am', though the Revised Standard Version margin reads 'I will be what I will be'. To say simply that Yahweh means the self-existent nature of God, being itself, is to reduce Jewish theology to static notions of essence. Yahweh is not the god of the philosophers. The Hebrew denotes not so much a static idea (being) as a dynamic process (becoming). 'I become what I become', or 'I will be what I will be', are closer to the underlying sense of the moving, living God. Yahweh is revealed as the God who *will* bring Israel out of Egypt, and who *will* be with Moses (Exod. 3:7–10): he is the God of the future, the God of creative history.

The revelation of the name of God is a kind of self-emptying, an act by which Yahweh surrenders himself. The true name of Pharaoh was kept secret, yet Yahweh, the God of all the earth, reveals his identity to Moses. Before Moses the goodness of God passes, and in his hearing the name of Yahweh is pronounced (Exod. 33:19). At the same time, the inner essence of Yahweh remains unknowable, for he is a God who hides himself (Isa. 45:15; Job 11:7; Ps. 97:2; Exod. 33:10). God cannot be described directly, but only in his relationships and in action. The recognition of this fact, that God cannot be portrayed or directly seen, is a fundamental principle of Yahwism, and of the Christian mystical tradition which grew from its roots. Jewish theology came to be wary even of uttering the name of Yahweh, and substituted Adonai, the Lord, in public use of the divine name. In Greek versions of the Old Testament, *kurios* translates both Adonai and Yahweh. In the period of the second Temple, the name Yahweh was pronounced once a year, by the High Priest on the Day of Atonement; but after the destruction of the Temple in AD 70, the priests forgot the form of the name, and it ceased to be used.

Yahweh is God of nature and of the historical processes, and yet is superior to them and beyond them. Unlike the pagan deities, Yahweh is not identified with the forces of nature, but is in control of them. Thus earthquakes and volcanoes are the fingers of Yahweh, he appears in clouds and stars, and he speaks through the thunder. The wind is his breath. But these natural phenomena are all his creatures, essentially distinct from him. Yahweh is no storm god or volcanic deity, nor does he have his permanent home within the mountain. He descends upon it, but speaks from heaven. He is distinct too from the gods, for there are many *elohim*, but Yahweh is one. There can be no rival. Thus to sacrifice to the *elohim* is a capital offence (Exod. 22:20).

So in the Old Testament the name of Yahweh is the expression of his character, his holiness, his power and majesty. Holy and terrible is his name (Ps. 111:9). Yet this name, the revelation of transcendence, dwells upon the earth, in a specific place (Deut. 12:5, etc.), in Jerusalem (1 Kings 8:27–9), and among his people who are called by his name.

Salvation in Christ[3]

That God has destined men and women for salvation is assumed in the New Testament (1 Thess. 5:9). He wills all people to be saved, and to come to knowledge of the truth (1 Tim. 2:4). And this salvation is the work of divine grace (Titus 2:11), it is 'the gospel of God' (Rom. 1:1), the 'power of God for salvation' in which 'the righteousness of God' is revealed (Rom. 1:16–17; 3:21–5). And this righteousness, like salvation itself, is not primarily a personal but a social reality. The Pauline letters are saturated with the language of social salvation. It is important to stress this social understanding of salvation, for it has been eroded by centuries of western individualism which has reduced the common salvation to a purely personal experience.

The letters speak of God's salvation as a past event: he saved us (2 Tim. 1:9; Titus 3:5; etc.) 'The death he died he died to sin, once for all ...' (Rom. 6:10). Yet it is also seen as present and continuing: we are 'being saved' (1 Cor. 1:18). And there is a future aspect: 'we shall be saved' (Rom. 5:9; cf. 13:11; 1 Thess. 5:9). In the history of salvation, the death of Christ is of central significance. The events of his passion and death dominate the Gospels – one third of Mark's account is devoted to the final week of the life of Jesus – while Paul shows little interest in Jesus' earthly life, but only in his death, resurrection, and presence in the Church.

Salvation according to the Pauline letters comes through Christ. He came into the world to save sinners (1 Tim. 1:15). He is the one mediator between God and men (2:5). He was put to death for our transgressions and raised for our justification (Rom. 4:25). We have been justified by his blood (5:9). It is in the writings of Paul that the saving work of God in Christ is described and explained most clearly, and therefore these writings are of central importance for understanding the Christian teaching about salvation. In the letters, the work of Christ is described by a variety of terms. It is *justification*: we are justified by the faith of Christ (Gal. 2:16; Rom. 3:26–8; 4:25; 5:18). It is *salvation* (2 Cor. 7:10; Rom. 1:16; 10:10; 13:11). It is *expiation* by the blood of Christ (Rom. 3:25). It is *redemption*: in Christ we have been ransomed, bought back (1 Cor. 1:30; Rom. 3:24; 8:32). It is *sanctification*, a word closely associated with redemption, cleansing, and justification (1 Cor. 1:2, 30; 6:11). It is *freedom*: in Christ we have been set free from bondage (Gal. 5:1, 13; Rom. 8:1–2, 21; 2 Cor. 3:17). It is *transformation*: we are being changed from glory to glory, being renewed in our whole beings (2 Cor. 3:18; Rom. 12:2). It is *new creation* (Gal. 6:15; 2 Cor. 5:17; Rom. 6:4; 1 Cor. 15:45). And it is *reconciliation* (2 Cor. 5:18–20; Rom. 5:10–11; 11:15).

Paul sees the relationship of human beings to God as having been radically changed by the work of Christ. Having been previously enemies, we have now been reconciled to God by the death of Christ, and we will be saved by the life of Christ (Rom. 5:10–11). Through the cross, peace has come to the disordered world (Col. 1:19–22), and those who were afar off have been brought near to God (Eph. 2:13). The fundamental idea in Paul's understanding of Christ's saving work is that of participation. Through Christ's dying and raising, a new system of relationships has been brought about. We have been changed as a result of what has happened to Christ. Christ is the first-fruits, the foretaste of the harvest of the dead (1 Cor. 15:20–23). Paul explains: 'If the dough offered as first fruits is holy, so is the whole lump; and if the root is holy, so are the branches' (Rom. 11:16). Thus the purpose of Christ's death was to bring about life in us (1 Thess. 5:10).

In describing the saving work of Christ, Paul draws on the sacrificial language of Israel. In 1 Corinthians 10, the Exodus drama is recounted. But, says Paul, these events were described for the Christian era: 'Now these things happened to them as a warning, but they were written down for our instruction, upon whom the end of the ages has come' (1 Cor. 10:11). Christians are living in 'end-time', in the time of fulfilment of the ancient hopes of Israel, the fulfilment of the sacrificial symbols of the past, the time of the new Passover.

> For Christ, our paschal lamb, has been sacrificed. Let us therefore celebrate the festival, not with the old leaven, the leaven of malice and evil, but with the unleavened bread of sincerity and truth.
>
> 1 CORINTHIANS 5:7–8

Christ is the *pascha*, the new Passover Lamb, the 'lamb without blemish or spot' (1 Pet. 1:19). Elsewhere, other sacrificial terms are used of Christ. He is described as a sin offering, who 'has appeared once and for all at the end of the age to put away sin by the sacrifice of himself' (Heb. 9:26). He is compared to the scapegoat of Leviticus who bears the iniquities of the people (Lev. 16:22). So Peter writes of Christ: 'He himself bore our sins in his body on the tree that we might die to sin and live to righteousness. By his wounds you have been healed' (1 Pet. 2:24; cf. Isa. 53:5). Similarly, Paul says that God 'made him to be sin who knew no sin, so that in him we might become the righteousness of God' (2 Cor. 5:21).

In Paul's theology, salvation and righteousness are inseparable. Salvation is the work of the righteous God. Through his saving acts we are delivered from slavery (Rom. 6:20; 8:15, 21), from unrighteousness (6:13), from condemnation (5:18; 8:1) and from hostility (Eph. 2:15). We are restored to freedom (Rom. 6:7; 8:21; Gal. 5:1), and reconciled to God (Rom. 5:10; 2 Cor. 5:18–19). God's righteousness is manifested (Rom. 1:17; 3:26), and Paul even asserts that we *become* the righteousness of God (2 Cor. 5:21). And this salvation is a social and cosmic event: it is the world, the *kosmos*, which is reconciled to God in Christ (2 Cor. 5:19).

A key idea in the Christian doctrine of salvation is that of reconciliation. Through Christ, Paul says, we have received reconciliation (Rom. 5:11). The group of reconciliation words have as their basic meaning the changing of a relationship. To reconcile is to make otherwise, to alter a state of affairs. In secular language, the words were used of social and political change. Reconciliation is similar in meaning to the English word 'atonement', a word with no equivalent in other modern European languages. There is, however, no connection with the themes of expiation or propitiation.

It has been suggested that the theme of reconciliation is a minor one in the New Testament. But this view can hardly be sustained. It is true that the actual words 'reconcile' and 'reconciliation' do not occur frequently in the New Testament as a whole. Apart from Matthew 5:24, most of the references are in Paul (see Rom. 3:24–6; 2 Cor. 5:18–21; Col. 1:15–20; Eph. 2:21–7). But the idea is a much wider one and pervades a good deal of New Testament teaching. In Paul, it is always God who reconciles and human beings who are reconciled. The good news of the reconciliation which has been accomplished in Christ, and the 'ministry of reconciliation' (2 Cor. 5:18) which is a continuing work, are central to the work of the Church. On one level, the work of reconciliation has been done: God was in Christ reconciling the world to himself. And yet, 'there can never be an end absolutely to this reconciliation, for it is the living God at work, and it is part and parcel of the fellowship which issues from his work and in which it is perpetuated'.

Much Christian preaching, however, has emphasised only the finished work of Christ, and has done so in a 'substitutionary' way. Christ took my place, he died instead of me. It would be wrong to claim that there was no basis for substitutionary ideas of atonement in the New Testament, but the support is very slight. In Paul, the stress is rather on the restoration of relationship: because we are justified by the blood of Christ, we will be saved from the wrath of God. For in Christ we are reconciled (Rom. 5:9–10). There are in fact only three passages in Paul which can be cited in support of a substitutionary view. First, in Romans 8, Paul writes that God sent his Son 'in the likeness of sinful flesh' (8:3) to fulfil the just requirement of the law. Christ was sent, moreover, 'for sin'. This usage 'for sin' indicates *purpose* (cf. Lev. 4:3). Christ comes to deal with sin.

There is a second passage in 2 Corinthians 5:21 in which Christ is said to have been made to 'be sin' for us. The point which is being made is that Christ became fully human: he who knew no sin shared in human nature, became human.

Thirdly, Christ is said to have become 'a curse for us' (Gal. 3:13). But the context makes it clear that the reference is to the legal curse upon a hanged man (Deut. 21:23). There is no real support in any of these passages for the doctrine of substitutionary atonement.

At the centre of the discussion of the nature of Christ's work is the theme of redemption. Originally the word *lutron* meant the price paid for one's freedom. But the verb *lutrousthai* came to be used, with God as its subject, to mean the securing of release by the power of God. Often in the New Testament the language of redemption is used without any reference to price. Thus God has redeemed his people (Luke 1:68). Anna spoke to those who awaited the redemption of Jerusalem (2:38). Christ secured an eternal redemption (Heb. 9:12). Christians have been redeemed by the precious blood of Christ (1 Pet. 1:18). In all these cases the words used are redemption (*lutrosis*) or the verb, to redeem (*lutrousthai*). The word *lutron*, which originally conveyed the notion of price, occurs only once in the New Testament, in Mark 10:45 and its parallel verse Matthew 20:38. (A similar word *antilutron* occurs in 1 Timothy 2:6.) It is not a Pauline word at all. In Paul's writings, there are only four references to purchase: two uses of the phrase 'You were bought with a price' (1 Cor. 6:20 and 7:23), and two references to redemption in Galatians (3:13 and 4:5). In none of these cases is there any reference to the person to whom the price is being paid. It seems reasonable to conclude that the terms are being used to describe the achievement of liberation and release, not a literal activity of payment of a ransom.

In Romans 3:25 Christ is described as an 'expiation' (*hilasterion*). It is possible that this means a propitiation, though it is unlikely. Certainly it cannot be seen as a kind of bribery, for 'the notion of a process of celestial bribery is entirely absent from the New Testament'. It is more likely that *hilasterion* refers to the place of cleansing. Through Christ, we have been cleansed from sin. This has been accomplished, not by a legalistic payment, but by 'an absorption by the very God himself of the fatal disease so as to neutralize it effectively'.

The very God himself: that is the heart of the gospel proclamation, the astonishing truth that God is himself the Saviour. It is in the later New Testament writings, particularly in the Letters to Timothy and Titus, that the notion of 'God the Saviour' is explicitly stated. The word 'Saviour' itself is rare in the New Testament, apart from the Pastoral Epistles and 2 Peter. However, on two occasions, we find the expression 'God and Saviour' (Titus 2:13; 2 Pet. 1:1) with the clear sense that the two are the same. On five occasions we find 'God our Saviour' (1 Tim. 1:1; 2:3; Titus 1:3; 2:10; 3:4). So, it is asserted, God is directly involved in the work of salvation. Jesus is also described as the Saviour in these writings (2 Tim. 1:10; Titus 1:4; 3:6), while the expression 'Lord and Saviour' is used of Jesus in 2 Peter (1:11; 2:20; 3:2; 3:18). While these terms are almost unique in the New Testament, they state in a precise and clear form the fundamental truth of Christian faith, that God was in Christ reconciling the world to himself. In the suffering of Jesus, we see the suffering of God. God suffered and was crucified, and in these saving acts his glory was revealed. Thus the gospel of reconciliation is the 'centre of all Christian knowledge', the revealing of the God who became human.

Spirit and Word[4]

In Hebrew thought, the spirit is 'the motive power of the soul ... the strength emanating from it'. Like the wind, from which the word *ruach* is derived, God's breath is powerful and mysterious. *Ruach* means both wind and breath, and in the Old Testament the wind is seen as the breath of God (Ps. 18:15; cf. Ezek. 14:21; 15:8), the breath which gives life to men and women and to the creation (Gen. 6:17; 7:15; Num. 16:22; Judg. 15:19; Ps. 104:29; Eccles. 3:21; 9:21; 12:7; Isa. 37:6, 8; Zech. 12:1). The Spirit of God, his power and life, was present at the creation of the world, transforming chaos into cosmos as it hovered over the primeval waters.

Genesis tells us that God 'breathed' the breath of life into man (2:7). A clear distinction is made between men and women, and the animals. Only into human beings did God transfer his own life force, his breath, *neshamah*. *Neshamah* and *ruach* are sometimes used interchangeably (cf. Isa. 30:33; Ezek. 37:1–10). There is thus within human beings a divine spark, the Spirit, which is not of this world but formed by God (Zech. 12:1). God himself is *ruach* (Isa. 31:3). The Spirit therefore is 'at all times plainly superior, a divine power within the mortal body, subject to the rule of God alone'. It is contrasted with the flesh which stands for the natural world (Isa. 31:3). And, like the holiness of God, *ruach* is explosive and unpredictable. Early Old Testament writers use *ruach* to describe abnormal occurrences or qualities. So Gideon's courage is due to possession by the Spirit of the Lord (Judg. 6:34), while Samson's strength is ascribed to the fact that 'the Spirit of the Lord began to stir him' (Judg. 13:25) and 'came mightily upon him' (14:6, 19; 15:14). Saul and his messengers were possessed by the Spirit and prophesied (1 Sam. 19:23–4). Balaam's oracular utterance is due to the fact that 'the Spirit of God came upon him' (Num. 24:2). Spirit is thus linked with power. It is through the Spirit that lions are torn in pieces (Judg. 14:6), kill thousands of people (15:14), and execute beautiful works of craftsmanship (Exod. 31:3–5).

Such possession was relatively rare, but it was regarded, at least by some writers, as desirable that the Lord's people as a whole should become prophets, and that he 'would put his Spirit upon them' (Num. 11:29). At the same time, possession by the Spirit could have harmful effects and still be attributed to Yahweh. Thus we are told that 'the Spirit of the Lord departed from Saul and an evil spirit from the Lord tormented him' (1 Sam. 16:14). For even evil forces were seen as being subject to God and incapable of independent activity.

To speak then of God's *ruach* is to speak of the mystery of life itself.

But the combination of the sense of the universal breath of life with the Israelite belief in Yahweh as personal led to a stress on the work of the Spirit as intensely personal rather than as some pantheistic life force. In many accounts the Spirit seems to assume personal characteristics, speaking (1 Kings 22:21), capable of movement (2 Kings 2:16), able to depart (1 Sam. 16:14). The Spirit was outside human control and could rush upon them and overpower them. Its operation, like that of the wind, was essentially erratic and unpredictable. It could not normally be bequeathed or transferred, and its power passed on, although there are hints of an association of Spirit with office (Num. 11:14ff).

For the prophetic movement of the ninth century BC, 'the presence of the "spirit of Yahweh" was absolutely constitutive'. The early prophetic scene was dominated by an experience of God as Spirit. However, the word *ruach* fell into decline in the period before the Exile. The pre-Exilic prophets wrote little about the Spirit. So we have 'the astonishing fact that in the line of divine messengers from Amos onwards, there is absolutely no mention of the *ruach* as the power that equips and legitimates the prophet'. The decay of the idea of *ruach* was probably due to a reaction against false prophets, and the consequent growth of a process of reinterpretation in prophetic spirituality. Later the term was to be readmitted to the prophets' vocabulary. But the early writing prophets rarely attribute their inspiration to *ruach*. Amos, Zephaniah, Nahum, and Jeremiah never mention the Spirit of Yahweh or link their work with it. Isaiah does not associate the Spirit with his prophetic ministry. Where spirit-inspired speech is alleged, there is the suspicion of false spirituality or of Canaanite influence. Amos denies that he is a *nabi* (7:14), the term used to describe the earlier ecstatic prophets, and this suspicion of the *nebim* (plural of *nabi*) extends to all the writing prophets. Only in Hosea, Micah, and possibly Habakkuk are there hints of *ruach* (cf. Mic. 2:7; 3:8; Hos. 9:7). There is no use of *ruach* in Deuteronomy, while the account of Elijah's experience of Yahweh in Mount Carmel is very explicit that Yahweh was not in the *ruach* (wind) or in the earthquake or in the fire, but rather in the still, small voice (1 Kings 19:11f). There are some references to *ruach* in Isaiah where the Spirit of Yahweh is seen, not as an occasional and extraordinary manifestation, but as a permanent presence in the person of the Messiah (11:1). Elsewhere *ruach* is seen as the imperishable life of God as contrasted with the perishable life of the Egyptians (31:3). The 'spirit of justice' is identified with the glory, beauty and strength of Yahweh (28:5), preparing Israel for Yahweh's visible presence in her midst (4:4).

However, *ruach* reappears in Ezekiel and Second Isaiah as a major idea, the power of the coming new age. In Ezekiel, the Spirit is not so much evidence of the authenticity of his message as an explanation of his experience. It is as a result of listening to the Word of the Lord that *ruach* becomes the power of resurrection. In Ezekiel, the Spirit assumes a place which is unknown elsewhere in the prophetic writings, and it is closely linked with his awareness that 'the hand of Yahweh' is upon him. But while *ruach* occurs over fifty times in the book, the 'Spirit of Yahweh' is only mentioned twice (11:5; 37:1) and the 'Spirit of God' once (11:24).

In Ezekiel, the Spirit enters into the prophet and sets him on his feet so that he may hear the words from one identified as 'the likeness of the glory of the Lord' (1:28—2:2). It lifts him up alongside the glory of the Lord (3:12), carries him away in bitterness of spirit with the hand of the Lord upon him, to the place of exile (3:14–15), where later it again enters him and sets him on his feet (3:24). Later, the hand of the Lord comes upon him, and the Spirit lifts him up between earth and heaven (8:1–3). The liftings up are repeated (11:1, 24, etc.). Spirit is associated with movement, but also with inner renewal. So the Lord tells him:

> And I will give them one heart, and put a new spirit within them; I will take the stony heart out of their flesh and give them a heart of flesh, that they may walk in my statutes and keep my ordinances and obey them; and they shall be my people, and I will be their God.
>
> 11:19–20

The promise is later repeated and is linked with purifications and cleansing of heart (36:25–7). In chapter 37, the Spirit is the power which raises the dead, the dry bones. The Lord tells the bones that he will cause *ruach* to enter them so that they may live (37:5). By this act, they will know that he is Yahweh. In Second Isaiah, Yahweh is he who 'gives breath to the people upon [the earth] and spirit to those who walk in it' (42:5). The abiding presence of the Spirit is the sign of Yahweh's covenant (59:21). In particular, the Spirit is seen as the power which guided Israel in the past, preserves her in the present, and will be her future hope of renewal. Similar ideas appear elsewhere in the prophets. The Spirit is seen both as the force which inspired the prophets (Zech. 7:12) and as an abiding presence with the people of God (Hag. 2:5). Joel writes of a new outpouring of the Spirit before the Day of the Lord (2:28–9).

Closely connected with the theme of God's Spirit is that of God's Word, *dabhar*. The Word of God goes forth and prospers (Isa. 55:10–11), it goes forth in righteousness (45:23). Like *ruach*, the Word comes forth from the mouth of God (1:20, etc.). It is endued with God's life, and communicates his character. As the Spirit of God is the breath of life, so the Word of God is the breath of his mouth (Isa. 11:4; Ps. 33:6). Often in the Old Testament it would seem almost as if the Word had acquired a separate identity. Yet the Word remains God. Moreover, Word and Spirit are inseparable (Hos. 9:7; Isa. 59:21). Like the Spirit, the Word is close, within mouth and heart (Deut. 30:14).

Zechariah links Word and Spirit together. So the angel announces: 'This is the word of the Lord ... Not by might, nor by power, but by my Spirit, says the Lord of hosts' (4:6). He describes the delivery of both Law and Word as the work of the Spirit through the prophets (7:12). In Nehemiah, an association is made between the indwelling Spirit and the food of manna (9:20). Again, like the Spirit, the Word is powerful. Jeremiah writes: 'Is not my word like fire, says the Lord, and like a hammer which breaks the rock in pieces?' (23:29). It is like 'a burning fire shut up in my bones' (20:9). The Psalmist sees the Word as the agent of creation (Ps. 33:6) and of its renewal (147:15–18). The Word brings healing (Ps. 107:20). For the prophet, the Word was a compelling presence which could not be ignored. 'The Lord God has spoken who can but prophesy?' (Amos 3:8). In fact, it was the Word, rather than the Spirit, of God which was seen as the primary source of the prophetic ministry and message. It was a dynamic force, an extension of Yahweh's own being, which was communicated to the prophets. It was the conscious, inner possession of the Word which distinguished the true prophet from the false. To the prophets, the Word of God was both external proclamation and internal presence, received into the mouth, inwardly digested and sweet as honey (Jer. 1:9; Ezek. 2:9—3:3). It was 'no mere thing' but rather 'the living, personal and free God'.

God of justice[5]

The relationship between the pursuit of justice and the knowledge of God is basic to Old Testament theology. To know God is to seek justice and to correct oppression. The Law and the Prophets are largely taken up with the issues of justice in society. Worship without a concern for justice is denounced as evil and unacceptable. For the God of Israel is a just God who has made humanity in his image, and has made men and women responsible for the just ordering of the earth. Nowhere does the Old Testament tradition make a separation between the 'social' and the 'spiritual' of the kind to which we have become accustomed in the modern western world. Such a division is in fact quite alien to biblical thought. The spiritual-ity of the Old Testament writers is a justice spirituality, in marked contrast to the false division between issues considered as spiritual and those considered social or political. Union and communion with God cannot be achieved apart from the achievement of earthly justice and shalom, peace, and this peace is not compatible with wickedness (Isa. 48:22). On the contrary, the breaking of the covenant with God has consequences which are earthly and material: a broken covenant leads to a broken and devastated earth (Isa. 24).

The divine justice is to be expressed within the context of earthly societies, however faltering and imperfect human efforts to achieve it may be. To disassociate the divine justice from the struggle for justice within the human community is to make nonsense of the biblical record. Thus we find, for example, a profound concern in Palestine after the conquest for the achievement of equality, and 'excavations in Israelite towns bear witness to this equality in standards of living'. Under the monarchy, as the prophet Samuel had warned, inequality increased, and the prophetic writings are filled with condemnations of the oppression of the poor. It is quite impossible to read the prophets and fail to see the way in which, in their thought, the spiritual and the social were united. Equally it is impossible to make any sense of the ministry of Jesus without taking account of the Old Testament background to his teaching, for he came to fulfil the Law and the Prophets. The view, commonly expressed today, that the Church has been traditionally concerned with the condition of the inward soul, and has recently begun to deal with matters of social justice, is utterly incorrect. Orthodox Christianity has never taken such a narrow and purely inward view of religion. We need therefore a 'return to biblical Christianity' if we are to move away from the false spirituality which is gaining popularity, and if we are to recover the centrality of the divine justice.

The biblical faith in the divine justice is rooted in a realistic optimism about the possibilities of human and social change, an optimism which is different from naive idealism (of which it is often accused) and different also from the fatalistic pessimism which is often mistakenly identified with 'the Christian position'. Much of the criticism of Christian concern with social justice has drawn on the insights of the late Reinhold Niebuhr who rightly insisted on the need to take human sinfulness into account in social programmes. However, a naive devotion to Niebuhr has led many to overdraw the contrast, thus making a sharp contrast between personal and social morality. It has also led to an ethical stance which pays more attention to sin than to grace, stressing the social and cosmic dimensions of the fall, yet paying less attention to the social and cosmic effects of the work of redemption. The late Martin Luther King once commented that Niebuhr was 'so involved in diagnosing ... sickness of sin that he overlooked the cure of grace'. A Christian realism does not ignore sin; indeed it is precisely because of its sense that the effects of sin are social and cosmic that it insists on the non-necessity of all imperfect structures, and the need to work towards a society which is more in accord with the divine character. It is motivated not by a theology which seeks to baptise a current social order but by a theology of dissatisfaction with *all* current social orders, a theology of the God-inspired future which draws future vision into present reality.

In fact, far from neglecting sin and the fall, Christians who seek to follow the God of justice have a higher doctrine of sin than do their critics. It is because they see that sin is more than the sum total of personal sins, and that the fall has distorted the whole structure of human society, they see the need for a theology which is concerned with more than the removal of personal failures and which takes seriously the embodiment of sin in social structures. The notion of 'social sin', though its roots are in Scripture, is unfamiliar to many people. In its simplest form, it recognises that it is not only individuals but whole societies and their institutions which have been twisted and warped by sin, and that any approach which concentrates purely on personal change will be inadequate. Many of those who claim to hold a high view of sin in fact neglect these social dimensions, and so locate sin only in personal misdeeds. As a result, they become uncritical of their societies and incapable of exercising any critical judgement upon them. Worse than this, their sense of the seriousness of sin, in itself defective, is not matched by any sense of the power of grace to overcome the effects of the fall. So it is that many of these Christians who constantly point to the fall seem to regard it as the only Christian doctrine! Their view of sin may even be social and cosmic, but their view of grace is personal and limited.

Jesus in context[6]

We cannot expect to make sense of the death of Jesus without an attempt to understand his life and background. He was born into a double system of exploitation in Palestine. While the Roman empire imposed economic control through taxes and political control through its officials, the Palestinian state operated through the Temple which demanded economic contributions in the form of tithes and other funds.

Jesus came from the most troublesome of all the Jewish districts, Galilee, with its unique social and political character. The word means district (*gelil*) and was used specifically of the district beyond the River Jordan ('Galilee of the nations', Isaiah 9:1), but it was far more than a geographical description. The term 'Galilee' was associated in popular consciousness with Judas the Galilean and with other leaders of insurrections. From Galilee arose all the revolutionary movements which disturbed the Romans. It was the scene of guerrilla warfare and of nationalist uprisings. The years from AD 30 to 70 were seething with revolts. To be a Galilean at all was to be suspect. Pilate had mixed the blood of Galilean rebels with sacrifices (Luke 13:1). Yet we are constantly misled by hymns which speak of 'Sabbath rest by Galilee [and] calm of hills above' when in fact Galilee meant trouble. As a child, Jesus would have witnessed the destruction of the town of Sepphoris, a few miles from Nazareth, and the annihilation of its population.

This was the geographical context of Jesus' birth. He was born in the specific circumstances of a census which had been set up in order to implement the poll tax. Ninety per cent of the population of Galilee were peasants. These oppressed peasants were 'the people' who, according to the gospels, heard Jesus gladly. The burden of taxation was the central economic fact of life, and led to class conflict with the priestly aristocracies, so much so that in AD 66 rebels burnt the record of debts in the Temple. There was high unemployment, with many looking for work, and the violence went far beyond Herod's slaughter of innocent children.

It was out of this deeply disturbed climate of alienation, upheaval and resistance that the 'marginal Jew' called Jesus came. The climate of colonial rule, oppressive taxation, accumulating debt and bank-ruptcy, forced migration and revolutionary uprisings, formed the background to Jesus' proclamation of the Kingdom of God (Mark 1:14).

So Jesus had a context, a base. In fact he had several bases. His geographical base was Galilee and the resistance movements against the Roman oppressors. His religious, or ideological, base was that of progressive Pharisaism, respectable religion, the movement for a holy nation, not all that different from the Church of England at its best. He was called rabbi. He recalled his hearers to the 'weightier matters of the law'. It was this group which he challenged most fiercely and repudiated most totally, probably because he realised that his follow-ers throughout the ages were most likely to revert to Pharisaism – as indeed they have done and continue to do. It was for this liberal religious culture that Jesus reserved his fiercest and most uncompro-mising language.

Against this he set his personal base, the apostles and the band of faithful women, the culture of the dispossessed whom he trained, radicalised and endowed with the power of the age to come. And that power was not seen merely as a future prospect but as an active present force. Salvation meant bread and forgiveness from debt.

So, gathering around him a rabble of fishermen, Zealot sympathis-ers and various riff-raff, he moved through this troubled region, teaching, healing, setting people free. The early chapters of Mark's Gospel show him healing, exorcising, cleansing lepers, and forgiving sins. He ate with sinners and tax collectors, and broke the Sabbath, claiming that the Son of Man was Lord of the Sabbath. The common people heard him gladly. The religious authorities saw him as a serious threat and, as a result of his activities, conspired to destroy him (Mark 3:6). The Romans saw him as subverting the lawful rule of Caesar. The picture that we find is not of a 'gentle Jesus meek and mild' but more like that given by Conrad Noel when he described Jesus as 'a rebel born in the shed of a public house, who called his king a silly jackal, who broke the conventions of society, who defied the world, broke the law, was hunted by the police, and was destroyed by the coalition of the worldlings and the next worldlings'.

We are in danger of missing all this because the form of the gospel that we have inherited in the west has been diluted, individualised and interiorised. Two texts have been used in support of this process of reducing the range and impact of the gospel. One is the phrase 'the Kingdom of God is within you' (Luke 17:21, King James version). It is argued, or rather assumed without argument, that Jesus taught a belief in a kingdom within the heart of the believer, an entirely interior experience, perhaps of warmth and peace. It is extremely unlikely that *entos humon* could mean 'within you', and it is normally translated as 'amongst you' or 'in the midst of you'. In any case, 'you' is plural, so even 'within' would refer to the presence of the Kingdom within a community. An interior understanding makes nonsense of the gospels and shows the influence of post-sixteenth-century western ideas. The notion of an interior 'spiritual' kingdom would have been wholly without meaning to the people of Jesus' time.

The other text is from John, where Jesus apparently claimed that his Kingdom was 'not of this world' (John 18:36). The phrase 'this world' was unusual and uniquely Christian. It is not found in classical writers or in the Old Testament. Here there is only one world, including heaven and earth, but not two worlds. But as used in John and Paul, the term refers to two ages, two realms. The Kingdom of God stands in contrast to, and in conflict with, the structures and values of this age. When Jesus says that his Kingdom is not of (or, more accurately, from) this world, he does not mean that it has nothing to do with this world, but that its origins and values originate elsewhere, that it stands over and against this world (or age) as a symbol of judgement upon it.

In fact the good news of the Kingdom of God is revolutionary news. The Kingdom is 'otherworldly' in the strict sense that it operates as a critical process within human history, a constant symbol of the other world, a sign of transcendence. It is a source of change and transformation for this world, a vision and impulse for a new world. For many years this message has been evaded and its impact ignored. In 1923 Percy Widdrington, a prophetic figure in the

Church of England, said that the recovery of the Kingdom of God as a hope for the transformation of this world and as 'the regulative principle of theology' would bring about a reformation in the Church compared with which the sixteenth-century reformation would seem a small event. Today we are witnessing part of the fulfilment of which he spoke. One of the most encouraging features of recent Christian history has been the recovery of this sense of the conflictual and world-transforming dimension in Kingdom theology and vision. For too long the Church has evacuated the good news of the Kingdom of God of all its dynamic content. Now we are seeing a recovery of the biblical message that the Kingdom will transform the structures of this world and will stand for ever. Once this has been recovered, simplistic divisions between religion and politics collapse.

A turning point for many evangelical Christians was the Lausanne Conference on World Evangelisation in 1974. At this gathering Billy Graham, a well-known 'evangelist' and close ally of the Nixon regime (and of earlier presidents) in the USA, claimed that social justice was 'not our primary concern'. The rejection of his dualistic theology, in which evangelism and justice were separated, marked a crisis in evangelical thought and a moment of renewal. It was part of a process of recovery of biblical wholeness which had been going on for some time. Two years earlier John Howard Yoder had published his important study *The Politics of Jesus*, in which he argued both that the message of Jesus offered a revolutionary political vision, and also that the Church, the community of the followers of Jesus, was the primary social structure in which the gospel was to be manifested. Soon afterwards Richard Mouw, another leading American evangelical, claimed that political activity was an integral part of evangelism. The phrase 'radical discipleship' entered the vocabulary of Christians. And soon Jim Wallis, who, as the key figure in the Sojourners community in Washington DC, had played a major role in the recovery of biblical radicalism, was pointing out that the gospel as preached in most conventional western settings had been moulded to suit a narcissistic culture. It sought to bring Jesus into our lives instead of bringing us into his. The gospel as preached in the west no longer helped to turn the world upside down but rather served to reinforce its false values and structures. This was to a large extent because the content of the message had changed. Indeed, Wallis argued, the gospel as preached in most churches 'bears almost no resemblance to the original evangel'. Evangelism, as a call to a new way of life, should lead to the spread of social deviance and undermine the economic and political system; the impact of the conventional message was rather to reinforce conventional life-styles.

Recently we have seen the 'Kingdom Manifesto on the Whole Gospel' which has emerged from a conference of evangelical, charismatic and pentecostal movements held in Malaysia in March 1994. The overall impact of this movement has been that many Christians have come to see that the gospel of Jesus Christ cannot be divorced from politics. An apolitical Jesus has no meaning. Such a view cannot cope with his life and ministry, with his teaching, with the cross, the death reserved for political agitators and threats to the *status quo*, or with the radical lifestyle of the Early Church.

Fire and Spirit [7]

We are in the midst today of a long-overdue renewal of belief in, and stress upon, the role of the Spirit of God in the Christian community. Much earlier reflection on the doctrine of the Holy Spirit (pneumatology) in both Catholic and Protestant traditions was heavily dominated by interest in personal piety. But in order to make sense of the place of the Holy Spirit in the Christian understanding of God, we need to widen the perspective. It is necessary to place our doctrine of the Spirit within the context of the history of salvation and of the struggles of the world, and specifically within the context of the empowering of the Christian community. For in the New Testament 'Holy Spirit' is the name given to the experienced presence of the living God in the Christian community. The subsequent history of Christian thought has seen a deterioration in understanding of the Spirit so that the Spirit has come to be seen as an impersonal force, an 'it', a power of presence, but not the personal power and presence of God.

Of course, the category of power (*dunamis*) was an important one in the New Testament description of the work of the Holy Spirit. Moreover, there is no direct ascription of personality to the Holy Spirit in the New Testament itself. Both in the New Testament and in the writings of the early church, we are confronted with attempts to express an overwhelming, shattering experience. So unspeakable is this experience that the early Christian writers 'lack the power to clothe it in precise language'. For the Holy Spirit is the very atmosphere within which prayer and theological reflection are possible at all. And the early Church was marked by an overpowering sense of the Spirit's presence. As a community, it was 'essentially charismatic and enthusiastic in nature, in every aspect of its common life and worship, its development and mission'. The experience of the charismatic gifts was seen as due to an act of God, its purpose being the building up and nourishing of the common life of Christ's body in the world.

The results of the neglect of the Holy Spirit by many sections of the Church have been utterly disastrous. Deprived of the sense of power and of the experience of God's life, religion deteriorates into a lifeless and dreary system of rules and ceremonies. It becomes content with a 'diminished mode of consciousness'. So religion ceases to mediate the world of the Spirit, and become a second-hand account of what was once experienced by people long since dead. And this, as R. D. Laing saw in 1967, produces a condition of spiritual famine. Laing wrote during a time of spiritual confusion, a time when many young people were seeking spiritual experience by discovering the disciplines of the eastern non-Christian traditions, as well as in a variety of other ways. But during the same years, there was a remarkable renewal developing within the Western Christian world, both Catholic and Protestant, a renewal associated with the recovery of the centrality of the experience of the Holy Spirit.

As the Second Vatican Council opened, Pope John XXIII prayed that the Church might relive the experience of the apostolic age, might experience a new Pentecost. He prayed: 'Renew your wonders in our day, as by a new Pentecost.' The documents of the Council lay a new stress on the Spirit as the source and instrument of perpetual renewal in the Church. In the Church 'Christ, through his very flesh, made vital and vitalizing by the Holy Spirit, offers life …' Later, Pope Paul VI emphasised that the recovery of the study of, and devotion to, the Holy Spirit was 'the indispensable complement of the teaching of the Council', and, in announcing the Holy Year of 1975, he stressed the need for a 'truly spiritual (pneumatic), that is, charismatic movement' among Christian people. This sense of continuing, empowering and renewing activity of the Spirit has been expressed in the renewal of the liturgy. At the same time, the charismatic renewal has been affecting many thousands of people all over the Christian world.

At the centre of the renewal has been the recovery of the sense of power. In the Old Testament, the spirit is not so much the centre of a human personality as the strength which emanates from it. Sharing a common origin with 'word' and 'breath', the spirit is described in terms of power and mystery. The *ruach* (breath, word, spirit) of God is strong and life-giving (Gen. 6:17; 7:15; Num. 16:22, etc.). Equally, the prophets of the Old Testament, people possessed and driven by the spirit, were powerful and violent figures. The early word for an ecstatic prophet, *nabi*, literally signifies a 'bubbling forth'. However, ecstasy was always somewhat suspect in the prophetic tradition. The prophets never appealed to inner experience to prove their authenticity. On the contrary, the ecstatics were likely to be seen as belonging to the category of false prophets.

At the same time, while it its probably a mistake to see ecstasy as the fundamental experience behind all types of prophecy, the historical accounts of prophecy in the Old Testament do contain strong evidence of personal, inner upheaval, disturbed patterns of behaviour, and uncontrollable passion. Sometimes similar behaviour is seen as originating in an evil spiritual force. Thus an evil spirit seized Saul, and he fell into a frenzy, or as the New English Bible translates, into a 'prophetic rapture' (1 Sam. 18:10). The prophets were regarded as sometimes being mad (Hos. 9:7; Mic. 2:11; Jer. 5:13; Zech. 13:3). But *ruach* was associated with great strength, as in the case of Samson (Judg. 14:6), with leadership, as in the case of Joshua (Num. 12:18), and with wisdom (Prov. 1:23). Moreover, the power of *ruach* can bring abut social, not only personal change. So Ezekiel speaks of the renewal of the community of Israel (Ezek. 11:19–20; 37:4–6). The result of the activity of the Spirit of God was thus seen as involving a revolutionary change, nothing less than resurrection from death to life.

The prophets, those extraordinary individuals who were set on fire by the Spirit of God, were people of tremendous power. They were 'some of the most disturbing people who have ever lived'. The prophetic temperament is very far removed from Wordsworth's 'emotion recollected in tranquillity'. It is marked more by agitation, protest, lack of poise, and a sense of alarm. The prophet's language is charged with fire, it is explosive. We are in the presence of fire.

The later Old Testament prophets looked forward to a new age of the Spirit. This would be a time when the Spirit would be poured out, the wilderness would become fruitful, and justice would dwell there

(Isa. 32:15ff). The pouring out of the Spirit was seen as the manifestation of God's face (Ezek. 39:29). In the prophecy of Joel, it is associated with visions and dreams (Joel 2:28–9). It is this prophecy which is taken up in the Acts of the Apostles when the Holy Spirit equips the Church for proclamation and for fullness of gospel living. The day of Pentecost is of central importance for the early Church's awareness of the presence and power of God in their midst, and later there is a second Pentecostal empowering of the Gentiles (Acts 10:44ff). So the coming of the Holy Spirit was seen as a time of newness, a renewal and re-formation.

In the accounts of the experience of the Spirit of God, a number of elements appear. There is the sense of power. There is the sense of intoxication. The apostles were accused of being 'filled with new wine' (Acts 2:13), and the association of spirituality with drunkenness is evident in the language of 'sober intoxication' which entered the spiritual vocabulary with Gregory of Nyssa, and is evident in the hymn of St Ambrose:

> *Laeti bibamus sobriam*
> *Ebrietatem spiritus.*

'Let us joyfully drink of the sober drunkenness of the spirit'. There is too the stress on freedom in the Spirit. Where the Spirit of the Lord is, there is freedom (2 Cor. 3:17). Scholastic writers claim that only God can move people from within, while at the same time preserving their freedom. Similarly, Pope Paul VI, in an address in 1969, spoke of the freedom of the Spirit in the future Church. The coming of the Holy Spirit is thus experienced as profound personal liberation.

There is the sense of great love. It is through the Holy Spirit that the love of God is inflamed within us. God's love has been poured into our hearts through the Holy Spirit (Rom. 5:5). Love is seen as the greatest of the spiritual gifts (1 Cor. 13). To know the love of Christ is to be filled with God's fullness (Eph. 3:19). St John, in the First Epistle, writes of love as the nature of God. Mutual love is the sign of the resurrection (3:14), the person who loves is born of God and knows God (4:7). Moreover, the gift of the Spirit is the proof that God dwells within us (3:24).

The experience of the Holy Spirit is thus described in terms of power, of intoxication, of hope, of freedom, of love. Throughout the literature of spirituality from biblical times onwards, a recurring symbol for the divine activity is the symbol of fire. The fire is one of the earliest symbols of divine presence and action. In the covenant with Abraham, a smoking fire pot and a flaming torch were the signs given (Gen. 15:7). In the account of the sin of Nadab and Abihu, the fire of the Lord came forth and devoured them (Lev. 10:2). Similarly, in Elijah's struggle against false religion, the fire of the Lord fell both on the altar of Baal (1 Kings 18:38) and on the messengers of Ahaziah (2 Kings 1:10, 12). Elijah was particularly seen in later Jewish thought as a prophet of fire (Ecclus. 48:1) who would appear before the great and terrible Day of the Lord, the day burning like an oven (Mal. 4:1, 5).

The fire symbolises the power of God, but it also is used of his glory. The angel of the Lord appeared to Moses in a flame of fire (Exod. 3:2). The Lord descended upon Mount Sinai in fire, and the people were warned not to 'break through to come up to the Lord, lest he break out against them' (19:18, 24). We are told that 'the appearance of the glory of the Lord was like a devouring fire' (24:17). After the encounter with the divine glory, Moses' own face shone with glory (34:35). In the writing of Ezekiel, fire is again used as a symbol of God's glory and splendour (Ezek. 1:13–14). He then looked and saw a throne upon which was seated 'a likeness as it were of a human form' (1:27–8). In the similar vision in Revelation, there are flashes of lightning, and seven torches of fire burn before the throne of God (Rev. 4:5). God, the Scriptures assert, is a devouring fire (Deut. 4:24; Heb. 12:29). And when, on the Day of Pentecost, the Spirit of God fell upon the apostolic community, it was in tongues of fire (Acts 2:3). Fire symbolism is also used in relationship to the last time, the Day of the Lord, the day of judgement, and the experience of hell. In the Old Testament, there are twenty-four occasions on which fire language is used in connection with God's wrath, though there is only one instance where it is used directly of hell (Deut. 32:22). In the Synoptic Gospels, however, *pur* is used twenty-two times, of which fourteen are with reference to eschatological judgement. In these cases, the fire represents the wrath of God, the converse of his glory. In the mystical writers, fire comes to be used of the intensity and burning love of God, while the Pentecostal movements have laid great stress on the power and inexpressible joy brought about through the 'baptism of fire'.

At the heart of the language of fire in relation to God is the sense that any encounter with the divine is marked by terror, awe, and the possibility of being consumed. For no one can see God and live (Exod. 33:20). And yet, in a strange and terrifying way, Moses saw the face of the Lord (Num. 12:8), spoke mouth to mouth and face to face with him (Deut. 34:19) as one speaks with a friend (Exod. 33:11). In all experience of God there is this mingled sense of terror and intimacy, as we encounter the fire which warms and heals while it holds out the possibility of danger and death.

2

The Political Kingdom

*My view is that the Kingdom must stand in
judgement over all social orders, though clearly
some are closer to it than others.*[1]

The Christian Left[2]

I want to examine the various strands which have gone to
make up the 'Christian Left' in the past; to look at some recent
influences; and to point to some present needs and present dangers.
The Christian socialist tradition historically has drawn on a number
of models and themes. There is, first, the theme of the church as an
alternative society, a theme which was strong in the apostolic period
and which was the impetus behind most forms of monasticism. It
reappears in the 'radical Reformation' among the Anabaptists. Taken
alone it leads to the religious ghetto, the world of isolated radical sects.
In my view, the real parallel here is with Trotskyism where one sees the
same ghetto pattern of those who, at all costs – including that of total
irrelevance – preserve the purity of the faith. In a different form, this
model appears in the Catholic Worker movement in the US and in
the Christian anarchist tradition. The role of the church is seen in
terms of creating pockets of resistance, withdrawing as much as
possible from the capitalist system. The recent discussions on 'alternative socialism' also provide some modern parallels.

A second model is that of the church as not merely set apart from,
but also in *conflict* with, the fallen world order. It is seen in the
Levellers of the Cromwellian era, and in the Diggers, in the Midlands
Uprising against the Royal Enclosures of the common land of 1607.

A third stream is that of Anglican social thinkers with their stress
on the Incarnation and the sacraments as leading to a new order. The
main thrust of these movements has been *reformist* – Headlam's paper
was actually called *The Church Reformer*. Thus the Guild of St Matthew, formed at Bethnal Green in 1877, stressed that the use of
sacraments both represented and created equality. Thus Westcott in

1890 said that 'individualism and socialism correspond with opposite views of humanity'. Individualism, he held, saw humanity as warring atoms, but socialism saw the human race as an organism. An incarnational and sacramental theology clearly fitted in with the latter and not with the former. This whole tradition was continued with Gore, the early Lambeth Conferences, William Temple, and thence into secular groups. Christians were urged to move into the world, to baptise society, to redeem the social order, and so on.

Closely associated with these movements was a fourth model, that of *Kingdom-theology*. Fr Lionel Thornton CR told the 1920 Anglo-Catholic Congress that the crucial task was the recovery of the idea of the Kingdom of God to be realised on earth, and this was a dominant theme of Percy Widdrington and his League of the Kingdom of God at this time. It was Widdrington who wrote that the Kingdom was the regulative principle of all theology. The Catholic Crusade under Conrad Noel was dominated by the centrality of the Kingdom of God in Christian belief, and so later was Stanley Evans.

Overlapping with the Kingdom theme was, fifthly, the explicit commitment to *socialist political thought*, as in the Council of Clergy and Ministers for Common Ownership of 1942 and other similar groups.

Two final themes from the past with important and lasting contributions to the growth of a Christian left-wing tradition were, sixthly, that of the *non-violent movement* (Ghandi, Tolstoy, the Quakers), and of liberal protestantism and its doctrine of progress and of the *social gospel*. Jesus became the social prophet, and this view of Jesus still influences much current 'Christian socialism'.

These then are some of the streams and themes from the past. In recent years some of them have reappeared in different forms, while newer themes have also been added. I would note eight important movements which have helped to shape the 'New Christian Left'. (1) Liberation theology, associated with Latin American thinkers such as Gutiérrez, Alves and Bonino. (2) The 'black theology' of James Cone. (3) The revolt of many Lutherans against the 'two Kingdoms' theology of their own tradition. (4) Feminist theology in which the struggle for women's liberation is set in the context of radical theology. (5) The ecological movement. (6) The social and political thought of the World Council of Churches. (7) The resistance movement of the 'underground church' in the US. (8) The new evangelical radicalism which was evident at the Lausanne Conference of evangelism and is particularly marked among third world evangelicals.

The Christian Left as we see it today is thus a result of the coming together of a number of streams and ideas in the Christian historical experience. There are major changes occurring at present. What are the needs which are evident? The first, I believe, is that for serious *theological work*. Theology needs to be rescued from its associations with the irrelevant and the academic. It is essential to examine the mistakes of past thinking, and not to blur the serious errors of the past. A great deal of serious work has to be done if the Christian Left of the future is not to be vague and woolly.

Secondly, there is an urgent need for *thorough analysis* of current events and trends in the light of the Gospel. There are many areas which can be isolated here and I simply mention four. We need to give much attention to the issue of private ownership. The risen life was one of common ownership. Another area where I see the need for serious Christian thought is that of the state and the nature of fascism. Today we need to turn our attention not just to the growth of the new Nazi-style groups (National Front, National Party, National Assembly, etc.) but more urgently to look to the phenomenon of the omni-competent 'corporate state'. There are other important areas: the arms economy, the examination of what is happening to people at local levels and relating this to the wider picture, socially and theologically, the quest for a contemplative spirituality which is capable of nourishing a revolutionary faith.

Finally, some dangers. First, that of a *'reds under the bed'* theology. The term 'Marxist' is again being used to describe loosely connected miscellaneous political groups. We are being told simultaneously that Marxism is dead and out of date, and also that it is undermining us. (It is hard to see how both theses can be true, but the same people seem to hold both!) On the other hand, there is a danger of ignoring the fact that it is precisely the ill-informed, but well-developed fear of Marxism which does in fact lead to fascist regimes. The Italian and German forms of fascism and the regime in Chile were built on precisely this fear. There is abundant evidence of subversion and conspiracy in the Chilean experience, but they derive not from Marxists so much as from people adhering to the views of the Milton Friedman Chicago School of economics. Very dark blues indeed are under lots of beds.

But the conspiracy and bedroom models are not conducive to serious analysis. I note a trend among certain bishops today to write and think in conspiracy and subversion slogans.

Secondly, we need to beware of certain dangers in the *charismatic* movement, particularly the tendency to the irrational. There is often in the movement a combination of bad theology and a reduction in the critical faculties which makes it very easy for people to be taken over by dangerous and irrational views. It can be an easy way of coping with a failure of nerve, of opting out of complex situations. Christians need to test the spirits: not all is as it seems.

Thirdly, we need to recognise the popularity of pseudo-radicalism which seeks to reform the church rather than challenge the world. So often 'radical theology' means diminished theology, theology deprived of its power. There are many today who seem to hold the allegedly radical view that you can believe anything provided you don't rock the boat. A century ago Marx mocked this view when he said, in the 1867 preface to *Capital*, that the Church of England would tolerate an attack on 38 of its 39 Articles rather than on one-39th of its income. Today, he said, atheism is culpa levis compared with the attack on property relations. Today his words remain; more than ever we need to remember that ideas are themselves threatening. Theology is toxic.

Throughout these trends, there is a marked fear of extremists. Note *fear* and *extremists*. Fear: for our society rests on a very fragile basis, we need bombs to defend us, we think in terms of conspiracies, as if the power of God were ineffectual and needed protection. What sort of Christian civilisation is this which rests on so frail a basis? We need Christian confidence and need to avoid the propaganda mentality for it is based on fear and not on truth. Extremists: yet if we call someone moderately honest, it is not usually reckoned as a compliment. Christianity is *per se* an extremist movement. Yet here lies its danger, the danger of the fanatic and the arrogant. Ghandi said only the spiritual person can remain non-violent. Can we not say that only the contemplative can remain an extremist?

Christians and fascism[3]

The danger in meetings of this type is twofold: first, that we speak only to the converted and committed, and, secondly, that we do not talk about fascism at all. The first does not matter provided that the result is some clearly thought out strategy. The second is a real danger, and we need to be clear what we are talking about. Fascism is not racism, it is not racial violence, not any authoritarian or repressive regime, not any dictatorship, not increased police power. Emphatically fascism is not a conspiracy or the result of a conspiracy. All of these may be elements within the process of 'creeping fascism'. But fascism is more than all these: it is the inevitable development of capitalist society if it does not move towards socialism. Fascism is not a plot: it is the logical result of certain processes of development. It is a phenomenon of industrial society in severe socio-economic crisis, confronted with the threat of socialism and containing a very frightened and threatened middle class.

The essential point to grasp is that in the initial stages it is not at all obvious that we are dealing with a movement or a process which is evil, sinister or nasty. It can appear very plausible and highly moral. So early fascism appeals primarily to the middle class and the inhabitants of suburbia. It is a popular and plausible appeal, and it has a great attraction to those decent people who are prepared to exchange justice and freedom for a measure of decency and security. It has a particular appeal to those who feel betrayed by mainstream politics, and it is into the vacuum that fascism will quickly step.

The churches and religious people may be particularly vulnerable to the appeal of fascism at two points. First, when religion degenerates into quietism and sentimentality. Lutheran pietism at the time of Hitler's rise was otherworldly, drawing a sharp distinction between the Kingdom of God (otherworldly, spiritual) and the affairs of this world. Secondly, when religion is allied with a dying social order so that it comes to care more about its privileges than its theology. A church which is otherworldly and which has lost a grip on the theology of justice and freedom is an easy prey for fascism. So at Charlottenburg in 1941 German evangelicals sent the notorious telegram to Hitler, assuring him of their 'unshakeable loyalty' and hailing him as the saviour of Christian civilisation. Hitler himself said that he had come to complete the work of Luther, and many good decent people believed him.

So the record of the church vis-à-vis fascism is ambivalent. One has on the one hand the long history of compromises and support for repressive regimes – Hitler, Mussolini, Salazar, Franco, the present regimes in Latin America, and on the other the record of witnesses and martyrs, many of them clergy and bishops, in resistance to these regimes. Perhaps one sees two types of Christianity which indicate the really fundamental divide within the Christian world.

I stress very strongly the appeal of fascism to the decent because it is easy to be carried away by the need to oppose and expose the really vicious forms of Nazi ideology which are now being revived. There are Nazi groups operating. The Crusade Church of Tunbridge Wells, for example, will supply you with the *Protocols of the Elders of Zion*, as well as the works of Goebbels and Heinrich Hoffman's *Hitler Was My Friend*. The British Movement, whose slogans are around the Bethnal Green area, may be thought to be a patriotic and even Christian group (with its badge of a cross in a circle) but this organisation advertises in its journal Nazi songs, cassettes of William Joyce's 'Germany Calling' and the Battle Songs of the Third Reich – £2 each – and *Mein Kampf* at £3. Very British! But the real danger does not lie here but among those good people who, when the real evil became apparent, would throw up their hands in horror and admit – too late – 'This is not what we meant at all!'

I want to suggest that there are five areas of activity which contribute to the growth of a fascist movement, often unintentionally, and which call for careful analysis and scrutiny. The first is that of religious movements which confuse Christianity with western society and its values. There are many Christians who are willing to exchange justice for decency, and who, because although highly moral, they lack theological depth, can be easily conned by apparently moralistic movements. It is here that the stress on the sexual area can be very dangerous. A stress on 'cleaning up the streets' and on anti-permissiveness seems to accompany the beginnings of fascist-type regimes. So the Greek colonels cleaned up the cities and saw naked tourists bathing as a threat to national morality. Genitals were not for public viewing but for police torturing. So in South Africa, that highly moral nation where a husband and wife cannot make love without committing a crime if their colours happen to diverge, the mini-skirt is seen as sinful and sordid. So Hitler cleaned up the permissive Berlin of the 30s and forbade the pure race to be sullied with Jewish blood. How easy it is for some Christians to be led astray by this kind of appeal.

Secondly, there are movements which attempt to identify and

attack minorities and lay blame on them in a blanket way. It is not just blacks and Asians but a whole scapegoating process which can be extended to squatters, the Irish, the mentally ill, youth, the unemployed, the poor – anybody, in fact, who forms a threat. In Sir Keith Joseph's notorious 'remoralisation' speech in 1974 we saw how this trend could move towards a wholesale attack on social classes 4 and 5. Again, this scapegoating mechanism does not depend on numbers: the Jewish population of Germany was 1 per cent when Hitler decided that zero per cent should be the maximum tolerable level.

Thirdly, and perhaps most dangerous because most financially powerful, there is the activity of those strong vested interests which organise to defend the established structures and to resist threats to their security and power. These may include anti-trades union groups, attacks on the welfare state, and para-military defence organisations.

Fourthly, there are the international anti-communist movements, often financed from Korea, Taiwan and the United States.

Finally, there are the grass-roots racialist and 'populist' organisations which exploit fears and resentments as well as entirely genuine wrongs at the local level and organise them into racial hatred and intolerance. They are important, but the point I want to stress is that they are not the sum total of the problem. The problem of the respectable suburban appeal of fascism is far, far greater.

Finally, four tasks which are urgent in response to creeping fascism. The first is the need for rigorous and continuous analysis of what is happening, for disciplined monitoring of the activities of racist and fascist groups. No response can be effective which is not based on accurate data.

Secondly, a recognition that one cannot fight fascism without building socialism. Some will dissent from this view, but I stand by it. If there is not a movement towards socialism, then fascism of some kind, given the character of our capitalist society, is inevitable. Nor is it enough to say that we fight fascism first and build socialism afterwards. Fascism flourishes in the absence of socialism: the creation of a socialist society is the only really effective way to defeat fascism.

Thirdly, there needs to be local action in the deprived and neglected areas which are the breeding ground for fascist groups. Often anti-fascists appear in these districts to be do-gooders and political activists from elsewhere who come for a season but are uninvolved in the real day by day lives of the people. Sometimes the fascist groups seem to them at least to understand their plight. To be a professional anti-fascist is no good: there needs to be a deep involvement in such issues as health care, tenants' rights, the care of the old and lonely, and so on. We need to be people who care more about the social evils which provide the raw material for racism and fascism than the racists and fascists do. Fascism cannot be defeated from a distance by people who are remote form the problems it manifests.

Finally, the message to the churches must surely be that at a time of growing anti-Semitism, the church must rediscover its essentially Jewish roots and the Jewish basis of its Gospel. Enshrined in the Law of Moses is the theme of the 'Year of Jubilee', the expression of a hope for justice and freedom for this earth, its land and its people. In this 'jubilee year' we are likely to hear a great deal of sentimental rubbish and are unlikely to hear the true meaning of Jubilee. It is useful therefore to recall the words of Father Stewart Headlam, once a curate in Bethnal Green, on the Golden Jubilee of Queen Victoria:

> The Queen's Jubilee is good: but the People's Jubilee is better … For the Jubilee of the Hebrews … was the Jubilee of a whole People … 'Liberty throughout the land unto all the inhabitants thereof.' That is the ideal of a true Year of Jubilee … restoration to the disinherited of their share in the land which the Lord their God giveth them and of which … injustice … has despoiled them.

A church with that vision would be no breeding ground for fascism.

Simplistic prophets[4]

The time is perhaps right for some warnings not to accept the communitarians without question, and it is worth beginning with a warning about the word itself around which there is much confusion.

The only feature that the people called 'communitarians' have in common is a rejection of liberal individualism with its lack of commitment to civic values, and a commitment to the rebuilding or rediscovery of 'community'. One crucial difference between MacIntyre and Etzioni lies in the attitude to moral consensus and to faith traditions. The 'common values' and 'moral unity of the nation' hich

Etzioni proposes, and about which we have heard a good deal recently from educationalists and others, is precisely what MacIntyre (in *After Virtue* and later studies) says is impossible. So deep is the moral confusion and fragmentation of the western liberal democracies that the only hope for the moral life and civic values is through the renewal of faith traditions. And even if MacIntyre has overstated the degree of moral confusion, his conclusion that the quest for moral consensus apart from traditions of faith is inescapable. That is not a pessimistic message, but it is a hard and realistic one.

It is, of course, Etzioni who has made communitarianism a vogue word and who, having been around in the USA for many years, seems to have set his eyes on Europe in recent years. His main English popularisers are Geoff Mulgan and the Demos think thank, and through their work, Etzioni's work has filtered through, albeit in a very populist and simplified form, to the speeches of Tony Blair. It has been argued that an earlier influence on Blair is the socialist Christian thinker John MacMurray who was also concerned about community: Blair seems to have taken the community aspect of MacMurray but neglected the socialism which is integral to it. There is nothing particularly religious in Etzioni's thinking (in contrast to MacIntyre who is a Catholic Thomist) but it is obvious that the word 'community' evokes all kinds of memories and visions in the religious mind. It is not surprising that Jim Wallis of the Sojourners Community in Washington, for whom community is also a key theme, should have been invited to address Etzioni's organisation recently.

While communitarianism is new, it does connect with much earlier activity – laments about the 'collapse of community' (particularly common in such areas as East London or Deptford and often echoed in the utterances of clergy from these areas), but also in community studies (which go back to Young and Wilmott in Bethnal Green in the 1950s), community development, youth and community work, community health councils, community policing, the community charge, and (God help us) community care – and now even community theologians! Community is a warm word, few would like to be heard opposing it, and on the surface it would seem to be desirable. Yet, as the above list indicates, it is capable of a vast range of usage. George Hillery in 1955 examined 95 definitions, the only common feature being a concern about people!

I want to suggest that 'community' and 'communitarianism' may be mixed blessings, and need critiquing very carefully. Much of the rhetoric of community, and many communities in practice, have been strong and supportive at the cost of high rates of exclusion. Much current communitarian thought is very anti-feminist and pays little attention to the role of women, apart from regular attacks on single mothers. Many of the tightly knit urban villages of London such as Hoxton, Bethnal Green and Notting Dale (all of them areas where I have worked) were districts with low rates of movement, strong patterns of kinship, and fierce levels of xenophobia and racism. It is not surprising that it was in these areas that Sir Oswald Mosley found much of his support for the fascist movement, and the first two are still targets for fascist activists. Community can turn to fascism very quickly if it does not connect with other values such as diversity and minority rights. Yet Etzioni wants a moratorium on civil rights, and much of his thinking seems to assume a normative view of sameness. Nor are these thinkers strong on economics. Yet it is the globalisation of capital which is the biggest threat to community.

This is not of course to deny that the communitarians are addressing real issues: the moral confusion and fragmentation, the sense of hopelessness, the rising crime rate, the influence of individualism (in part sponsored by recent governments). But to recognise problems is only the beginning and some 'solutions' can make the problems worse as Germany in the 1930s saw. The church has a tendency to latch uncritically onto some new movement in each decade. Before it latches on to Etzioni (who is hardly new in fact), it is right to urge caution and critical scrutiny.

Perhaps we need to remember the words of Martin Buber: 'Community should not be made into a principle; it should always satisfy a situation rather than an abstraction. The realisation of community, like the realisation of any idea, cannot occur once and for all time: it must always be the moment's answer to the moment's question and nothing more.'

Feminist voices[5]

Contemporary feminism did not arise from nowhere. It has roots both in the earlier movements for women's emancipation and in the counterculture consciousness of the 1960s, with its rejection of conventional middle-class lifestyles, its focus on the personal aspects of liberation, and its concern for justice. The theme of the personal as political, though it is rightly associated with the women's movement, in fact antedated it and was an integral part of the thought of Jean-Paul Sartre, R. D. Laing, and Herbert Marcuse as well as other writers of the late 1960s. But the specific origins of modern feminism in Britain are usually located in the four demands of the Women's Liberation Movement, a feminist network that began in 1970: equal pay, education, and job opportunities; free contraception; abortion on demand; and free twenty-four-hour nurseries. Later a number of other demands were added: legal and financial independence; an end to discrimination against lesbians and the right to define one's sexuality; and, in 1978, freedom from intimidation, violence, and sexual coercion. Behind these demands lay a deeper concern for an end to the oppression of women within Western social, political, and economic structures.

The women's movement arose out of such concrete and practical struggles. The year 1971, which saw the effective origin of the movement in Britain, was also the year in which Chiswick Women's Centre was formed, the first of a number of refuges throughout the country. By 1975 the National Women's Aid Federation had been formed, a federation of thirty-five such centres. In the same year the first Rape Crisis Centre also appeared. Modern feminism had its origins in such responses to specific examples of sexual and domestic violence and economic exploitation. To say that it was a practical movement before it became a literary and reflective one would be to oversimplify the position. It would be more correct to say that it was a movement rooted in a unity of practice and theory. From its early years there were organs of feminist opinion and debate. In 1972 the best-known British feminist magazine *Spare Rib* began. Since then there have been many debates about white domination of the movement. In 1982 Outwrite, a multiracial collective, was formed, and black feminist groups have grown significantly during the 1980s. In addition to the changing racial character of feminism, four other developments within the recent movement are important: the growth of political lesbianism after 1978; the rise of eco-feminism; the rise and decline of socialist feminism; and the growth of the women's peace witness, particularly since the creation of the peace camp at Greenham Common in Britain in 1981 and the numerous movements of women against nuclear violence in the United States.

If I, as a male writer, am to reflect on, and respond to, the challenge of feminism, I need – as do my readers – to be clear about what I am doing and to be aware of some dangers. Most male writing on this and other issues is based on the very notion of neutral objectivity that feminists reject. Thus male writers will discuss 'feminism' in a lofty, complacent, and detached, though 'concerned', way as if it were simply another subject on the academic (male) agenda. To contribute to this process would no doubt earn me a reputation for scholarly objectivity – and it would be to misunderstand totally what the feminist challenge is about. However, most male writers, and especially those within the churches, seek to respond to feminist issues in this classical liberal way: by seeking to identify specific demands and then campaigning to have them placed upon the existing agenda. In this way feminism can, it is assumed, be absorbed into the already fixed framework of the (male) establishment. I have placed 'male' in brackets because it is a feature that is normally hidden. The fact that an agenda, or an establishment, is male-dominated is not normally seen as more than an incidental feature of its status. It is simply part of the way things are: it is not questioned, and a whole range of issues (including feminism) are discussed and debated within its accepted framework. In this way an illusory objectivity is created, the male viewpoint being seen as the norm. This phenomenon has its liberal form: today it is not at all uncommon to find writings by men that purport to summarise, evaluate, and contain movements of thought (such as feminism) within their already formulated agendas. It is not unknown for male writers to extol the virtues of feminist thought with virtually no reference to any feminist thinker.

I believe that one of the most important contributions of feminist thinking is its recovery of the concrete origins and character of knowledge and its rejection of the abstract self of the Enlightenment. Notions of a 'received correctness' are rejected, along with those familiar ideas of complete objectivity that merely lead to isolation and estrangement from lived consciousness. I believe that feminism has contributed greatly to any understanding of liberation in the current climate, and so, encouraged by Beverly Harrison, who urges men to do feminist theology, and by other feminist thinkers, I offer the following reflections.

Feminism offers an alternative vision of the self to that of liberal individualism: a view of the self as foundationally social. As women and men, we are historical beings and can only be understood in terms of that history and of the relationships that have developed within it. In the early years of the women's movement, this social consciousness was communicated in the concept of sisterhood. Since those years there has been much criticism of this notion, with many pointing out that, though it has been a valuable rallying cry, it has obscured important differences between women through an overemphasis on middle-class white lifestyles. In spite of this, the themes of solidarity and friendship as basic to politics and spirituality are among the major contributions of the women's movement to contemporary understandings.

The slogan 'The personal is political' (which antedates feminism) has been a crucial element in challenging a politics that treats people as agents rather than subjects. In emphasising the central place of the personal in politics, feminists have demanded more of themselves and have called for more exacting inner standards of political commitment. In a feminist perspective, politics absorbs more of one's being than has been the case in political life since the early days of the labour movement.

Of course, there are real dangers in so strong an emphasis on personal awareness and identity. Though fragmentation need not follow, the power structures are always ready to absorb and marginalise such groups, so concern for liberated lifestyle can replace the struggle for liberation as such. Yet in the recovery of the personal dimension in politics, there has come to the surface a feature of liberation struggle that is vital and yet is all too easily forgotten in much fashionable militancy; the value and dignity of every human being, however degraded and broken. Feminist politics arises from very basic and painful experiences of oppression, and it is this rootedness, this solidarity in pain, and the organised response to it, that makes the commitment to the least powerful so passionate and so persistent.

For liberation does not occur at the level of ideas and feelings but at the level of actual people and of concrete institutions and structures. At the core of contemporary feminism is a profound commitment to people combined with a critique of existing institutions that oppress and damage people. Its analysis of the family is of critical importance and is basic to all feminist analysis. Feminists rightly see the family as a central site of oppression and reject the dishonesty and hypocrisy that surrounds much idealising and ideologising of the family within Western societies. A critical approach to the family is particularly necessary for Christians, who have often naively accepted the modern nuclear family as if it had appeared fully grown from the Garden of Eden, though it is in fact extremely modern and Western. No one can take feminism seriously without understanding how central is its critique of the family as the basic material structure that embodies formal dependence on the male and of the dominant ideology of motherhood and domesticity. It is, in short, the embodiment of domination, and any critique of domination has to begin there.

But feminist social and historical criticism goes beyond the nuclear family to include 'an enormous interrogation of the past'. There is a concern to recover the lost voices of women, to reclaim lost history, to let suppressed voices from past and present be heard. There is a concern to unmask the history that has been written from the perspective of its male participants. Here the resistance to violence, whether at Greenham Common or in the large number of refuges for victims of rape, incest, and domestic violence, plays a crucial part in the shaping of the contemporary women's movement for liberation. A feminist spirituality of liberation involves the healing of lives that have been disfigured and crushed by the cycle of male violence and cruelty.

In recent years I have played a small part in bringing to public attention two studies, one of rape and one of violence against black women. I believe that it is essential for men to hear these voices and take account of these struggles and not to seek either to contain them within an acceptable, male-absorbed form or to listen only to the gentler, sanitised voices of the reformist liberal feminists who are often encountered in churches. By failing to let the movement speak for itself, we miss the pain and anger of the feminist liberation struggle. Some of the most powerful influences on my thinking have come from socialist feminists, those women who seek to pursue the struggle for women's equality within the framework of the socialist tradition. The socialist feminist voice is currently muted, as feminists share in the general confusion and perplexity of the left in the 1990s. Yet there is much that feminists have to contribute to current discussions about the future of socialism, about the state and society, about the inadequacies of the Leninist tradition, about the need for vision and for the utopian dimension in radical thought, about unexplored dimensions of Marxism, and so on. It could be argued that the future of the left in Europe and North America may depend on its ability to hear the feminist analysis and critique.

Feminists within the church too stand in a critical relationship to the tradition. Beverly Harrison has made the point that in the church women have heard 'a story of liberation that we were not intended to hear.' Christian feminists represent a neglected, suppressed, marginal tradition of Christianity and are under no illusions about the degree of hostility toward their testimony and about the weight of the historic tradition that is held against them. The language that sees women as 'the devil's gateway,' as the 'advance post of hell', as misbegotten males, the tradition of Tertullian, Jerome, and John Chrysostom, of Augustine and Aquinas, is not easily overcome. Even much so-called progressive or radical theology ignores both the position of women and its own gender base. At the Second Vatican Council no women were allowed to give papers, and there were strong attempts to ban women journalists from attending the Council Masses and from receiving communion.

It is not surprising that many women, and probably most feminists have abandoned the Christian tradition as irredeemably patriarchal. Those who have not, and have chosen to remain, have set about interpreting the Bible as a liberating source and researching Christian origins to identify the egalitarian roots of the movement.

I doubt if most men realise the courage and persistence, not to mention the capacity for coping with weariness, that is required for such women to remain faithful to a church in which they constantly find themselves 'overwhelmed by a linguistic form that excludes them from visible existence'. For such women the Eucharist, which is meant to be a focus of unity and solidarity, becomes a point of paradox and contradiction. It is desperately important that men try to understand the intensity of the darkness into which many women are plunged in their encounter with the Christian tradition. In Carolyn Osiek's words: 'It is a death experience, a dark night, to which all the descriptions of such abandonment and desolation in the spiritual classics are applicable ... It is a spiritual crisis of enormous proportions and must be understood and treated as such.' One of the characteristic features of the dark night of the classical tradition is that all concepts and assumptions go into solution, all existing securities and certainties are purged and re-evaluated. There is a thorough ascesis of soul and society in which everything has to be looked at afresh. Reality is never the same again. I believe that the feminist revolution is of such a character, and it is necessary for men to learn to listen, to hear, and to reflect on the significance of this revolution. It has to be part of our liberation too.

Gays and lesbians[6]

The word *homosexual* owes its origin to the Hungarian physician Karoly Benkert in 1869. From its first use in the nineteenth century it was not a neutral or value-free term but reflected the current ideology within biology and psychology as well as the social need to classify a new type of deviant. On the other hand, *sodomite* and *bugger* had been in use from medieval times. An act of 1290 decreed that convicted sodomites were to be burned alive, and, although Henry VIII in 1533 changed the mode of execution, death remained the penalty in Britain until 1861 and life imprisonment until 1967. To this day the death penalty for homosexual activity is still demanded by some American Christians. Homosexuals have been among the most persecuted and brutalised groups within 'Christian' societies, not least as victims of the Nazi holocaust. From the perspective of a theology of liberation, therefore, the central issue is very simple. Whatever the moral status of 'homosexual genital acts', the evidence shows that this community has been among the most oppressed, persecuted, and victimised groups in human history. Any theology of liberation must be tested against the response to this community and its struggle against such oppression.

The modern gay liberation movement is usually dated to the police raid on the Stonewall Cafe in New York in 1969, which led to an annual celebration of 'gay pride'. However, there had been activity within the Christian church prior to this, including the founding of Dignity, the gay supportive and pressure group within the Roman Catholic church in the United States, and the Metropolitan Community Church, a gay Christian communion, in 1968. Later came Integrity, the American Episcopal group, and the Gay Christian Movement (now the Lesbian and Gay Christian Movement) in Britain.

The gay liberation movement arose as a resistance movement against the persecution, stereotyping, and prejudice directed against gay people. Since those days the arrival of the AIDS epidemic, wrongly associated by many people exclusively with gay men, has further stigmatised this community. Gays are increasingly portrayed by sections of the media, and viewed by many people, as a contaminating influence within society. They have joined the ranks of the scapegoats. For many centuries people have sought scapegoats, particularly when confronted with disease or disaster. The Jews were blamed for the Black Death and later (by Hitler) for syphilis. In England the Tudor and Stuart plagues were blamed on 'blasphemers', and the nineteenth-century cholera on 'the great unwashed'. The attack on gay people today could be extended to other vulnerable groups. Such stigmatising and victimising presents a major challenge to Christians as disciples of Christ the victim, who, like the scapegoat of Leviticus, bore our sins in his own body to the tree (1 Pet. 2:24; cf. Lev. 16:8–10).

At the present time people with AIDS suffer a multiple stigma. They suffer as gay people or as drug addicts (another group among whom the virus has spread). They suffer as a result of physical marks – the blotches of Kaposi's sarcoma and other skin lesions, as well as the loss of weight, the general physical deterioration, and the enforced isolation from 'respectable' circles. In a real sense they have become the equivalent of the ancient lepers, the unclean and despised, the outcasts of society.

However, it is not simply people with AIDS but people in the lesbian and gay community in general who have suffered in the recent upsurge of what is, somewhat misleadingly, termed 'homophobia'. In particular, they have suffered the effects of a frightening increase in violence and harassment within the 'Christian' nations of the United States and Britain. The documentation of such attacks in recent years is considerable and terrifying: an attack on two gay men with garbage cans in Greenwich Village on a crowded Friday night in 1986; two gay men decapitated in Queens in 1986; two men cut up and set on fire in a garbage can in New York City in February 1986; six to ten reports of violence each day in New York City in 1987; swastikas with antigay slogans on the Episcopal chaplaincy at the University of Chicago, with signs saying 'Fight AIDS, Castrate All Gays', and so on. In the United States, recorded attacks grew from 2,042 in 1985 to 4,946 in 1986 and have continued to rise. At Yale, nearly half the lesbian and gay students in one survey said that they had experienced harassment, and other surveys have shown similar results. In Britain there were seventeen murders of gay men, or men believed to be gay, in two years; three gay men were murdered in west London in 1990. The increasingly hostile attitudes of the media and sections of the government have helped to create a climate in which violence can flourish. In Britain the notorious Clause 28 of the Local Government Act of 1988 attacked those who were 'intentionally promoting homosexuality' and what was termed the 'pretended family relationship' of lesbian and gay couples. There is no doubt that the atmosphere has become increasingly oppressive.

The growing climate of intolerance and hatred has not left the Christian community unaffected. Indeed, in some respects the attitude to gay and lesbian people within some sections of the churches is more hostile and more rooted in fear and loathing than it is in the wider community. The call by the Moral Majority for a 'war against homosexuality', with its injunction to 'stop homosexuals dead in their tracks', has been followed only too literally by some people. The ferocious hatred that one finds in some types of fundamentalism is one facet of our religious problem, and it is clear that lesbian and gay people have most to fear from the recent upsurge of the Christian Right. In Britain one observer has spoken of the resurgence of homophobia as 'the most sordid and squalid campaign of bigotry and scapegoating which this country has seen since the heyday of Mosleyite enthusiasm'.

In the Church of England, the response to homosexuality has been more genteel and hypocritical, lacking in both pastoral sensitivity and theological seriousness. In 1988 the legal officers of the Diocese of London, a diocese with very large numbers of homosexual clergy, including many in very senior and influential positions, initiated proceedings to evict the Lesbian and Gay Christian Movement from its premises in Saint Botolph's Church, Aldgate, a church with a long record of compassionate and caring ministry. The saga of the proceedings, and the behaviour of the officials, makes very sad reading. At one point seventy clergy wrote a letter pointing out that 'members of the LGCM are our brothers and sisters in Christ, and the rest of the church should listen to them with respect and love, especially at this time of increasing hostility to gay people. But again the church has been seen as intolerant and rejecting, driving gay people out both physically and symbolically.' But the letter made no impression, and the church bureaucracy and hierarchy colluded with the secular mood to reinforce the growing bigotry.

I want therefore to argue that the movement for the dignity of lesbian and gay people, and the history of their treatment at the hands of violent and oppressive forces – both inside and outside the church – is a critical test case for Christian spirituality and Christian concern for justice. It raises many issues that go far beyond the confines of the homosexual community.

It raises, first, the binding obligation upon Christ's disciples to stand by the stigmatised and the afflicted, following Christ's own example of solidarity with outcasts. Wherever men and women are despised, rejected, and abused, there is Christ. Such solidarity with the victims of injustice and oppression must always override any temptations to judge or condemn. It is a critical test of fidelity to the way of Christ.

Second, the struggles of lesbian and gay people pose in a fundamental and painful way the whole issue of honesty within the church. It is well known that churches have contained 'practising' homosexuals for centuries and that many of these members have been ordained to the ministry. Yet bishops and senior church officials continue to speak as if this were not the case. As a result, lesbian and gay people within the churches are often forced into a position of silence and secrecy and may feel obliged, under pressure, to vote against their own identities as a way of protecting themselves. Indeed, many parts of the church seem to encourage concealment and dishonesty and to reward effective concealment with promotion, while handing over to the bigotry and cruelty of the secular press those who do not succeed in this charade. This climate of doublethink undermines the church's claim to be a zone of truth; honesty becomes impossible within the church community, with tragic consequences not only for lesbian and gay people but for the integrity of the entire community. A spirituality of liberation cannot be built on dishonesty and the refusal to confront the realities of human life.

These struggles, and the responses to them, reveal a third issue of enormous concern for the future of spirituality: the resurgence of right-wing fundamentalism in a specifically homosexual form. At the heart of the fundamentalist tradition is a posture of utter certainty and an exclusion of doubt and darkness, and it is not surprising that intolerance of dissent and deviance should form a central part of the movement, particularly when it is allied to a conservative political crusade. Biblical fundamentalism has normally been accompanied by manifestations of bigotry, intolerance, and often violence, and there is little doubt that in the present climate fundamentalism and antigay politics go hand in hand. Fundamentalism of this kind is a serious danger to Christian spirituality as well as to the health of any community in which it is present. It is a pathological growth upon the Christian movement, and it calls for very serious and thoughtful responses. The worst kind of response would be a reverse intolerance by which fundamentalists became the new outcasts and a demonology was created around them. Indeed, there is considerable evidence that many of those attracted by fundamentalist claims are people who feel left out, undervalued, insecure, people whose voices have not been heard. The resurgence of fundamentalism is a challenge to all Christians to re-examine the roots of their faith and discipleship.

Fourth, the struggles of lesbian and gay Christians raise a central issue for spirituality: the relation between orientation and practice. It is curious that in most areas of the Christian life – social justice, political action, the life of prayer, for instance – the unity of being and doing, inner disposition and outward practice, are stressed. The test of our devotion is practical action, faith is manifested in works, and so on. Only, it seems, on the matter of homosexuality is a sharp moral division made between being and doing. What we seem to be saying is that God has created a community of people whose psychosexual identities are such that they can have no physical outward manifestation, a community for whom orientation and practice must for ever remain divided. The tragic feature of this approach is that, though promiscuous and irresponsible relationships can always be forgiven, and so 'pastoral care of the homosexual' can be sustained as a Christian norm, the real victims are those people in stable, loving, and responsible lesbian and gay relationships, people who feel no need of repentance. These are the people for whom the church has nothing of positive value to say: they remain 'intrinsically disordered', their condition one of 'symbolic confusion'. Surely Christian spirituality can offer a more hopeful path to perfection.

There is a fifth issue that is raised specifically by the spread of AIDS. In bringing AIDS into the discussion at this point I do not wish to reinforce the view that it is a 'gay plague' or that only gay men are affected by it. Indeed, the point of raising the question is to emphasise the creative and positive response of the gay community to the disease and the transforming effects within those sections of the Christian church that have responded, not with panic, fear, and loathing, but with compassion, love, and gentleness. It has been said that the Roman Catholic Holy Redeemer parish in San Francisco came to life through its experience of AIDS, and the responses of love, compassion, and understanding that resulted. There are many other examples from those who, through the experience of HIV and AIDS, and through ministering to those affected, have been drawn into a more profound spirituality, an encounter with the mystery of dying and rising, with the very heart of our faith. They have come to experience what Christian preachers have always said, that there can be no way to resurrection except through the encounter with death. To speak of such mysteries and to experience their reality are quite different, and it is of the nature of *krisis* and *kairos*, as the Scriptures see them, to make these truths real in all their disturbing nature.

Finally, the struggles of lesbian and gay people point us to the problem of difference and to the need to see the response to difference as central to our politics and our spirituality. The issues that arise around difference and diversity have been a major concern of the black American thinker Audre Lorde. In her book *Sister Outsider*, Lorde writes of the inability of our society to relate to difference in a way that is based on equality and respect. The project of 'relating across our human differences' is really basic to Christian life. Nothing was more striking about the ministry and teaching of Jesus than his insistence on the need to move from differences and strangeness to solidarity and communion. Instead of seeing one another as threats or as sources of contamination, we need to learn to recognise, value, and support one another as sharers in a common life and partners in a common struggle.

For these and for other reasons, I believe that the recent history of the movement for lesbian and gay rights carries important lessons for the practice of Christian spirituality and for the Christian commitment to social justice. Here particularly we see the coming together of the quest for personal identity and the need for political struggle. Yet here too we see how so much of the confusion about sexuality in the Western world has been projected upon the gay community, so this history also brings to the surface with a renewed significance and urgency the very old issue of the relationship between sexuality and the life of the spirit.

Peace not violence [7]

All thinking about human liberation today takes place within the context of violence: violence against the environment, violence against Third World peoples, violence against the poor, racial violence, violence against women, and so on. Violence is not an aberration within our society: it is endemic, it is normal. Yet we persistently ignore the systemic violence of the state, manifested in so many forms, while we deplore the violence of individuals against the state machine. Here the tradition of Catholic social thought is important in recalling us to foundational principles. The notion of systemic or structural violence is not new. Saint Thomas Aquinas taught that unjust laws were acts of violence; the French Catholic personalist thinker Emmanuel Mounier, writing in 1933, pointed out that attention to acts of violence tended to deflect attention from the more fundamental problem of states of violence – unemployment, dehumanisation, even death. The claim made by the bishops at Medellín in 1978 that Latin America was a 'continent of violence' was well within this traditional way of thinking.

Religion, and Christianity in particular, has been linked historically with violence. The church of the medieval West blessed the warrior class that emerged from the twelfth century. Indeed, the military orders, such as the Templars or the Knights of St John, a fusion of the Germanic warrior and the Latin *sacerdos*, were central to medieval culture. They had been blessed by the church from the start and were a major factor in undermining the whole idea of the just war. The just war theory, concerned with means and limits, grew up *within* Christendom. But if one is fighting for absolutes, as in the 'religious wars' of the sixteenth and seventeenth centuries or the ideological wars of the nineteenth and twentieth centuries, all means become legitimate. Churches often claimed that wars cleansed and created a new and more religious society. In fact, the opposite was the case. The contribution of war to the erosion of spiritual and moral values is very great.

Our history since 1945 has been dominated by the memory of violence on a more massive scale. Beginning with Auschwitz and

Hiroshima, it has been within the political and spiritual climate created by the violence of the death camps and the bomb that we have had to struggle to live out our Christian discipleship. There are many who have questioned whether Christian faith can be maintained with integrity after the holocaust, just as there are many who have found that the 'way of life' structured around the philosophy of nuclear deterrence has made any life of faith impossible.

Auschwitz took place in total silence, away from the sight of humanity. Only a few cried out, and their voices were not heard. Hiroshima took place with greater clamour for all the world to hear, yet the scars and deep wounds of the Nazi holocaust are in some ways more abiding than even the effects of the bomb. We still live under the shadow of the total violence and destructive power of these two evils. At the basic physical level, ours is an age in which great damage has been done, and continues to be done, to the planet, damage greater than at any time in the previous sixty-five million years. There have been scientific blunders, industrial crimes, numerous errors of judgment. The creation itself suffers violence, and is in travail, awaiting its deliverance from this slavery and oppression. We now have the materials to wipe out the world one hundred and fifty times over.

But alongside the physical contamination and other damage there is the growing insecurity that the nuclear arms race and its spin-offs have created. From the Mershon Report of 1960 to the study by Professor Norman Rasmussen in 1974, the danger of nuclear accident has been well documented. The dishonest and increasingly incredible claims for the adequacy of 'civil defence' made by successive governments in Britain and the United States no longer convince people. Britain, which has one of the highest concentrations of nuclear bases, would fare very badly in a nuclear attack. Even a one-megaton bomb on one city would kill one-third of the population of Great Britain immediately; it has been estimated that a 167-megaton attack would lead to 6.8 million deaths in the first month and 38 to 40 million in the first year. The seriousness of nuclear damage is recognised by virtually all scientists as well as by leading military historians and experts on war. Thus Sir Michael Howard has written, 'Few of us believe that there would be much left of our highly urbanized, economically tightly integrated and desperately vulnerable societies after even the most controlled and limited strategic nuclear exchange.' So we live in a climate marked by both accelerating expenditure and accelerating insecurity. Not only has insecurity increased as a reality, but the consciousness of insecurity has also increased, and as a consequence intensified despair and hopelessness.

In moral and spiritual terms, what is most alarming about the nuclear state and the culture of deterrence is the combination of secrecy, lying, and linguistic corruption. The nuclear industry was raised in secrecy, though it is only recently that the degree of this structural secrecy has been appreciated. In Britain, from the Atomic Energy Act of 1946 right through the 1950s, the growth of the industry took place beyond the sphere of democratic control and accountability. Even today the British government denies the existence of some US military facilities (though they are listed in British Telecom directories!). The climate of secrecy and deception is not an accidental accompaniment of the nuclear weapons industry but is fundamental to its nature.

The nuclear state is a repressive and authoritarian state by its nature. But it has increasingly become a state in which lying, and the corruption of language have been institutionalized. A climate of illusion has been created in which our leaders are no longer believable. The importance of this for spirituality is clear, for a central task of spiritual tradition in the past has been to uphold the integrity and moral credibility of language. In the climate created by 'nukespeak', a climate alien to all spiritual values, this task can only be pursued as a subversive one, for nukespeak has made ordinary straightforward and honest talk a virtual impossibility.

So oppressive and degrading is this climate that increasingly those who seek to follow and serve truth, as well as justice and peace, find themselves turning to, or being led to, 'holy disobedience'. Through their obedience to Christ they become part of that network of 'dissident groups' about which the Home Office *Training Manual for Scientific Advisers* warns its readers. The nuclear issue has presented Christians with a real diagnostic test of spiritual fidelity. 'Blessed are the peacemakers' has today to be worked out in the framework of a spiritual formation that seeks to disaffiliate from the dominant culture of violence and destruction. Within this culture of total violence, with its threats to the planet itself as well as to human life and human values, the many signs and symbols of localised violence, whether in terrorism, vandalism, or urban uprisings, are not surprising. It is not odd that some young people should wish to smash up decaying and dehumanising buildings when they have been brought up to accept the threat to smash up the world as a matter of course. Violence is indivisible: it cannot be condoned at one level and attacked at another. Planetary violence has its localised spin-offs because patterns of destruction have an increasingly global character. Yet much spirituality and church life lacks this global perspective and seeks to resist cosmic forces of destruction with weapons derived from an earlier, preglobal perspective.

I believe, therefore, that one of the contributions of the nuclear climate to Christian consciousness lies in the recovery of the meaning of nonviolence, not simply as a tactic but as an expression of what it is to follow Christ today. It is interesting to recall that the ancient writer Celsus's main complaint against the Christians was that they refused to fight in the army, and he saw this as being related to their claim to possess some special revealed truth. Certainly Celsus was correct to see that the refusal to fight was more than a rejection of the Roman imperial claims to obedience. Nonviolence was a manifestation of obedience to the teaching and example of Christ. In a similar way today the Christian community is called to practise and manifest nonviolence at the heart of its spirituality.

What does this involve? Those who seek to practise the nonviolent life must have faced the reality of violence, both within themselves and within the society of which they are a part. Nonviolent spirituality cannot be built on innocence or on a failure to deal with the roots of violence; it can only be built on the foundations of a recognition of, and transcendence of, both the power and the limitations of violence. Only those who have faced, recognised, and rejected the violence in themselves can be truly nonviolent. Only those who have understood the pressures that lead to violence can credibly struggle to be nonviolent. For it is struggle, liberating struggle, with which we are dealing, struggle that calls for a greater degree of love than does the commitment to violence. As Simone Weil observed, if we are merely incapable of the same degree of brutality as our enemies, there is no guarantee that we will prevail. A greater intensity and power of countervailing love is called for. Nonviolence is rooted in such intense love, in purity of heart and interior struggle. It is a whole way of life, the only way of life that is compatible with Christian discipleship.

A life of nonviolence cannot then be a passive life. In his 'Letter from Birmingham Jail', Martin Luther King described nonviolent action as a crisis force whose aim was to bring a community to confront issues that it would rather avoid. Earlier Ghandi had written of it in terms of liberating force, that force of truth which is the original meaning of *satyagraha*. For truth and peace are integrally connected. Peace can only be achieved through the transforming power of truth. Stanley Hauerwas is therefore right to say that nonviolence is integral to the shape of Christian conviction and stands at the heart of the Christian understanding of God. Christian theology is the theology of the Prince of Peace; Christian spirituality is a spirituality of peacemaking, of nonviolent struggle to bring about God's will on earth as in heaven. That struggle cannot be pursued by violent and destructive methods that, though they may rearrange the structures of power, do not effectively change the nature of power. The Second World War did not bring an end to fascism. That struggle is still with us, as is the struggle for peace and justice. It is a struggle that goes to the very heart of Christian faith, a warfare of the spirit, the conflict with principalities and powers, calling for the most heroic discipleship.

At the heart of the nonviolent tradition is the conviction that politics is not simply about method and organising, but also about lifestyle, identity, and supportive solidarity. To practise nonviolence is to be a particular kind of person, to be part of a nonviolent community, a community of peace.

Transfiguration and disfiguration[8]

> ... a cloud came and overshadowed them: and they were terrified as they entered the cloud.
>
> LUKE 9:34

There is an Anglican Church in New York City called the Church of the Transfiguration, but it is much better known locally as 'the little church around the corner', a title which is even printed on the notice board. A North American student who did a placement with me in the East End of London over ten years ago told me that, after a month, she had come to mistrust two English expressions which she had encountered when asking for directions to places. The first was 'You can't miss it'. This, she said, translated meant 'It is very difficult to find'. The second was 'It's just around the corner'. This, she said, meant that it could be anywhere from five yards to ten miles away.

But the Church of the Transfiguration 'around the corner' witnesses to the truth that transfiguration, the dazzling light of the glory of God, can occur anywhere. We sense that glory in the midst of the common and the ordinary, as Francis Thompson said 'between heaven and Charing Cross'. It is in the midst of the common life, not apart from it, that we experience the glory which dominates this feast. The late Bishop Ian Ramsey was always saying that there are moments 'when the penny drops'. He would then add: 'This is what I call a cosmic disclosure situation'. It usually happens in ordinary places, often in unexpected places and at unexpected times. Transfiguration happens 'around the corner'.

Very little attention has been paid in the Western Church to the Transfiguration. While St Leo the Great in the fifth century, and St John of Damascus in the seventh century preached on it, it was not until 1457 that Pope Callistus III introduced the feast into the universal calendar of the Roman rite. Among Anglicans, it did not survive the Reformation, and its celebration did not figure in Anglican liturgies from 1549 to 1928. I would be interested to know if there are any Anglican churches in England dedicated to the Transfiguration, though there are many in the US. There is one Roman Catholic church in Kensal Rise in West London, but I am not aware of others.

Nor does the centrality of glory, so important biblically, figure much in the collects for this feast. The collect prescribed in *Common Worship* calls on us to 'bear our cross' but says nothing about our transfiguration. The Roman collect is certainly better with its reference to 'the splendour of your beloved sons and daughters'. *The Book of Common Prayer of the Episcopal Church* in the US prays that we may be 'delivered from the disquietude of this world', though, apart from death, I am not quite clear how this is to take place! By far the best is that in the *Book of Alternative Services of the Anglican Church of Canada*: here we pray that God would deliver us from darkness and change us into his likeness from glory to glory.

It is also depressing that there has been little theological writing about the Transfiguration apart from Bishop Michael Ramsey's book *The Glory of God and the Transfiguration of Christ*. It is significant that Ramsey was greatly influenced by Eastern Orthodoxy. In the Orthodox churches, there are almost always three icons present in the smallest church – the Baptism of Christ, the Transfiguration, and the Resurrection. In this tradition, the stress is on both the glory of God and the glory of humanity as central, while sin is viewed as, literally, accidental to human nature (which is why, rightly or wrongly, the Orthodox do not like Augustine very much!).

To turn from Mount Tabor to the horror of Hiroshima might seem obscene, while to suggest that there were similarities might seem blasphemous. Yet there are twisted, demonic similarities between the two. In each event there was brilliant and dazzling light, and Robert Jungk entitled his book on the Hiroshima bombing *Brighter than a Thousand Suns*. There was a cloud, and I cannot imagine that those who experienced the bombing of Hiroshima could not have identified with my text – 'a cloud came and overshadowed them: and they were terrified as they entered the cloud'. But the mushroom cloud of Hiroshima was a kind of demonic antitype to the cloud of transfiguration: it could be described as a cloud of cosmic disfiguration – of God's 'beloved sons and daughters' as of the earth itself.

And there was revelation. I am struck by the frequency with which commentators on Hiroshima (including Noam Chomsky) use terms such as 'apocalypse' and 'apocalyptic'. Apocalypse means unveiling, revealing. At Mount Tabor it was the glory of God in the face of Jesus Christ which was revealed and, by implication, the potential glory of human beings made in God's image. At Hiroshima it was the human potential for destruction, for cruelty, for incalculable violence, which was revealed. Each event told us a story about our potential for good and for evil.

This feast, so neglected in the west, is rooted in the gospels and in the testimony of early Christian writers. Both Matthew and Mark use the word 'transfigured', while Luke does not, preferring the word 'changed'. What is often missed is that, first, transfiguration precedes resurrection: it occurs in the midst of perplexity, imperfection, and disastrous misunderstanding. Within a few verses of Luke's account of the transfiguration, the disciples are urging Jesus to call down fire from heaven to destroy his enemies. At this late point, they still haven't 'got it'. Secondly, transfiguration does not apply to Jesus in isolation but to us. The two crucial texts here are Romans 12:2 and 2 Corinthians 3:18. Few, if any, English versions translate the word used as 'transfigured', though it is the same word used in the account of the event on Mount Tabor. In Romans, Paul urges us to 'be not conformed, but be transformed', or, literally, 'transfigured'. In 2 Corinthians we are said to be in process of being transformed (transfigured) from glory to glory. In each case, the Greek word is the same: 'metamorphosed', transfigured. It is this emphasis, on our own transfiguration, on our sharing in the divine glory, which is missing in so much of our western Christian thinking.

Transfiguration can and does occur 'just around the corner', occurs in the midst of perplexity, imperfection and disastrous misunderstanding. The hope of glory does not lie in a return to a lost paradisal innocence, but in a movement forward towards the Kingdom of God, which is only manifested through the encounter with evil, injustice and frailty.

The theology of revolt [9]

The conflict between the rulers of the darkness of this world and the Church of God is an issue which must concern pacifists immensely and the need for a theological basis for resistance is underlined by recent activities of the Committee of 100. I believe that traditional Catholic orthodoxy teaches us three vital truths here whose consequences are tremendous. First, that the Kingdom of God is not an otherworldly kingdom but is to appear on the earth, that it is to transform the kingdoms of this world (Rev. 11:15). The hope of the Kingdom of God is neither an otherworldly hope, nor a wholly future hope. In Colossians 1:12–13, verses which are used with great effect in the Office of Christ the King in the Roman Breviary, we read that God 'hath delivered us from the power of darkness and hath translated us into the Kingdom of His dear Son'. The stress is on the present – '*hath* delivered ... *hath* translated' – the last days have come upon us (1 John 2:18) and the Kingdom of God has been inaugurated, as one of the Little Brothers of Jesus has written, 'in the physical brutality of the Cross-gallows'.

This is the Kingdom of which Daniel says that it will 'break in pieces and consume all kingdoms, and it shall stand for ever' (Dan. 2:40). This is the Kingdom described in the Roman Missal as 'an eternal and universal Kingdom: a Kingdom of truth and life: a Kingdom of sanctification and grace; a Kingdom of justice, love and peace' (*Preface of Christ the King*). It is a present Kingdom, though there is more to come. St Paul speaks of two phases, first, the present period of Christ's rule at the right hand of God who has 'put all things in subjection under His feet' (1 Cor. 15:27); secondly, the eventual subjection of the powers of this world – 'when he shall have abolished all rule and all authority and power' (1 Cor. 15:24). We are living 'between the times', in the birth-pangs of the Kingdom, in an age of crisis. Upon us the ends of the ages have come (1 Cor. 10:11).

The second relevant assertion of orthodox faith is that the Word became flesh. God entered the world, not to make a way of escape from it but to redeem it. Social action is rooted in the Incarnation because it proclaims the essential sacredness of the secular order. Moreover, the Word of God comes as Messiah to fulfil the hope of the Hebrew prophets. In St Luke's Gospel, our Lord applies to himself some words of the prophet Isaiah: God, he says,

> ... hath sent Me to proclaim release to the captives,
> And renewing of sight to the blind,
> To set at liberty them that are bruised.
> To proclaim the acceptable year of the Lord.

The Revised Version marginal note refers us here to the Year of the Jubilee in Leviticus 25: the year of the restoration of the land to the people, the year of freedom for the oppressed and of the return of the captive peoples to their inheritance.

The third truth is that the social redemption inaugurated in the Incarnation is fulfilled in Calvary and perpetuated in the Church and sacraments. Here bread and wine are not only the signs but also the instruments of world-redemption. Archbishop Temple stressed that in the Mass we offer bread and wine, not corn and grapes: we offer the products of labour to be transformed into the life of God and to transform the life of the world. But because particular bread and particular wine are thus transformed, all bread and all wine are brought before the altar to be transformed, it is the whole world which awaits the redeeming hand of God. The eucharistic offering must be at the heart of Christian politics, because it is the realisation of a new force at work within the world which is recreating and transforming the face of the earth, lifting it up into the cosmic offering of the Son of Man. 'The bread and wine at the Offertory set forth structures in history which have been brought out of the fallen world into the first stage of its redemption.'

The premises from which any theology of revolt must be worked out then are these. (1) The Kingdom of God is here and now bursting in upon and penetrating the present age. (2) The Word of God has entered into this age to inaugurate the New Age. (3) The Church and the Sacraments are the instruments of the Divine revolution, the vanguard of the Kingdom, the germs of the New Creation.

> Fulfilled is now what David told
> In true prophetic song of old.
> Amidst the nations God, saith he,
> Hath reigned and triumphed from the tree.

English risings[10]

> You shall proclaim liberty throughout the land to all its inhabitants.
>
> LEVITICUS 25:10

It is exactly 600 years ago today, on 14 June 1381, that the peasant army met at London Bridge and marched to Mile End. The first thing to recognise is that the term 'peasants' revolt' is in some sense a misnomer, for not all the rebels were peasants. They included a substantial section of the urban London poor. Nor is it correct to call it exclusively a 'bourgeois' revolt: of the 148 who were refused pardon, 33 had no occupation and no skills. Workers and the lower clergy played a major part in the leadership – at least twenty priests are known to have been involved. At Mile End, the central demand was the demand for *freedom*, for the abolition of serfdom and service. At Smithfield, this was extended to the call for the abolition of *lordship* (they included in this the abolition of 'lord bishops', asking for one bishop and, for the rest, equality). They wanted the disendowment of the church. So the call for freedom was linked with that for equality. Unfortunately, forgetting the Psalmist's injunction, they put their trust in princes, and the rising was crushed. But its inspiration remains and its deeply Christian demands have not lost their urgency and importance in the intervening centuries. They called for liberty throughout the land to all its inhabitants.

The more closely one examines the 14th century in general, and the events of 1381 in particular, the more one is struck by the parallels with our own time. It was a century marked by social upheaval and conflict in the cities and in the countryside. Taxation was the initial factor behind the rising, but behind this lay deep social and economic factors. There was poverty and unemployment, and, while simplistic parallels must be avoided, there are parallels with the recent Peoples' March for Jobs and the 'riots' in British cities this year. There were many 'drop-outs' in the 14th century as the refugees from oppression fled to the growing sectarian religious movements. Among these, there was (as today) a growth of Adventist and Millenarian groups, and many believed that the end of all things was at hand, seeing in the risings indications of the time of the end. Some interpreted the earthquake of 1381 as the wrath of God in the rebels. There was also an upsurge of false mysticism, meditation schools, the occult and astrology. Venereal disease rates were high and so moral doomwatchers were common.

The specific parallels with 1381 are significant and depressing. In Gravesend, the second phase of the rising was sparked off by an arrest of one runaway serf. As at Brixton in 1981, it was one incident which ignited the fire. Then, just as today, much of the spontaneous rising against injustice was blamed on the work of 'extremists' and 'outside agitators'. Today clergy who are concerned about social justice are often described as 'Marxists'; in 1381 they were called 'Lollards' or heretics, and Wycliff was blamed for infiltration. John Ball was seen in this way though it is clear that his theology was rooted in Catholic orthodoxy, while Wycliff had little time for social radicals and wrote a tract on the proper relation of servants to masters. Finally, it was an 'army of occupation' which surrounded the peasants and finally crushed the rebellion. 'What absolute nonsense! What an appalling phrase,' exclaimed Mrs Thatcher on television after Brixton on 13 April. 'I condemn the person who said that!' Three months later, yesterday, the person who first warned of the danger that the police might come to be seen as an army of occupation, the Chief Constable of Devon and Cornwall, was awarded the CBE!

The events at Blackheath and Mile End took place in this season of Trinity and Corpus Christi. It was at the Feast of Corpus Christi 1381 that John Ball preached his famous sermon on Blackheath.

> Good friends, things cannot go well in England, nor ever shall, till all be held common, till there shall be neither bond, nor serf, but all of us are of one condition.

His words are even more relevant in the Thatcher era when inequality and poverty are increasing, when all things are not common, and where clearly things are not going well in England. John Ball rooted his social radicalism in the doctrine of God and in the creation of men and women. As in the Holy Trinity, 'none is afore or after other, none is greater or less than another', so this equality must be expressed in human society too, for human beings are made in the image of the social God. At the original creation, Ball claimed, there was equality:

> When Adam delved and Eve Span
> Who was then the gentleman?
> Hierarchy and inequality was the result of the fall. At the beginning it was not so.

What then can we learn from the rebels of 1381? First, we can recognise that revolt is often part of the purpose of God. The Old Testament begins with the account of a bricklayers' strike in Egypt and ends with a successful insurrection in the Maccabean period. The New Testament begins with the proclamation of the Kingdom of God, bringing not peace but a sword and casting fire on the earth, involving crucifixion and subsequent martyrdoms, and ends with a song of triumph over the collapse of Rome. There is no support in the Bible for the view that God only works through 'peace and quiet' or that the Church must always 'support' peace and stability. 'Woe to those who cry "Peace, Peace!" when there is no peace!' So we need to look for the hand of God in social upheaval and revolt.

Secondly, we can learn from John Ball the explosive power and importance of orthodoxy. A genuine Christian radicalism cannot be built upon woolliness of belief, vague liberalism, or the assumption that theology and dogma do not matter. Theology is highly toxic and nothing could be more disastrous for Christian rebels than the kind of 'theological striptease' which divests itself of as much belief as possible. When we are confronting monsters, we need all the theological and spiritual resources we can get. We need more theology, not less.

Thirdly, we can learn the painful truth that to struggle for freedom and equality is to put us in the position of a resistance movement. To do so seriously will not increase the popularity of the church, it will make us more isolated, increase the opposition of the powerful, and so we will need to support and nourish each other more and more.

Finally, we can learn from her 1381 rising that the church can only speak with credibility for the poor and marginalised if it is itself pushed to the margins of society and more identified with the poor.

So on this Feast of the Holy Trinity, the social God, the God in whom all is common, the God who became poor and little, and whose Mother rejoiced in the putting down of the mighty from their thrones, let us uphold the truth of 'all things in common' and say 'As in the Holy Trinity, so in earthly society, none shall be afore or after other, none shall be greater or less than another.'

Part Two

The Visible Church

3
Church and Society

*The Church should be the primary social struc-
ture through which Christians seek to effect transformation – revolution – elsewhere in society.*[1]

Church and state[2]

If you had told any typical Christian thinker in any century
from the 12th to the 16th that religion had nothing to do
with economics, and that bishops must not intrude in these
matters upon the deliberations of laymen – propositions
which to many of the correspondents to our newspapers
appear to be axiomatic – he would either have trembled for
your faith or feared for your reason. He would have
regarded you, in short, as either a heretic or a lunatic.

Thus wrote the veteran Anglican social thinker Maurice Reckitt in
1935. In the same year Bishop Bell commissioned T. S. Eliot's *Murder
in the Cathedral* for the Canterbury Festival. On this day we celebrate
Becket, the martyr of Canterbury, murdered as a result of a conflict
between church and state, over eight hundred years ago. In 1935 the
focal point of church–state crisis was not Britain but Germany. Hitler
had come to power and the key internal issue facing the church was
that of its freedom. The Synod of Barmen of 1934 had asserted that
freedom against the intrusion of the Nazi state. Karl Barth, the major
theologian behind the thinking of that synod, wrote: 'I saw my dear
German people beginning to worship a false god ... a pure consistent
nihilism destructive and hostile to the Spirit ... and aimed at the
eradication of Christian belief and its expression.' It is a far cry from
the Constitutions of Clarendon to the Nuremberg Laws, from Becket
to Barth, but in different ways the same issue was at stake, that of the
spiritual freedom of the church within the state.

Reckitt and Becket. Reckitt is reminding us that separation
between religion and the economic and political order is a modern

notion, unknown to the medieval church. Becket, the chancellor turned archbishop, represented on the one hand the unity of sacred and secular: the chancellor concerned with the administration of civil law. As archbishop, however, the crisis which faced him was that of the spiritual independence of the church, its freedom from the state, and especially royal interference. The conflict came to a head with the question of the taxation of the criminous clerks. It was a crisis which was to rumble on. In 1215 Magna Carta asserted: *Ecclesia Anglicana libera sit.* The Church of England shall be free. At the Reformation the secular power again assumed control. The crisis remains unresolved in our own day with bishops appointed by a secular state machine, and continuing signs of church–state conflicts.

What can we learn from this obscure and distant controversy? First, that we cannot and should not try to recover the Middle Ages, the ages of 'Christendom', of a church–state union, the age of the two swords. That order has gone. Nostalgia for the 'ages of faith' is a form of illusion and reverse utopianism which can only lead to despair. The medieval synthesis will never be recovered in that form.

Yet with the passing of the Middle Ages has gone the whole idea of an integration and interdependence of spiritual and political realms. Today the church is a minority group within post-Reformation states, ruled by the autonomy of the economic. To assert, in this context, the primacy of spiritual and moral values is a subversive act: for our culture is built upon that very division which the Middle Ages rejected. To commemorate Becket is to assert that religion and politics cannot be divided without disastrous results: and to recognise that this has happened, and indeed is the basis of our culture.

The second 'word' from Becket is complementary: that if religion is *subsumed* into politics, 'politicised', then the essential liberating element of the gospel is lost. The church becomes a mere religious department of state. That is what Henry II wanted just as it is what the British government wants today. It is what all governments want from Hitler, Franco and Salazar to our modern quasi-Christian states. They see the role of religion to be that of nurturing souls, keeping things calm, providing ideological reinforcement for and support for the status quo, and preserving 'traditional' moral values – though morality does not extend far beyond the personal and sexual realms. But for the Christian community which seeks to be faithful to the gospel, such a church–state alliance is idolatrous and apostate. It is a modern form of worship of the Golden Calf. Not for nothing is the restaurant in Church House, the heart of the Anglican establishment, called Vitello d'Oro!

Against such pagan views the Christian community is in perpetual and unrelenting conflict. Like the three holy children in the Book of Daniel, the church, confronted by the demand for its soul from modern Babylon, can only reply:

> If there is a God who is able to save us from the blazing furnace, it is our God whom we serve, and he will save us from your power, O King. But if not, be it known to your majesty that we will neither serve your god nor worship the golden image that you have set up.

Today we are in conflict with a Mammon-worshipping world order which pays lip service to the residue of a Christian vocabulary, while denying its meaning and significance at every important point. There is an urgent need for a Confessing Church movement which will help to keep alive the liberating symbol of faith through the new dark ages.

St Thomas of Canterbury, pray for us.

Disestablishment [3]

For the first time in years, we read in *The Economist* last week, 'politicians and newspapers of all stripes are discussing whether disestablishment of the Church of England might benefit monarchy, church and nation.' But the case for disestablishing the Church of England has nothing to do with the marital affairs of Princes Charles and Princess Diana, or even with the Church's periodic clashes with the governing political regime. It is a case which touches the very heart of Christian faith and discipleship and the nature of the Church itself.

It can, of course, be argued that given the devotion of a majority of the population of a country to a particular faith, some form of legal recognition of this fact is defensible. If this were so, the current position, in which around 10 per cent of the English population are practising members of the Church of England, would hardly justify such an arrangement. In terms of this kind of claim for establishment, it should be fairly clear that the basis for it is long past.

This seems to have been recognised in recent years even by arch-bishops. Michael Ramsey, after he had retired as Archbishop of Canterbury, became utterly convinced of the need for disestablish-ment. Robert Runcie, as Bishop of St Albans in 1977, expressed the wish that the Church of England should be disestablished, and in 1984, as Archbishop, said that it was inevitable though not imminent.

I believe that we need to move beyond such pragmatism. There is a more fundamental argument which is about the nature of the Christian church and its gospel.

It is not clear when the Church of England became established, though Canon 3 of 1604 refers to it 'established under the King's Majesty'. Richard Hooker held that those who were members of the Commonwealth of England were automatically members of the Church of England, and this view was to prevail for centuries. The original establishment was initiated by the Emperor Constantine in the 4th century. It was then that the church made its peace with the civil power and abandoned its fidelity to the gospel of the Kingdom of God. It is the Constantinian project which must be undone and ended.

Those who argue for the continuation of the establishment say that without it the Church of England would no longer be the church for all people, would cease to be present in every neighbourhood and would become an elitist sect. As someone who has lived and/or worked in inner-city areas for the whole of my life, I find this a strange claim.

If the Anglican presence is only sustained by a legal structure, is it worth anything? Experience in the US suggests that presence in and commitment to an area has more to do with fundamental belief, with theology, than it has with legal apparatus.

Bishop Trevor Huddleston has claimed that when he was Bishop of Stepney he found the establishment 'a perpetual hindrance to mission'. Were it to be disestablished, the Church of England might well lose some of its more expensive buildings and much of its status, but what it might gain in credibility is enormous.

In fact, credibility is at the heart of the whole debate. Establish-ment might have advantages, might bring benefits, might be irrel-evant, and so on. But is it honest? Is it not a pretence, a mystification, a fudge? Does it not deny both the reality of the church's position now, and the meaning of the church in its origin? In the New

Testament, Christians are described as 'strangers and pilgrims' in the world. As Father Stanton asked in the last century: 'Who has ever heard of established strangers and endowed pilgrims?'

Even the word 'disestablishment' puts the issue in negative terms. A better and more biblical word is liberation. For what is at issue is the freedom of the Church to be itself. A free church would be a church devoted to God and to the call of the gospel. As it stands the Church of England is a compromised, captivated and Constantinian church, a church in bondage to Babylon, a church which is bound to have safe leaders: its bishops are state nominees. Charming and pleasant as they are, they bear the mark of the beast.

Of course, liberation is a process, and disestablishment would be one small stage in that process. It would be one facet of the wider goal of disaffiliation from bondage to 'the powers'. A truly disestablished church would be a poor church, a church with less material resources, a church on the margins. But, at the end of the day, what resources does a Christian church need? Memory, vision, and, if possible, water, bread and wine.

For the church to hide behind the structures of Caesar is a betrayal of the Gospel. Whatever the church might lose by disestablishment would be of minor importance compared with the tremendous gain in respect and credibility. To perpetuate the establishment is to maintain the idea that the Church of England is the church of the English people (as it is in law) rather than a minority among minorities (as it is in fact). Those who argue that disestablishment would make this church into a sect ignore the fact that, in sociological terms, that is precisely what it is.

Disestablishment would liberate the Church to be what it is in gospel terms: the body of Christ, the community of gospel freedom, the herald of the Kingdom of God.

Church and class[4]

The Church of England as an institution is an integral part of the ruling class, maintained and administered by the middle class and seeking to minister to the working class and the poor. Yet in spite of the fact that this is widely recognised, little serious attention to class issues is found in the thinking and writing which emanates from the Church and its leaders.

There have, of course, been many studies of Church and class, particularly in relation to the nineteenth century. It was, many argued, during the process of urbanisation which occurred then, that the churches 'lost the working class'. Nor was this belief peculiar to members of the Church of England. 'The greatest scandal of the church in the nineteenth century', claimed Pope Pius XI, 'was that it lost the working class.' On the other hand, Bishop Winnington Ingram in the early twentieth century argued that 'it is not that the Church of God has lost the great towns: it never had them.' Disraeli had apparently believed that 'it will be in the great towns that the greatest triumphs of the church will be achieved', and Bishop Blomfield, Bishop of London in the mid-nineteenth century, held the view that the working class did not attend churches because there were not enough churches for them to attend. So he initiated a period of promiscuous church building, building ten churches in Bethnal Green in ten years.

But the underlying problem was, and is, that the Church does not relate in any fundamental way to the needs of working-class people. It was, and for the most part remains, an alien institution, which seeks to minister to a community which it does not understand and with which it has never really identified. In 1898 a clergyman called Fry wrote:

> The church is mostly administered and officered by the classes; her influential laity belong almost wholly to the class; she is doing a great and growing work among the masses; but the deep sympathies of the clergy with the poor are largely obscured in the eyes of the masses by the fact that social rank and social position count for so much in her service, both among clergy and laity.

His words remain as true today as they were in the nineteenth century.

The very presence of the Church in the new urban areas was an afterthought of the Industrial Revolution. Apart from the medieval churches and those built under an act passed in the reign of Queen Anne, there was no church building in the cities and new towns until the act of 1818. In 1843 the Church of England had seats for only 40.3 per cent of the population. So as the Victorian city grew up, healthier than its predecessors and less dependent on migrants, it grew up relatively churchless and, on the whole, irreligious. The Church of England in particular, as it grew in parochial terms during the nineteenth-century epoch of church building grew as a middle-class agency in areas which were entirely working class and poor. Areas such as the East End were virtually colonised by the Church of England in the mid-nineteenth century. And the pattern was repeated elsewhere. Between 1824 and 1880 over six hundred new churches were built in urban areas. But the model which dominated the growth was a model derived from an agrarian society, the parish based on territory within a mainly rural environment. The urban church grew up using a rural pattern of organisation, and led by those with no real urban experience. Of 104 bishops between 1783 and 1852, only 17 had any experience in urban ministry.

This is not to deny that the nineteenth-century Church, in its motivation and its pastoral zeal, both cared for the poor and often campaigned for social justice. There is considerable documentation of the contribution of church groups and individuals to the reform movements, and of the contribution of some of the heirs of the Tractarians to the emergence of Christian socialism as a powerful force. Yet the overall impact of the Church's mission was to maintain and reinforce the class structure of which it was itself an integral part. The life, culture and spirituality of the Church of England in particular remained essentially alien to the working class, and so it is not surprising that 'in the modern urban environment, the act of worship did not become customary among most working class people'. The 'rites of passage' were observed, though diminishing over the years, but the church as such never became part of working-class culture in the way that, for example, the Labour Party did. A study in Middlesborough in 1907 showed that more people went to the pub than to the church on Sundays: nearly seven times as many men, two-and-a-half times as many women, and twice as many children. While, as is often pointed out, village communities often grew up around the church and the pub, in the cities it was the pub rather than the church which became the focal point of working-class neighbourhood life.

The general failure of the Church of England to make any profound impact on the urban scene is brought out in report after report from the later years of the nineteenth century. 'The church is nowhere in East London,' complained Bishop Walsham How of Stepney in 1897, while south of the river a local newspaper announced: 'Christianity is not in possession in South London.' A writer in *John Bull* described the East End as 'teeming with people who are almost as remote from Christian influences as savages in the wilds of Africa.' At the turn of the century, both the Booth and the Mudie Smith surveys bore witness to the weakness of all the churches in working-class areas of London.

The period of what has been described as 'the Church condescending' is manifested with particular visibility in the East End of London. Here, apart from the medieval church of St Dunstan, Stepney, and a number of churches (Spitalfields, Bethnal Green, Limehouse, Poplar and St George's in the East) built in Queen Anne's reign, most of the parishes date from the nineteenth century. The ritualists concentrated much of their pastoral energy on East London, building great basilicas such as St Columba's, Kingsland Road, and St Peter's, London Docks. The public schools and the universities established settlements: Toynbee Hall, Oxford House, St Hilda's East and the quaintly named St Mary of Eton, Hackney Wick, among many.

It is not my purpose here to condemn this upsurge of concern and goodwill, and there is no doubt that, in terms of benefit to individuals, the Church condescending has a great deal to its credit. But the whole enterprise was based on a refusal to question and attack the class system. Canon Barnett, the Warden of Toynbee Hall, was a fervent believer in the class organisation of society. Years later, George Lansbury wrote that the purpose of Toynbee Hall – and by implications of the other settlements – was 'to bridge the gulf between rich and poor by the use of smooth words and ambiguous phrases'. The settlements, like the Church as a whole, sought to ameliorate the worst aspects of the system, to make it human and tolerable. The poor were worthy of care and compassion, but they had to be kept in their places. One of the motivating forces behind the Hoxton and Haggerston Church Extension Fund was the fear that something similar to the French Revolution might occur in London. The Church of England in the East End of London was first and foremost an instrument of social control.

The pattern of church life in the East End, where a powerful and wealthy Church sought to minister to the working class, was not unique, but it exposed the reality in an unusually stark form. This was because on the one hand, the East End was – and, in spite of some gentrification in the riverside areas, for the most part still is – an entirely working-class community, and on the other hand, because it was here that Oxbridge and the public schools put in so much effort over a century. But the reality which was so visibly portrayed in the East End was present in every city and town. Nowhere did the Church of England become an indigenous part of working-class culture. Those who sought to 'missionise' the East End in the nine-teenth century made much of the fact that the population consisted exclusively of the working class or 'the poor'. Thus the Rector of Spitalfields informed the Ecclesiastical Commissioners in 1859 that the population of the new parish of St Stephen would be of this character: 'in the district there will *not* be *one* gentleman living, *not one* professional man of any description'. A year later, the Rector of the nearby parish of St George in the East explained that his parish consisted entirely of 'those very classes who are alas! almost universally alienated from attendance upon the services of the Church'. The history of that church, a Hawksmoor edifice of enormous propor-tions, rebuilt in the 1960s at great expense for a tiny congregation, shows that the population remained alienated down to the present. Its own essentially alien character was symbolised by a notice which remained on its main door until 1939: 'No dogs or women without hats allowed in.' The attitude of benevolent (?) contempt indicated by such a notice is one which has characterised much of the Church's presence in working-class areas. The local people are seen as objects of the Church's care and concern – and as a pool of potential members. They are there to be done good to. But the Church does not belong to them. Its true home is elsewhere.

Its true home, in fact, has always been among the upper and middle classes in the wealthier parts of town, and more recently in the growth areas of suburbia. It is here that its interests lie, and where, in statistical terms, it is still largely 'successful'. The composition of the General Synod brings out very clearly the built-in bias of the Church towards the world of Oxbridge, the public schools and the profes-sional middle class. In 1970–71, 49 per cent of the male lay members of the Synod had attended public schools, and 35 per cent had Oxbridge backgrounds. A further study in 1975 showed that the composition of the Synod was 99 per cent middle class and 79 per cent upper-middle class. And the 1980 Synod, not surprisingly, was found to be 'still essentially a bastion of male, middle-aged and middle-class Anglicans'. By 1980 96 per cent of lay members had upper-middle-class professional or managerial backgrounds. There had in fact been 'a further entrenchment of the upper middle class within the Synod'. The public school and Oxbridge backgrounds of the bishops are well known. Of course, most of these men are more at home in the House of Lords, the Athenaeum Club and the homes of 'the great and the good' than they are in an East End pub. They represent the ethos and culture of a Church of the wealthy and the genteel. It was this Church of the wealthy and the genteel which was exported to the United States where, although the Episcopal Church accounts for only around 3 per cent of the population, a study in 1976 found that 48 per cent of its members had incomes over $20,000, 94 per cent were white, and 20 per cent of big business concerns and one third of the banks were run by Episcopalians.

In the London borough of Tower Hamlets, however, one of the poorest and most deprived districts in Britain, and one with a long history of Anglican missionary activity, only 1 per cent of the population in 1973 were on electoral rolls of the Church of England. A report in that year, commissioned by the Bishop of Stepney, was still referring to the East End as a 'mission area'. And there is no doubt that the Church has sent many devoted individuals as part of its mission into this and similar areas. But the people there know and realise that they come from elsewhere, they do not belong. The Church of England not only speaks the language of class; its interests clearly lie in the preservation of the present arrangement of society. Actions speak more loudly and more accurately than words, and nothing speaks more loudly in the inner urban areas than the concern of the Church, visibly represented in the property world by the Church Commissioners, to make as much money out of its land as possible. Thus the scandal of the sale of church property for luxury flats in areas of acute housing shortage, homelessness and deprivation is defended on the grounds that such commitment to the forces of the market enables the Church's mission to the poor to be maintained elsewhere. Working-class people are unlikely to be convinced by arguments such as these.

It is difficult to see how this situation can become very different without so fundamental a restructuring of the Church of England that it could hardly be said to be the same body. For its entire ethos is bound up with the preservation of the stable order, with the monarchy, with the 'establishment' and with the structure of capitalism. In a class society, a racist society, a society rooted in hierarchy and inequality, this is bound to mean that the Church of England will be a class Church, a racist Church, and a Church which, in its own life reflects and reinforces the inequalities of the dominant society. Yet most church documents seem not to be aware of this. They are filled with apparently 'radical' calls for an attack on inequality, for campaigns against racism and so on, but seem strangely blind to the structural reality of the position from which they themselves speak.

Social holiness[5]

Was Wesleyanism a radical movement? It is a question which has occupied historians and theologians for many years. Superficially, the early evidence seems to be clear. Politically both John Wesley and George Whitefield were extreme conservatives, opposed even to the liberal and radical reforms of their day. And the suspicion of organised working-class movements of protest extended into the nineteenth century. Jabez Bunting, who virtually managed Methodism in the years after 1814, claimed that Methodism was 'as opposed to democracy as to sin', and refused to conduct the funeral of a Luddite who had been shot at Cleckheaton in 1812. 'Fear the Lord and the King', he proclaimed, 'and meddle not with them that are given to change.'

Yet the image of Methodism as a radical and even socialist movement has survived. It is often claimed that British socialism 'owes more to Methodism than to Marxism' (though it is difficult to recognise any greater knowledge of John's than of Karl's writings among most Labour MPs today). Undoubtedly Methodism did inspire in many leaders of working-class movements a zeal for justice, a spirit of persistence, and a biblical basis for their commitment. It made them better rebels. That many became socialists also is probably incidental to Methodist theology: it was rather a consequence of the rootedness of both Methodist and labour movements in the same areas.

Methodism is, of course, only one of the strands within Christian socialism in Britain. The two main groups of Christian socialists from the 1920s to the 1960s were the nonconformist radical group, heavily influenced by Methodism, and the Anglo-Catholic group. When in 1960 the Christian Socialist Movement was formed as a merger of some older bodies, Donald Soper became its president, and the

Methodist influence probably became the dominant one. Nevertheless socialists have remained a minority among Methodists, as they have in every other Christian church.

The social record of Methodism is, as one would expect, a mixed one. Yet there are two elements in the Wesleyan tradition which have greater potential for future developments. The first is the stress on social holiness. Of course, Wesley's social teaching is ambivalent. The most typical stress both in Wesley and in later Methodism was on the fact that individual salvation would inevitably bring social evils to an end. Yet Wesley did say that 'the Gospel of Christ knows of no religion but social; no holiness but social holiness'. It is doubtful whether by 'social holiness' Wesley meant more than relations with others. But the drawing out of the implications of his words is a major task for Methodists today.

The second element is the teaching about sanctification. By its insistence that holiness involved a real transformation, and that perfection was possible, the Wesleyan movement opened the door to movements of radical change which were not bound by the restrictions of the present, by the theology of 'no alternative'. Thus there is a clear link between the holiness movement and early resistance to racism, while the connection between the Wesleyan movement and the ending of slavery in the United States is clear. The holiness movement in Britain, on the other hand, never exhibited such radical aspects.

The contemporary dilemma for Methodist social theology is that, while the transition from individual to society may be an easy one, it is not inevitable. A crudely individualistic Methodism, shorn of its perfectionism and its biblical wholeness, can lead to the theology of Margaret Thatcher. It is up to heirs of Wesley to show that it need not end up there.

Church and social action[6]

This year is the centenary of the death of Josephine Butler, that 19th-century evangelical Christian woman, who cared for, but also campaigned for the dignity of, women involved in prostitution. Josephine Butler, in common with many 19th-century Christians, worked happily with the language of 'rescue', but she realised the need to go beyond rescue to reform, and she successfully campaigned for the repeal of the Contagious Diseases Act which helped to stigmatise and dehumanise prostitute women. A political campaigner, she was profoundly influenced by the mystic St Catherine of Siena: piety and politics went together.

Thinking about Josephine Butler, I realise that she, like many of us, moved from rescue to reform, from mysticism to politics, from care to campaigning. And not just 'beyond', for rescue and reform, mysticism and politics, care and campaigning hang together. As I reflect on how churches respond to such issues as homelessness, bad housing, prostitution, drug abuse, and so on, I believe that they tend to move between six modes of response: retreat, reinforcement, rescue, reform, revolution and resistance. I want to look at these six Rs in relation to our work in the field of homelessness.

First, Retreat. Usually this is a fundamental option. When I hear the statement 'Why churches cannot ignore poverty and oppression', my depressing response is that they often can and do. And they do so on the basis of a kind of theology: a theology which sees 'the world', not as the fallen order alien to God and the demands of justice, but as the material, life of the world – economic and political activity for instance – which is a source of contamination and a threat to the purity of Christians. Often the retreat posture leads to an obsession with internal church politics and a retreat into a pseudo-Christian piety. Retreat can also be a strategy of renewal, withdrawal in order to build up resources to advance, but it is not usually so.

My second R is Reinforcement. Here the church acts as an agent to reinforce inequality, injustice and oppression. It upholds the culture of wealth, the dominion of Mammon, the economic, political and social system which prevails. Again, there can be moments when reinforcement can be a positive force. Churches can, and should, give support to actions of governments which seek to support the common good. It would be interesting here to compare *Faith in the City* (1985) with *Faithful Cities* (2006). But the danger of Reinforcement is that churches come to sacralise the dominant order rather than challenge it, and there are many examples of this.

Thirdly, Rescue. Here churches see the need to rescue individuals from forms of bondage – alcoholism and other addictions, prostitution, and so on. The Salvation Army, the 'rescue missions', much evangelical work comes to mind. I worked in the 1950s with Fr Joe Williamson, the 'prostitutes' priest' in the Cable Street area of East

London. Williamson, like Josephine Butler, who inspired him, and about whom he wrote a small book, used the language of rescue constantly, yet he saw the close link between prostitution and bad housing. He campaigned so relentlessly against slum conditions that he got a good deal of his parish neighbourhood demolished. However, Williamson was not politically astute, and often failed to make wider connections.

However, there were Christians who saw the importance of Reform, my fourth R, and this involved careful research, documentation and political campaigning. One of these was the economic historian R. H. Tawney who once observed that what thoughtful rich people called the problem of poverty, thoughtful poor people called the problem of riches. Commitment to reform involves churches in policy issues and in legislation. Examples of such groups are the Christian Social Union in the 19th century, the various Boards for Social Responsibility in the Church of England, and, more recently, the Catholic Housing Aid Society, now part of Housing Justice.

The fifth R is Revolution, and conventional Christians may be surprised that this is the most traditional and most biblically rooted of the six. The word *dunamis*, power, often used if the power of the Holy Spirit, is the word from which we get dynamo, dynamite, and dynamic. It means revolution in its most literal sense. *Metanoia*, translated repentance in most English Bibles, refers to a complete change in values and in consciousness. Its closest Greek word is *paranoia* which means to be out of one's mind. Metanoia means a revolution of the mind, the personality, so that we see things utterly differently.

These words call for not only personal but structural change, for a new form of community. The call for revolution is always present, and essential, in Christian preaching and catechesis, but, in its political sense, it rises when, as Yeats said, 'the centre can not hold', when a political system is 'beyond patching', beyond reform. Many Christians believe that capitalism, based on the moral sin of avarice, is such a system. The Roman Catholic philosopher Alasdair MacIntyre ends his major work *After Virtue* with the claim that our predicament is 'so disastrous that there no large remedies for it'. His close friend and colleague Stanley Hauerwas calls the church to be an alternative form of community based on a different politics. Here we move towards my sixth R.

Resistance, according to Hauerwas, influenced by the Anabaptist tradition, is the normal condition of a prophetic, counter-cultural church. It seeks to offer a different model of being human together, moving beyond rescue and reform, moving beyond 'the servant church' towards one which, by its lifestyle as well as its proclamation, calls the principalities and powers to account.

Now I am not arguing that any individual or church can neatly be identified with one of these models. Most move between several of them, often trying to hold them together at the same time. For example, we spend a good deal of time in band-aid or ambulance style ministry, while at the same time trying not to lose sight of the prophetic ministry or of campaigning for legislative changes. We may believe that capitalism is not reformable, yet we still find ourselves putting forward what Trotsky called 'transitional programmes'. But my experience has been we usually, as churches and as organisations within or outside churches, usually move from one model to another when events, struggles or experiences bring about some sort of 'paradigm shift' in our thought and practice.

Thus, in 1880 the Whitechapel Board of Guardians reported that 'habitual vagrancy cannot be repressed by severe discipline and treatment unassociated means of pauperisation'. This marked a shift from a penal understanding of homelessness to a more structural one, a shift from a reinforcement model to one of reform. The shift in the 1960s from the highly localised provision of housing by groups such as the Notting Hill Housing Trust towards national campaigning led to the creation of Shelter: a shift from the rescue of individuals and families from housing distress towards a more political stance. About the same time, Anton Wallich-Clifford, founder of the Simon Community, wrote *Beyond Simon* (1968) in which he argued that the organisation needed to expose its own image and recover its Catholic identity. While I don't think this ever happened – Simon was never the same as the Catholic Worker in spite of being inspired by it – it did seem to make a shift from being a 'mission to the misfit' (an early Simon phrase for rescue work) towards something akin to Hauerwas's stress on the church as an alternative reality, rooted in a social and sacramental tradition.

When Anton and I and others founded Centrepoint in December 1969, we had both rescue and resistance in mind, as the name indicated. St Anne's Church, where the night shelter began, does stand, geographically, at the 'centre point' of the district of Soho. But we also had in mind another building of the same name, the Centrepoint tower by Tottenham Court Road, which stood empty as its value increased. It was Ruth Glass, Director of the Centre for Urban Studies in Gower Street, who said that, by calling our little project Centrepoint, we would be causing major confusion, and drawing attention to the scandal of 'this insolent building' which was an insult to all the homeless and badly housed people in London.

In 1991 the publication of Michael Fielding's study of homelessness projects in London and New York pointed to the fact that a number of them seemed to make little or no connection between their religion and their work. This helped to push some towards more theological reflection while not neglecting the needs of people. At the end of the day, the churches' authenticity and faithfulness to the gospel can only be judged in action. It is by our fruits, not our words, that we will be known (Matt. 7:16, 20). The Son of Man will repay us 'for what has been done [*kata ten praxin*, according to the praxis]' (Matt. 16:27).

The future of the Church [7]

A key issue for the Church of England, as for many parts of the Church, is the fact that, in many places, the Church has become a 'clerical reservation'. The laity has disappeared, except as consumers of sacramental and verbal ministrations, as customers and volunteers within the institution. This may seem an outrageous claim in the light of the immense involvement of lay people in church life, and of the clear increase in theological education involving what the Vatican once quaintly referred to as 'the non-ordained faithful'. There have been movements for, and books about, 'the liberation of the laity' for many years. My experience, however, is that lay people remain second-class citizens, devalued, not least within church congregations. They are seen as important and indispensable aids to the running of the business of the Church, which is basically controlled by clergy.

Yet 'the laity', the *laos*, *is* the people of God, and, if they disappear, the Church disappears. The use of the terms 'lay' and 'laity' bring out, and focus, the central issue: what is the Church? In popular discourse, laity means inferior, second-rate, untrained. Even Rowan Williams recently described William Stringfellow as a 'lay theologian' as if that were some peculiar kind of theologian, while John Habgood, former Archbishop of York, used the same term about Baron Von Hügel. Others write of 'lay theology'. This kind of language suggests that 'normal' theology is done by clerics, while 'lay theology' is some radical, unusual innovation. I believe that the exact opposite is the case: most theology is done by 'lay' people, much academic theology is now written by 'lay' people, and ordained persons perform an important, though statistically minor, role in this activity. The use of 'lay' as a euphemism for inferior continues to trouble me. One recent handbook for people seeking ordained ministry spoke about the need for the Church – that is, the clergy – to 'mobilise lay people', although the Church, for the most part, *is* lay people.

My experience in the Diocese of Northern Michigan is important here. This diocese is one of the largest and poorest in the USA. Indeed, many people in the USA seem unaware that Northern Michigan, or, as it is usually known, the Upper Peninsula, exists at all. They think Michigan ends at Detroit. But beyond Detroit, going up to the Canadian border, is a vast area, mostly rural, where the church has faced, and responded to, enormous problems. We have much to learn from them.

When I first went to speak in Northern Michigan, two things hit me. The first was that, in spite of the enormous geographical distances – fifty to a hundred miles between one parish and another – most of the people seemed to know one another. This seemed to be a community which was accustomed to co-operative work. The second was that I could not tell who were the clergy and who were the laity. When I mentioned this, and congratulated the people on it, an elderly woman stood up, and said, 'In this diocese we have abolished the word "laity".' Although they knew it was a biblical word, they felt that it was now so tarnished, so damaged, that, for the foreseeable future, it was unusable. It meant inferior, second-rate, untrained, and so on. So they only spoke of 'the Church' and of 'the people of God'. In Northern Michigan, there has been a real recovery of what is called 'total ministry', the ministry of all the baptised. Baptism is seen as more important than ordination, and this has led to a church in which all minister on a basis of equality. When I visited the diocese last, the number of paid clergy, including the bishop and archdeacon, numbered nine. What began as an economic necessity – the survival of the church – quickly became a theological renewal, a transforming rediscovery of the nature of the Body of Christ.

Northern Michigan is not alone. Local-based theological work goes on in all sorts of places. I visited All Saints, Pasadena, California, where they ran a reflection programme on their various projects entitled 'What in God's name are we doing?' The Education for Ministry (EFM) programme, which emanates from Sewanee, Tennessee, has been enormously successful in rooting theology in local communities. There are many examples in Britain also. I believe that our little experiment in Whitechapel has contributed to the essential work of local theology. This is not, and must never become, a special type of theology. It is rather Christian theology as it engages with the specific character and needs of local communities. If theology fails to do this, it withers and decays as a discipline.

The movement into the future is, literally, of critical importance. In the year 2000 there was a great flurry of interest in what was called 'the Millennium'. Much of it was confused, and at times absurd, and little is now left of it apart from the ill-fated 'dome' in Greenwich and other relics. In a largely non-Christian culture, it was hardly surprising that there was confusion. Churches, particularly those of the evangelical brand, displayed – and many still display – posters announcing that the year 2000 was the anniversary of the 'birthday of Christ'. What kind of theology was involved here is unclear, but, whatever it was, it made little impact on the mass of the people, and reinforced the idea that churches lived in a kind of backwater of ideas. The Jubilee Group and others tried to treat the issues of millennial hope seriously, and for us it raised the question of the place of the future in the activity and thinking of the present. This concern was at the heart of our thinking about the future of theology in the East End, but it seemed vital to locate it within the context of the future of humanity, the world and the universe.

Eschatology, the doctrine of the 'end', is often dismissed by Christians and others as the preserve of fanatics and of those who have abandoned any hope for this world. I want to argue that it is of the greatest importance to any creative theological work. Christians are called to be 'a people of the last times, the people of the new age'. The future of theology, in East London and elsewhere, can only be discussed within the context of the theology of the future. As Daniel

Jenkins once put it, 'it is the world to come which writes the agenda for the Church'.

Being Anglican[8]

What then of Anglicanism? Does this tradition have a future as a form of Christian presence and consciousness? I must confess that my relationship to Anglicanism has always been a marginal, and, in the strict sense, an eccentric one. Yet here I remain – troubled, irritated, often profoundly uneasy with this strange Church, this *église ridiculeuse* (as the late Hugh Maycock used to call it), yet not knowing where else I could go and be more at home. I find my relationship with the Church increasingly complex and ambiguous.

Yet the history of Anglicanism is itself complex and filled with ambiguity. The close links with monarchy, aristocracy and establishment, with national identity and state, are inextricable elements of dominant Anglican history, and I see them as serious obstacles to the future of Anglicanism as a coherent Christian tradition in the modern world. On the other hand, I look around at other parts of the Christian world, and am often relieved that I am an Anglican! Part of the relief is due to the fact that within Anglicanism there are deviant, dissident, minority traditions, some of them products of the Oxford Movement and its fusions with other forms and developments. One Orthodox writer used to say that the genius of Anglicanism was its ability to preserve for the Christian future the vision of unity in diversity, while others have seen Anglicanism as a form of 'Western orthodoxy' – an orthodoxy which takes account of the insights of modern and (postmodern) thought.

To be an Anglican intelligently is to enter into a particular way of doing theology which brings together pastoral and academic approaches as well as socio-political struggle. This is true in spite of the immense differences in the way such a theology is interpreted. Thus, at their best, and clothed in their right mind, evangelicals, liberals, Anglo-Catholics, and all the people who do not fit these increasingly problematic labels, do tend to have in common a broad view of pastoral care, a respect for the intellect and for freedom of thought, and a commitment to some kind of involvement in the issues of the wider society. Such a posture cannot be taken for granted in the same way in other Churches or traditions, and it is a major strength of the Anglican way.

It seems to me beyond doubt that there is a long and rich tradition of Anglican theological thought which goes back, at least, to the seventeenth century. At this time, for example, a school of Anglican moral theology grew up which was much closer to Thomas Aquinas than was much contemporary Roman Catholic thought. It was a tradition which integrated moral and ascetical theology, discipleship, and a theological vision of the final end of humanity in glory. Much nineteenth-century Anglican theology – F. D. Maurice is a clear example – shaped the thinking of Christians in many communions, while much of the thought of the Second Vatican Council was anticipated in Michael Ramsey's *The Gospel and the Catholic Church* (1936). This small Church has pioneered many areas of thought which have later become normative in the Christian world.

There has been debate for many years about whether there is a distinctively Anglican theology at all. Michael Ramsey, in a famous passage, stressed incompleteness, clumsiness, mess, and lack of neatness as central features and strengths of Anglicanism. Its strength, he claimed, lay in its very brokenness. In an article of 1945, Ramsey discussed the question of whether there was an Anglican theology, answering his own question positively. Anglican theology, he argued strongly in the post-war years, was sorely needed. It was not a confessional system so much as a method, a use, a direction – and only provable by its fruits. Ramsey stressed the need to prevent Latin scholastics dominating the Church's theology (a view which he re-emphasised in my presence during the papacy of John Paul II), but he was also highly critical of the neo-orthodoxy of Barth. For him, the Anglican sacramental and incarnational thrust was of crucial importance to the Christianity of the future.

Certainly the Anglican Church is one of the most pluralist Churches in the world, and the idea of a *via media* seems often to have a disintegrative rather than a unifying effect. Halevy, writing of the nineteenth century, commented that England was the only country in Christendom which did not require any theological knowledge from candidates for ordination. But the concept of the *via media* is usually misunderstood. It is not a broad path of vagueness, rather a precarious way of holding together paradoxical truths in an uncomfortable but creative dialectic.

I certainly do not believe that the civic tradition within Anglicanism, with its lack of any clear dogmatic belief or serious spiritual life, can make any creative contribution to the Christian future. I see the de-Englishing of Anglicanism as a major breakthrough, and it is certainly the case now that the most vigorous areas of growth of the Anglican form of Christianity are in Africa, Asia and Latin America. But I do believe strongly that there are elements in Anglican history – its rich sacramental life, its respect for scholarship and free enquiry, its commitment to biblical reflection and preaching, its liturgical discipline, and its emphasis on pastoral theology – which have enormous, and at times unique, contributions to make to world Christianity. Many people have come to Anglicanism as a result of their felt need for a deeper and richer liturgical and sacramental life; or as refugees from the Roman communion with its often slipshod and mechanical approach to worship, or its harsh and uncomprehending approach to sexuality; or because they find their intellects are respected here. There are all kinds of reasons why people become Anglicans. But in order for them to come at all, the Church has to stand for something.

The belief that the Anglican Church does not stand for anything has in recent years provoked a number of documents which have sought to recover 'Anglican essentials', or to restate the fundamentals of their faith. Some of these are very narrow, others are a needed corrective to much sloppy 'liberal' thinking. Some have lamented that today, orthodoxy is only one option among many; while others have suggested that the future of Anglicanism involves an increasingly orthodox theological profile.

The strength of Anglican Catholicism lies, first, in its ability to offer a form of Catholic faith and life which is compatible with intellectual freedom and with a creative engagement with contemporary thought. Secondly, its strength is in the fact that, at its very heart, it is deeply mystical, social, sacramental and thoughtful, offering synthesis and integration. Thirdly, its strength lies in its ability to offer a way forward for apostolic Christianity which avoids the ethnic captivity and pre-Enlightenment perspectives of Eastern Orthodoxy, and the narrow authoritarianism of the Vatican, while learning from, and absorbing, the best in these streams. Finally, its strengths is in its ability to offer a place of nourishment for Christians who are escaping from bigotry but who do not wish to abandon the positive and valuable aspects of the tradition.

At the heart of classical Anglican theology is a view of pastoral care which extends way beyond the confines of the congregation. In a moving essay on being Anglican in South Africa, Mamphela Ramphele speaks of her experience as one of pain and privilege. She lays particular emphasis on the opposition to rigidity and the openness both to people and to new ideas. For Ramphele, it was loving pastoral care which brought her into the Anglican Church, and this is a really important pointer for the future.

A final struggle in Anglicanism concerns the question of purity. Problems around purity have been central to religion since ancient times, and one of the radical contributions made by Jesus was to redefine the approach to notions of pure and impure. Anglicanism has to a large extent avoided sectarianism and its tendency to make sharp divisions between pure and impure, recognising the need to deal with impure and ambiguous realities. John Kevern has argued that the future of Anglican theology depends on its ability to take seriously the doctrine of analogy, to do for the twenty-first century what Aquinas did for the thirteenth. Whether Anglicans take the opportunities seriously probably depends on factors about which I have no knowledge and over which I certainly have no control.

4
The Catholic
Movement

*The Catholic movement in Britain and in the
United States has tended, particularly since the
1950s, to become an ecclesiastical ghetto, marked
by fear of change and by a defensive posture.*[1]

Catholic theology and social change[2]

Catholic theology, like society itself, is changing, and within
the broad spectrum of western Catholicism there are widely differing
and contradictory elements and emphases. In this paper I want to
look at the western Catholic tradition as a whole, and only briefly at
the Catholic movement within Anglicanism. Today, the Roman
Communion might be compared – as the 17th-century Latitudinar-
ian Cudworth compared the Church of England – to Noah's Ark, for
it contains almost every kind of animal. Within this fold are both
Marcel Lefebvre and the Berrigan brothers, the Warriors of Christ the
King in Spain and Christians for Socialism in Chile. The range of
social action includes the defence of established structures of oppression, and social rescue work within them, as well as Marxist and
anarchist groups, movements of non-violent protest, fighters for
racial justice, anti-abortion campaigners, radical feminists, and so on.
All of these will claim to draw on some resources within Catholic
theology. While Camillo Torres held that the Catholic who was not a
revolutionary was in a state of mortal sin, many of the supporters of
the Tridentine Mass see 'reds under the bed' even within the walls of
the Vatican.

However, while this wide range will continue to exist, it is the
official liturgical texts which will shape the future ethos of Catholic
Christianity, for *lex orandi, lex credendi*, the rule of worship is the rule
of belief. The new Roman Missal and Breviary form the daily worship
of the church, and the changes in emphases since the recent revisions

are striking. The Vatican document *Gaudium et Spes*, frequently quoted in the readings of the Office, sees the church as a serving church, and its service is in the cause of 'a new humanity', 'a new humanism'. Gone is the old language of the 'supernatural order' – in fact the word 'supernatural' is scarcely used in the Vatican texts at all. Instead we read of such concepts as integral development, humans as the centre and crown of all things, the universal destination of the world's goods. Social action is rooted in social theology. Again, the collects of the Missal are concerned to stress the social nature of the Eucharist of the people of God, and it is this language which replaces the language of the Council of Trent. The intercessions at Evening Prayer in the Breviary have a strong social flavour, referring to 'a community where justice and peace may flourish', prayers that 'human rights and freedom may be everywhere respected, and the world's resources may be generously shared', that the work of humanity may not disfigure the creation, and so on. There is a reduction in judicial and pietistic language, though the elements of prophecy and conflict are not apparent. The servant church seems to have replaced the prophetic church. The world is to be cared for and served, not to be challenged and renounced.

Now in principle, some kind of social theology based on Catholic theology was to be expected. For Catholic theology possesses certain characteristic features which would tend to lead in that direction, other factors being equal. First, Catholic theology is social theology, rooted in the theme of redemption for the world and for human society. Secondly, Catholic theology is materialistic, rooted in the crude materialism of Incarnation and sacraments, and totally opposed to the false spiritualising of both. Thirdly, Catholic theology is an inclusive theology, wide, rich, deep, and open to development and growth.

Now it would be dangerous to make a simple causal link between Catholic theology and specific commitment to social change. Many other factors – class, cultural influences, and so – are involved. But in principle Catholic theology is likely to lead to some kind of social action within the world, unlike Lutheran theology, for example, which contains within itself a violent separation of the material and spiritual kingdoms. The thinkers of the Christendom group in the 30s – Reckitt, Demant, Peck, and the young Mascall – were correct in claiming that what they called Catholic Sociology was deductible from Catholic dogma. Catholicism is incompatible with a totally irresponsible attitude to human society, it cannot assume a wholly other-worldly posture. Nor in fact has the Catholic tradition been content with a social caring or ambulance role, although that aspect has been evident certainly since the time of Gregory the Great. At the centre of the Catholic view has been the vision of the City of God which is, in Augustine's words, 'partly seated in the course of these declining times ... partly in that solid state of eternity.' The vision was of a unified society directed towards the vision of God, a renewed creation, and this vision has remained in spite of the most severe distortions of the tradition.

The changing emphasis of Catholic social thinking can be seen in the 'social encyclicals' which were initiated by Leo XIII's *Rerum Novarum* of 1891. Written against the background of 'the spirit of revolutionary changes', Pope Leo did not welcome them. In fact, he reads like a 19th-century version of Archbishop Coggan, speaking of 'crafty agitators' and condemning socialism's class war, and the various subversives who were threatening the stability of the Christian order. Pius XI's *Quadragesimo Anno* of 1931 reiterated the themes of its predecessor, stressing the rights of property, and condemning 'Christian socialism' as incompatible with Christianity. The most extreme of the Papal documents of this period was the encyclical *Ingravescentibus Malis* of 1937 which urged the recitation of the Rosary as an anti-Communist weapon, to 'rout these subverters of Christian and human culture.' This was the period when, dominated by the fears of Communism, the Latin Catholic bloc took sides in the class war against the workers, and allied itself with Fascism and reaction. So, we have Pius XI's concordat with Mussolini, the long alliance between the Roman Church and the Christian Democrats in Italy, the support of Franco and his followers ('dearest sons of Catholic Spain'), and the silence on Nazism on the grounds that 'the Pope is the Father of all the near and remote victims and culprits'. In Italy, the use of Catholic Action to ensure the victory of the Christian democrats has been a major factor in the decay of a true Catholic social conscience.

It is not simply the loss of any sense of perspective, but the apparent loss of vision of what is actually going on in the real world, which is so disturbing here. So in Italy, the Catholic social witness is often reduced to opposition to legal abortion, while the country continues to show one of the highest abortion rates in the world.

Throughout this entire period, the radical Catholic social voice was not totally silent. There were the 19th-century Catholic modernists, there was James Connolly and the Irish rebels of 1916, there was resistance to Franco from the Basque Catholics, and to Nazism from the French Catholic Left. There was the important influence of Jacques Maritain, and the Catholic anarchism of Peter Maurin, Ammon Hennacy, Dorothy Day and the remarkable Catholic Worker collective in the USA. It was in fact out of years of Catholic social thinking that there emerged in the 60s the encyclicals *Mater et Magistra* (1961) and *Pacem in Teris* (1963), the former dealing with 'socialisation', the latter with the issues of human rights, justice, equality, disarmament, migration, and so on. Pope Paul carried on from the social teaching of his predecessor, John XXIII. So *Populorum Progressio* (1967), denounced by the *Wall Street Journal* as 'souped-up Marxism', included the strongest condemnation of international capitalism and ignited the fires of revolutionary theology in Latin America. *Octogesima Adveniens* (1971), ironically issued on the 80th anniversary of *Rerum Novarum*, reduced its critique of socialism to the view that it is not 'a complete and self-sufficient picture', while Marxism was said to be 'a doctrine and method which furnishes some people not only with a working tool, but also a certitude preliminary to action: a claim to decipher in a scientific manner the mainsprings of the evolution of society'.

Nevertheless, while the general direction of the Vatican's social outlook has altered, there are still a number of distinct and conflicting theologies present in the Catholicism of post-Vatican 2. The old authoritarianism is clearly still there, as the recent disputes over the Latin rite has shown. Pope Paul brings together in his own actions the curious mingling of the progressive and reactionary elements. The same Pope who issued *Populorum Progressio*, in the same year, visited the shrine at Fatima, 'a devotion which subtly reinforced the political pattern of Salazarism', just as in 1944 Cardinal Griffin, in the context of the same cult, had broadcast to Portugal, and hailed them as the key nation who would lead Europe back to Christ. And now, with the Lefebvre movement, we see the surfacing of some very old and unpleasant aspects of Catholic social action. It is alarming that most observers have seen the dispute as merely liturgical, and ignored its close association with the resurgence of the Catholic extreme Right.

In his sermon at Lille, Lefebvre, the former supporter of Marshall Petain and opponent of universal suffrage, praised the junta in Argentina for their crushing of anarchy, and later added his praise for the regime in Chile. His supporters include many who see Salazar as the nearest to a Christian society, and for whom Mussolini and Franco were a shade too liberal. The new Catholic Fascism, like its predecessor, exalts order at the expense of freedom, opposes change and urges a return to the stable forms of the past, and fears the spectre of Communism which it sees everywhere.

On the other hand, tucked away in the pages of *Populorum Progressio* was a small section which, while it advised against revolution, accepted its legitimacy by applying the old Catholic principle of the *justum bellum* – that a revolution was unjust if greater misery would be produced afterwards than existed before. It was no doubt meant as a red light, but for the Catholics of Latin America, who were inspired by the encyclical, the Medellín Conference in 1968 issued guidelines for Catholic radicals in the Third World, and the 'Liberation theology' which has emerged from Latin America is still in its early stages. It represents a renewal of Catholic social theology, and a break with the false spirituality which has pushed the hope of the Kingdom into the next world. With St Bernard, it sings of 'the peace that is from Heaven, and shall be too for earth', sentiments which we are now inclined to sing – it is Hymn No. 495 in the English Hymnal – with a spirituality which St Bernard never intended.

Finally, what of Anglicans in all this ferment? In one sense, Anglicans are on the fringe of all the present movements, although much of the writing of the liberation theologians is reminiscent of the 19th century German Catholic socialists. Anglo-Catholicism has a mixed history as far as social action is concerned. While 'the radicalism of the original leaders of the movement is fairly easy to document', the radical stage did not last long. The Catholic socialists – Headlam, Hancock, Marson, Noel and the rest – were always a tiny minority. Certainly there were strong elements of social concern in Bishop Weston's famous speech at the Anglo-Catholic Congress of 1923 when he urged his hearers to 'come out from before your tabernacles': 'You cannot claim to worship Jesus in the Tabernacle if you do not pity Jesus in the slum ... If you say that an Anglo-Catholic has a right to hold his peace while his fellow citizens are living in hovels beneath the level of the streets, then I say to you, that you do not know the

Lord Jesus in his sacrament.' But that kind of language was soon to fade, and many have used the material improvements since 1945 as excuse for evading the task of identifying the wounds of Jesus in the new poor. Today little is left of the social radicalism of the Anglo-Catholic tradition, and the reasons for this are complex. I will merely suggest four in conclusion as pointers to discussion. First, there was published in 1933 – ironically, the year that Hitler came to power – a large book edited by N. P. Williams called *Northern Catholicism*, which put forward the thesis that there was a Catholic ethos peculiar to the countries of Northern Europe, a kind of spiritual regionalism. The thesis is now totally discredited, though the quaintly archaic and insular Anglicanism which it represented survives in such groups as the learned, but pastorally irrelevant, Alcuin Club. But the important fact, it seems to me, is that it left behind a type of nationalism which was hostile to social action, which associated Anglican Catholicism with the Union Jack and with John Bull. Secondly, and associated with this, Anglo-Catholics have become absorbed into the bourgeois and largely Erastian culture of 'Middle Anglicanism', and this has led both to a reluctance to challenge the established order, and to a decline in Catholic spirituality and Catholic prophecy, neither of which are happy bedfellows with conventional Anglicanism. Thirdly, the Catholic Movement in this country and the United States has become an ecclesiastical ghetto, marked by fear of change and a defensive posture. Ecclesiastical conservatism has become associated with political conservatism and the preservation of the old order. Finally, and most important, has been the loss of theological perspective, in which the 'regulative principle' of the Kingdom is relayed to a society in turmoil. Only when there is a dialectical relationship between these two realities can a Catholic radicalism emerge.

What is Anglo-Catholicism? [3]

When people use the term 'Anglo-Catholic' they may be referring to one of a number of movements or tendencies, and often the distinctions between them have become blurred. They may, first, be referring to something which is quite different from Anglo-Catholicism, but which is often confused with it: namely the Tory High Church tradition which derived historically from the Caroline period and which antedated the Oxford Movement of the 19th century. 'High Church' and 'Anglo-Catholic' are quite different although many people, both inside and outside the churches, assume they are synonymous.

Secondly, they may be referring to the Tractarian movement which began at Oxford in 1833: a movement which emphasised the catholicity of the Church of England, its identity with the pre-Reformation church, and its spiritual autonomy and independence of the state. The Tractarians opposed theological liberalism, and looked back to the patristic period more than to contemporary Rome as their source of authority and identity. ACism certainly grew out of Tractarianism, but the distinction between the early movement and later developments is important, historically and theologically.

Thirdly, they may be referring to what is known (incorrectly) as 'Ritualism'. (Ritual strictly is that which is related to rite, the language of the liturgy; the actions which accompany the liturgy are ceremonial, not ritual. Nevertheless the term 'ritualist' has stuck as a description of the practitioners of impressive and 'advanced' ceremonial.) The ritualist movement of the late 19th century flourished in new industrial towns, in old city slums, in seaside resorts (whence the nickname given to ACism of 'Brighton and South Coast religion') and in some very posh neighbourhoods. Ritualism contained within itself a number of different trends of which two were particularly significant and contrasted. There were those who looked to continental Rome for their inspiration both in theology and in rite and ceremony, and who became known therefore as 'Anglo-Papalists' or 'Romanisers' or, in C. B. Moss's term, 'ultramarines'. They ranged, and still range, from those who see the Church of England as two provinces of the Western Church which have become separated from the See of Rome by a series of historical accidents, to those who, while rejecting many of the Roman claims, nevertheless, in their liturgical and spiritual practice, draw heavily on Roman teaching and styles. The changes in the Roman Communion since the Second Vatican Council have meant that the kind of Anglo-Papalism which was, in a previous era, associated with such groups as the Catholic League, the Society of the Holy Cross and the Society for Promoting Catholic Unity, and journals such as *The Pilot*, *The Dome* and *Crux*, no longer exist except as a fringe oddity. However, the changed ecumenical climate has meant that a very wide range of people of differing theological emphases now feel free to draw on Roman theological, liturgical and spiritual developments in a way which has eroded much of the distinctive Papalist consciousness of the past. In this process of erosion, the 1960s was the crucial decade. In London, early Papalism became almost endemic in the Hoxton and Haggerston district of Shoreditch where it still represents the dominant version of Anglicanism.

The Papalist wing of ACism grew up at a time when the Roman Church itself was reviving its mission in England. This was the era of rococo Italian devotions, elaborate vestments, May as the 'month of Mary', and dramatic processions with banners. There was a profound devotion to the Blessed Sacrament, to Christ as 'the prisoner of the tabernacle'. Here, in the words of Father Faber, 'a helpless and captive God experiences a mournful universal solitude in the little dungeon of the tabernacle'. Much of the Catholic piety of this type was very genteel, precious and dainty. It was a form of camp/kitsch devotionalism in which the symbolism of the Sacred Heart (often portrayed as a somewhat feminine young man) and the Blessed Virgin (an agenital, almost androgyne, young woman) were almost interchangeable. Hymns to the Sacred Heart ('Sweet Heart of Jesus, fount of love and mercy', 'To Jesus' heart all burning' and so on) and to the Blessed Virgin would be high on the repertoire of these churches. Devotion to Mary the pure virgin was particularly important, and AC men and women would pray, in Faber's words:

> Thou who were pure as driven snow,
> Make me as thou wert here below.

A high mark of the Papalist movement within ACism was the restoration of the Shrine of Our Lady at Walsingham. Modern Anglo-Papalism, while it may include some of the features mentioned above, is likely also to have absorbed much of the healthier and critical theology, spirituality and social thought of Vatican 2. Many AC socialists come from this wing of the church. The widespread use of The Divine Office by ACs – to a vastly greater extent, and by a wider range of people, than was the case with the old Roman Breviary – is indicative of the different character of contemporary Roman influence in the movement.

A quite different trend within ACism was that which became known as 'English Use' or 'Sarum', often ridiculed by its opponents as

'British Museum religion'. This wing of the movement was fiercely anti-Roman, held that Anglican Catholicism was a purer and superior type of Christianity to that of the Vatican, and in its worship drew more on the medieval English ceremonial than on that of modern Rome. Within this group were both theological liberals of the Gore type, and somewhat rigid Anglican Catholics of the genre of the late Dr C. B. Moss. Moss was fiercely anti-Roman but even more anti-Protestant, and held that Anglican Catholicism was a unique and distinct species of Catholic Christianity.

A variant of these two positions which combines elements of both is found more in the Episcopal Church in the United States where Papalism of the English type never really existed. It is not uncommon in the US to find Anglo-Catholic churches which take no notice, theologically or liturgically, of the contemporary Roman developments, but which use Roman ceremonial from a previous age. Thus they continue to use books such as the English Missal or its variant the Anglican Missal which contain rites and ceremonies which were once authorised by Rome but which today do not represent the liturgical practice of any Christian church. So Anglo-Catholicism of this type represents a fossilised form of Christian presence, a way in which abandoned and obsolete forms and styles continue to exist in pockets of a sectarian kind.

Fourthly, people, particularly those within the 'Jubilee tendency', may be referring to the various forms of Catholic socialism associated with such figures as Stewart Headlam, Conrad Noel, Percy Dearmer or St John Groser. For some, the concept of ACism relates to this 'rebel tradition'. And certainly there are areas of overlap with the movements mentioned above. But the socialists drew more on the theology of F. D. Maurice than on that of the Tractarians, and in many respects it is misleading to call them ACs at all. Their theology was quite different, and there was little love lost between the Catholic socialists and the Ritualists. W. G. Peck told Maurice Reckitt that he had been rescued from 'lace and incense pietism' by the Catholic socialist movement. If one retains the term AC for the Catholic socialist tradition – and there may be good grounds for doing so – it is important to be clear that there were, and are, profound differences, theological and cultural, with other wings of the movement.

The Oxford Movement[4]

One hundred and fifty years ago, on July 14, 1833 John Keble's Assize Sermon on 'National Apostasy' began what we now identify as the Oxford Movement. The immediate occasion was the suppression of some Irish bishoprics, but beneath lay the deeper issue of the spiritual autonomy of the Church. The Tractarians rejected the whole notion of the Church–state alliance in which the Church was seen as a department of the secular power.

The movement was founded, as Newman wrote, on a deadly antagonism against Erastianism or Caesarism. Yet, while the ritualist priests from the 1860s onwards were almost all anti-establishment, within several decades the Oxford Movement had been absorbed into the 'middle Anglican' culture, and its rebel tradition had been absorbed. That situation has prevailed to this day.

This year many who celebrate this anniversary will do so with a backward-looking, romanticised view of the movement. Anglo-Catholicism today tends to cling to the ethos and rejoice in the victories of the past, but not to be easily at home in the present. Yet there are important insights in the Oxford Movement, and in the tendencies which developed from it, which are of permanent importance to the Christian consciousness.

First, the movement sought to recover the sense of the Church as a holy people, a community called to prayer and to holiness. It promoted the deepening of spiritual life, restored the Eucharist to its rightful place at the centre of Christian worship and amid violent controversy, urged the renewal of the practice of confession.

It had no time for conventional religion. Hence the emphasis on the spiritual, as opposed to the political, perspective of the movement.

Paradoxically, it was that rejection of political involvement which, in the climate of the Church–Tory alliance, made the movement most subversive. Spirituality, in a politicised Church, leads to disaffiliation.

Secondly, the movement sought to restore what Newman called 'the prophetical office of the Church'. By that he meant the teaching office, but he also wrote, in his study of Arianism, that the Church was created to meddle in the affairs of the world.

It was a later generation, the Catholic Socialists of the school of Charles Marson and Stewart Headlam, who took this seriously. They changed the course of the movement in a direction which would have horrified both the early Tractarians and the Christian Socialists of the time of F. D. Maurice. For a while their theology came from Maurice, they united that theology to a Catholic sacramental outlook. The result was a vigorous movement for social justice which, under the influence of Conrad Noel, John Groser and others in the Catholic Crusade in the 1920s, also began to grapple with issues raised by Marxism.

Thirdly, the movement was concerned with the urban poor. This can be exaggerated: the view of the slum parish as typical of the ritualist movement is certainly incorrect. In much of its manifestation, Anglo-Catholicism was a genteel, bourgeois, even dainty movement. Yet it is a fact that in many back-street districts, ritualism broke the identification of the Church of England with the middle class and with respectability. In the ministries of Lowder and Wainwright in Wapping, or Dolling in Portsmouth, we see a pastoral priesthood, committed to the poor, and unconcerned with ecclesiastical promotion. In the ministries of Headlam and Groser the pastoral becomes political.

The most valuable way to commemorate the Oxford Movement today is to work these three ends: a Church which is deeply spiritual and prayerful; a Church which will prophesy against the secular power; and a Church which will become identified with the struggles and longings of the poor and the downtrodden. But if these ends are pursued, it will mean a greater degree of seriousness in the area of spiritual discipline than prevails in most church life. It will mean a determination to work to end the Church–state alliance, for disestablishment is the logical end of the Tractarian demand. It will also mean a real commitment to social justice against those who decree iniquitous decrees and grind the faces of the poor. That may not be what Newman had in mind, but it would be a real recovery of the prophetical office of the Church.

Conrad Noel's Thaxted[5]

The strength and influence of Noel and the Thaxted movement is difficult to assess. The Crusade itself was always a small group. While there were concentrations of members and supporters at Thaxted itself, at Sneyd in the Potteries, at Ancoats in Manchester, and at Stepney, there is little in the archives to help us identify areas of support nationally or the extent of Noel's influence. There are lists of names and addresses which would merit further research. Certainly Noel was in regular demand as a speaker, and many of those who invited him identified themselves as socialist or communist. Thus R. W. Cummings, the Communist vicar of Hurst in a letter of 28 August 1920, inviting Noel to preach at a harvest festival, wrote 'we are out and out Bolshis here'.

One of the neglected aspects of the Thaxted story was the radicalism of other surrounding parishes, in particular the neighbouring village of Tilty where the Countess of Warwick had appointed E. G. Maxted. 'Tilty', Maxted wrote in 1909, 'is rapidly becoming famous as the first village in Essex to stand for socialism'. Thaxted itself, of course, exercised a remarkable attraction and power over those who came. There was something unique about it which led visitors, including many non-Christians, to write about it in a quite extravagant way. It was 'unlike any other parish church in the kingdom', wrote one reporter, while a guide to Essex described it as 'one of the few places in which it is easy to understand how religion can enrich ... life'. Here, in this spacious and beautiful church, Noel initiated a movement of celebration and thought which stressed gaiety, colour, movement, and the use of old dances. The dance was particularly important in the life of the Crusade and was seen as having a sacramental character. Noel's aim at Thaxted was to create an authentic religious culture. He believed that conventional religion, along with much in contemporary life, was shoddy and superficial. The Crusade's task therefore was one of reclaiming a lost heritage. Music was particularly associated with the envisioning of the new world.

At the heart of Noel's commitment was a profound and wide understanding of sacramental theology. In order to emphasise this sacramental understanding of reality, he felt it necessary to go back to an earlier tradition. Inevitably some were critical of this approach, seeing the style of Thaxted as nostalgic, a futile attempt to recover 'a world we have lost'. According to C. E. M. Joad, Noel 'sought to make religion a thing beautiful but apart'. Others saw Noel's attachment to the Middle Ages as a serious weakness.

In the liturgical life and celebrations at Thaxted, there was a strong democratic sense. So, for example, processions of all the people were important, and were in sharp contrast to the very clerical and hierarchical processions of the Anglo-Catholics. Services which did not depend on the priest, or where there was a central role for the laity, were stressed. Thus Benediction was valued as a 'people's devotion'. But it was the Mass that was central to the life and activity of the place.

Gin and lace[6]

It is arguable that changes both in the Roman Communion since the Second Vatican Council, and in the Christian world as a whole since the Second World War, have meant that ACism as an identifiable phenomenon has ceased to exist. Certainly many of the elements which were once the marks of the movement – the centrality of the Eucharist, confession, retreats, and so on – are now absorbed in to the culture and life of 'middle Anglicanism'. It is also arguable that, to the extent that ACism survives, it does so as an exhausted religious tradition, one which has fulfilled its historic role and is not capable of further creative developments. I am not concerned to argue these issues here. Nevertheless, one can identify a type of worship and Christian life within the Church of England which lays great emphasis on the sacrifice of the Mass and on Christ's 'real presence' in the sacrament, on the affinity with the Roman Communion, on the necessity of a recognised priesthood, and on the need for 'correct' celebrations of the sacraments. In spite of all the changes which have occurred, an AC church is still recognisable and distinctive. And the AC world has many of the features of a subculture, a minority culture within the larger cultures both of Anglicanism and of the wider society. There are certain aspects, or offshoots, of the AC movement which are worth noting at this point.

1. Its emphasis on the doctrine of the incarnation, on the material basis of all religion and spirituality. The AC stress on sacramental worship, on the place of art, music and beauty, on incense, statues and banners, was an inevitable byproduct of its theology of creation and incarnation and of the church and sacraments as the extension of the incarnation into the world.

2. The element of rebelliousness and 'nonconformity', evident not only in liturgical but also in social and cultural matters. George Orwell described ACism as 'the ecclesiastical equivalent of Trotskyism', an ironic observation since, although Orwell probably was

unaware of the fact, one of the reasons given for the expulsion of the early Trotskyists from the Communist Party was their association with Conrad Noel and the Catholic Crusade. Of course, it is also true that many Anglo-Catholics were, and are, to be found politically on the extreme right, and some have been associated with a fascist position. Yet the rebel tradition remains a significant element within the movement as a whole.

3. The phenomenon known as 'spikery'. The spike is usually a male, often a young male, who has the minutiae of ceremonial at his finger tips. Spikes are to be found in all AC churches. Their distinguishing feature is their obsessive concern with liturgical 'correctness', and at times their concern with 'doing things properly' takes precedence over the actual meaning of the liturgy and indeed of the faith itself. While there are parallels in the Roman Communion, spikery is essentially an AC creation, and does not exist in the same form anywhere else in the Christian world. It is one of the curiosities of ACism and it arises wherever that movement takes root.

4. The more or less psychopathic fringe of 'spikery' which veers off into the strange world of the episcopi vagantes, the range of curious sectarian groupings claiming valid episcopal orders from various sources. ACism and the world of irregular episcopacy have been associated since the days of Dr Lee of Lambeth and Father Ignatius of Llanthony in the 19th Century. It is easy to see how some of the elements described above might connect with the homosexual society, or at least might be seen to have connections. A religion based on the incarnation, the belief in the Word made flesh, might be expected to take human sexuality seriously, for if Christ has taken 'manhood [i.e. humanity] into God', as the Athanasian Creed claims, then that must include sexuality. Again, it might be suggested that nonconformity in one area would attract nonconformists in other areas, or that 'dressing up' in church would tend to attract male homosexual people. It is often assumed (wrongly) that all 'spikes' are gay, while the high proportion of male homosexuals among the adherents of the episcopi vagantes has provided material for the Sunday papers for many years.

Not from Oxford [7]

You cannot serve God and Mammon.

MATTHEW 6:24

It is exactly fifty years since the Anglo-Catholic Congress of 1923 at which Bishop Frank Weston delivered his memorable address. His words are even more relevant today than they were at the time.

> I say to you, and I say it to you with all the earnestness that I have, that if you are prepared to fight for the right of adoring Jesus in the Blessed Sacrament, then you have got to come out from behind your tabernacle, and walk, with Christ mystically present in you, out into the streets of this country, and find the same Jesus in the people of your cities and your villages. You cannot claim to worship Jesus in the tabernacle if you do not pity Jesus in the slum. Now mark this – this is gospel truth. If you are prepared to say that the Anglo-Catholic is at perfect liberty to rake in all the money he can get, no matter what the wages are that are paid, no matter what the conditions are under which people work; if you say that the Anglo-Catholic has a right to hold his peace while his fellow-citizens are living in hovels below the level of the streets, this I say to you, that you do not yet know the Lord Jesus in his sacrament. It is folly – it is madness – to suppose that you can worship Jesus in the sacrament and Jesus on the throne of glory when you are sweating him in the souls and bodies of his children. It cannot be done.

These words were typical of many uttered from the Anglo-Catholic pulpits of this period. Listen again, for this is also the sixtieth anniversary of the Church Socialist League's conference of 1913 when Canon Percy Widdrington said these words:

> The church has been too long the Church Quiescent here on earth, content to serve as the scavenger of the capitalist system. If it refuses the challenge it may survive as a pietistic sect providing devotional opportunities for a small and dwindling section of the community, a residuary solace for the world's defeated, administering religion as an anaesthetic to help men to endure the hateful operation of life, an ambulance picking up the wounded, entered on the Charities Register – an institution among institutions. But it will

cease to be the organ of the Kingdom, building up the world out of itself: it will have abandoned its mission and become apostate.

One could quote much more from the same period. At the 1920 Congress Father Thornton was saying that the greatest need was to rediscover the vision of the Kingdom of God on earth, and Canon Widdrington, in a volume which appeared a few years later, was claiming that such a rediscovery of the good news of the Kingdom would bring about a new reformation compared with which the reformation of the sixteenth century would appear trivial. Earlier Father Adderley was saying that the Mass was the weekly meeting of rebels against a Mammon-worshipping world order. 'You cannot serve God and Mammon' was understood in those days. They were the days of Dolling in Portsmouth, and of Stanton at St Alban's, Holborn. These men must be turning in their graves today.

What these early Anglo-Catholics possessed, and what we most manifestly do not possess, was a theology and a social conscience, and the two were inseparable. The conflict between God and Mammon grew out of their theology, for they were people whose lives and thought were rooted in the incarnation and the sacraments. Today we are part of a church which serves God weakly and Mammon strongly. But on the 50th anniversary of Bishop Weston's speech, on the 60th anniversary of Widdrington's, and on the 140th anniversary of the beginning of the Oxford Movement, where is the Anglo-Catholic movement now? It is a movement which has clearly lost its way, and which is obsessed with trivia. So, confronted with international racism and oppression, with war and injustice, with a situation where some two hundred multinational firms will soon control the bulk of the world's economy, we are discussing Series 3 and the ordination of women. I sometimes think that when the nuclear bombs have exploded and the world is devastated, somewhere on an island in the South Pacific the brave Anglo-Catholic remnant will sit amid radioactive dust discussing valid orders. We are more concerned with changes in the liturgy than with changes in the world. Ritual change has taken the place of social change. We would do well (if I may be spared another quote) to take to heart the words of another famous priest, Father Charles Marson, when he appeared before the ridiculous Royal Commission on Ecclesiastical Discipline in 1905, to answer charges of ritual atrocities, such as wearing vestments and bowing. After his evidence, Marson said:

> If the Commissioners wish for any further information as to our clothes, chandlery, or as to which of our joints we crook in worship, I shall be delighted to give them every information. But I beg leave to point out that the lives of Christ's poor are starved and stunted, that their wages are low, their houses often bad and insanitary, and their minds full of darkness and despair. These are the real disorders of the church.

At the risk of being dubbed an obscurantist I believe that we can learn more from these pioneer priests of the movement than we have done.

For if there is to be a Catholic revival in the Church of England, it will centre upon the recovery of authentic social prophecy and of authentic Catholic spirituality. The prophetic voice and the spirit of inner prayer are not two alternative ways of Christian witness: they are inseparable in a healthy Christian life, and history shows that where they are not held together, both decay. First, we need to rediscover the vision of the Kingdom of God and of the hope of the transformation of the earth. The real division among the Christians of the future is going to be about this vision: it will be the division between those who believe that the gospel has a hope for this world and for human society, and those who do not. Many who call themselves Catholic in this respect are only Catholic in externals: at heart, in their assumptions and their thought, they are protestant individualists. They have accepted the basic heresy that Christianity is only concerned with saving individual souls, and they have accepted the doctrine of the two kingdoms which are quite separate. This is not Catholicism. Catholicism is concerned with the redemption of the whole world, and it is this total vision which we need to recover. The early Catholic rebels realised that the clash between God and Mammon followed inevitably from their theology; that if they took seriously the doctrines of the incarnation, of the Kingdom, and of the Mass, this had revolutionary social and political consequences.

Secondly, there will only be a Catholic revival if there is a recovery of inner spirituality. In the last few years I have been in close touch with very large numbers of young people who have turned for spiritual guidance to eastern gurus, for spiritual guidance they assumed western Christianity was too superficial to provide. And this revival of the spiritual quest was occurring throughout the so-called 'trendy sixties', that decade when the church was at its most 'relevant' and activist, when deans were jumping in parachutes, when young curates were rushing about feverishly trying to be 'with it', and when many priests seemed to spend all their time doing every other job except their own. While all this was happening, many of the young were turning elsewhere for their spiritual strength: to Maharishi, Hare Krishna, and Guru Maharaj Ji. The most desperate need at present among priests is not for more socially active clergy, for more 'involved' clergy, and so on (although these things are important), but for more priests who are competent spiritual directors, for priests whose lives are steeped in prayer and contemplation.

We are on the verge of a spiritual revolution in the west. But the direction it will take is by no means clear. In many ways the similarities with the early Christian centuries are close. There were two great enemies of the early church: gnosticism, the false spirituality which divided the world from the 'spirit', and the totalitarian state, nicknamed in the Book of Revelation as 'Babylon the great, the mother of prostitutes'. Today we see a new gnosticism, esoteric spiritualities of all kinds, astrology, spiritualism, occult magic, and we see concentrated power and wealth, and a church which has long ago accepted and acquiesced in an unjust order. If there is to be a Catholic revival, we must recover a true spirituality and we must recover a prophetic voice, and the two are inseparable. As Daniel Berrigan says, the time will soon be upon us when the pursuit of contemplation will be a strictly subversive activity. A praying church will soon become a prophetic church, a dangerous church.

We need nothing so much as a new Anglo-Catholic revival, a new Oxford Movement. But we need not wait for it to come from Oxford, and it will not come from there. It could begin now, and it could begin here.

Holy Mary[8]

To speak of Mariology, the theology and spirituality concerned with the role of the Virgin Mary, as a problem is already to arouse suspicions or preconceptions in some minds. Devout Catholics will protest that, far from presenting a problem, Mariology is a most important and integral part of Christian faith, a gift to the Church, a priceless source of enrichment and of spiritual life. Hostile Protestant readers will be pleased to have the Marian issue presented in problem terms, for that is how they see it: a problem, a deviation, a distortion of the pure Christ-centred faith. In speaking of Mariology as a problem, I have no intention of denying its necessary place in the Church. Indeed, attitudes to Mary are a decisive test of Christological orthodoxy. Mariology does not, in my view, present a problem in the sense that many Protestants would suggest, but it does present a problem in relation to the theme of the feminine dimension in God. For the cult of Mary grew as the use of feminine images for God declined. Much of the Wisdom material in particular was transferred to Mary as were other attributes previously applied to God. So the Mother of God replaced God the Mother. Mary might be highly exalted, but she was not divine: the feminine dimension was now safely removed from the divine realm.

The main outlines of Marian theology are clear by the second century. It has been suggested that a major factor in the development of devotion to Mary was the fact that the Logos Christology tended to make Jesus a remote, heavenly figure. So the more intimate human figure of Mary compensated for the seeming lack of humanity in Christ. There is almost certainly some truth in this, though it was not what the doctrine of the incarnation was meant to uphold. At the same time, the emphasis on Mary grew as a by-product also of the christological emphases: so the question of how one saw Mary became a diagnostic test of one's understanding of the nature of Christ. 'This name,' wrote St John of Damascus of the term Theotokos (God-bearer, or Mother of God), 'contains the whole mystery of the Incarnation.' Mary also came to be seen as the embodiment of divine Wisdom, and the passage in Ecclesiasticus 24:9–10 which speaks of the origins of Wisdom came to be the standard reading in the Mass of Our Lady in the Roman rite. In the Eastern Church too Mary was seen as identical with Sophia. Thus the relationship of Mary to Christ is paradoxical. On the one hand, she is seen as the Mother of God, bearer of the incarnate Word. On the other hand, she is the recipient of titles and characteristics previously associated with divinity itself.

Another essential element in the development of Mariology was the link made by the early Fathers between Mary and Eve. Paul saw Eve as the source of sin (1 Tim. 2:9–15), and early Christian writers saw Mary as the new Eve, the woman who reversed the curse. Justin Martyr tells us that Eve brought disobedience and death, while Mary brings obedience. Gnostic writings, such as the *Gospel of Philip* and the *Gospel of Bartholomew*, also make the point that Christ was created from a virgin so that he might make good the false step made at the beginning. It is Irenaeus who most explicitly states the doctrine of Mary as the instrument of reversal of the curse of Eve. The human race fell through a virgin, and is now saved by a virgin. The knot of Eve's disobedience is loosed by the obedience of Mary. Already there is the idea of Mary as a co-redemptrix. And this theme of the reversal of Eve's work later entered into popular hymns.

> When the salutation
> Gabriel has spoken
> Peace was shed upon us,
> Eva's bonds were broken.
> As Eve, when she her fontal sin reviewed,
> Wept for herself and all she should include,
> Blest Mary with man's Saviour in embrace
> Joyed for herself and for all human race.

So Mary is seen as the mother of a new people, a free people. She comes to be seen as the first fruits of the new creation, the Church. 'Eve, Mary, Church: early theology always saw these three personages as it were through a single transparent image.'

The climax of the Marian debate in the early Church was the ascription to her by the Council of Ephesus in 431 of the title Theotokos: literally God-bearer, but more popularly Mother of God. The Antiochenes would have preferred the title Christotokos, mother of the human Jesus. Theotokos was seen as a decisive victory and a vital christological issue. To deny that Mary was Mother of God was to deny the truth of the incarnation. Yet, as Cyril of Alexandria was anxious to stress, the ascription of the title must not be understood to imply ascription of divine status to Mary. 'We ... who call her Mother of God have never at all deified any one of those that are numbered among creatures ... and we know that the Blessed Virgin was woman as we.' What was being asserted was the truth of God's taking of full humanity to himself. So fundamental was this truth to Christian faith that Gregory of Nazianzus could say that 'one who does not acknowledge Mary as Theotokos is estranged from God.' The title is therefore seen, particularly by Eastern Orthodox theologians, as the 'ultimate test of christological orthodoxy ... a key word to the whole of Christology'.

In much of the early Eastern devotion to Mary, a close link is made between Mary and the Eucharist. In both of them, there is an overshadowing of the Holy Spirit. As the Spirit, the power of the Most High, came upon Mary (Luke 1:35), so God overshadows the bread and wine in the epiclesis of the eucharistic rite. As Mary is the meeting place of God and humanity at a specific point in time, so the Eucharist is the meeting place of God and humanity throughout time. As Mary gave birth to the incarnate Word, so the sacraments give birth to Christ in us, we all conceive Christ, a theme which occurs in the writings of St Symeon the New Theologian and is later taken up by Eckhart. However, in medieval Western spirituality, there is no doubt that it was Mary who overshadowed both Father and Son! While in the Eastern Church, Marian devotion was located firmly, and to Western eyes at times shockingly, within the framework of Christology and of Eucharist, in the West Mary came increasingly to represent the tenderness and warmth which had been excluded from the transcendent Godhead.

Nor did the resurgence of the theme of maternal dimension in God from the twelfth century onwards diminish the devotion to Mary. In popular devotion, the two feminine-directed trends flourished together. Mary, wrote Aelred of Rievaulx, is the one 'who has given us life, who nourishes and raises us. She is our mother, much more than our mother according to the flesh.' More than that, in some forms of Marian devotion, Mary is our mother much more than the Trinity. In one sixteenth-century French statue, a seated Madonna holds in one hand a small world, and in the other a baby. The body of the statue is also a door, and when it is open, it reveals God the Father holding up the crucified Christ, while all the saints look on. The entire drama occurs within the womb of Mary the Great Mother!

The way in which Mariology has taken over crucial areas of divine experience is of fundamental importance for understanding the strength of the resistance to it, as well as the strength of its own grip on peoples and communities. For the opponents of Marian devotion have been right to sense that, in spite of protests to the contrary, elements formerly ascribed to God have been absorbed into the cult of Mary. It is highly significant that so orthodox a theologian as Hans Urs von Balthasar, whose influence on the thought of Pope John Paul II is considerable, can even suggest that Mariology is the only guarantee of the humanity of the Church. Von Balthasar may well be right. But what is disturbing in this passage is that Mary seems to be seen as a necessary corrective to the masculinisation of God. Mary is needed to make up for deficiencies in God, or perhaps in our theology. For it is 'without *Mariology*', not without a more holistic doctrine of God, that this writer sees the dangers of a masculine, functionalist Church. It is not therefore surprising that feminist critics of the Christian tradition such as Mary Daly, who once hoped for a reform of the Church and a reintegration of feminine insights into its theology, now suggests that Mariology be examined as a possible alternative to Christology. Mary, the Virgin, who conceived without the aid of man, stands for female autonomy, integrity, completeness; her Assumption stands for the reintegration of the divine androgyne. For if Mary can do what God the Father cannot, perhaps she can stand alone.

In orthodox Christian thought, Mary does not stand alone. Yet the exclusion of feminine understandings and symbols from the doctrine of God has meant that, on the one hand, Mary comes to carry much of the weight of deity, while, on the other, she remains firmly in her place, as an inferior being. The masculine God may be inadequate, and will need to be supplemented by devotion to the human mother, but the distance between masculine Creator and feminine creature must be firmly maintained. So it is that those who exalt Mary may at the same time be performing a major disservice to the cause of a more whole theology as well as to that of real women in the world.

Another related distortion of Mariology has been the idealisation of Mary so that she comes to represent, not real womanhood, but some 'pure', spiritual model of femininity, safely removed both from the power of sexuality and the dirt and violence of social life. In much nineteenth-century devotion in popular Catholicism, Mary becomes an asexual being. To her, men and women pray for deliverance from 'impurity'. So, taught by Father Faber, we ask:

Those who wert pure as driven snow,

Make me as thou wert here below.

These, and many other hymns of the period, identify sex with sin, Mary with purity, virginity with the Christian ideal. Mary the Virgin both symbolises and ratifies an ethic of sexual repression, seen very clearly in the effect of this devotion on the Irish manual workers' view of the world. But as a model, Mary cannot easily be imitated by women, most of whom are not called to virginity and are hardly likely to be virgin mothers, or by men. She becomes an impossible ideal, and, because of the gulf between the ideal and the reality of human life, we often find that the result is to widen the gulf between religious devotion and personal and social activity. Mary then takes her place in the grotto, the shrine, the cultic place to which we flee for a transitory escape from the real world. For men, devotion to Mary can all too easily become an escape from the demands of real women in the world.

If Marian devotion can deteriorate into a false purity, it can equally move in the direction of a weak and passive Mary. So it is not surprising that, in many statues and pictures, Mary assumes a posture of resignation, with her head tilted, her look melancholy, her entire posture one of female passivity and submission.

Against the background of the corrupt and sentimental Mariology of most of Western Christianity, the words of the late Pope Paul VI in his encyclical *Marialis Cultus* come as something of a surprise:

> The modern woman will note with pleasant surprise that Mary of Nazareth ... was far from being a timidly submissive woman. On the contrary, she was a woman who did not hesitate to proclaim that God vindicates the humble and oppressed and removes the powerful people of the world from their privileged positions.

In recent Marian writings, it is the Mary of the Magnificat who has been the theme. The Pope returned to this theme in his address at Zapopan at the time of the Puebla Conference of Latin American bishops. There he said:

> From Mary, who in her Magnificat proclaims that salvation has to do with justice, there flows authentic commitment to

the rest of humanity, our brothers and sisters, especially for the poorest and the most needy, and to the transformation of society.

This is a striking shift from most Marian devotion of past years.

Mary is no substitute for the living God, no compensation for inadequate and one-sided theologies, no escape from sexuality and from the rights and struggles of her sisters. Yet, as the small, poor Galilean woman, who became the God-bearer and sang that most radical of freedom songs, she is a central figure of hope for a Church which seeks to respond to the incarnation.

The politics of the Magnificat [9]

The Feast of the Assumption of the Blessed Virgin Mary, celebrated throughout most of the Christian world, is not a feast to arouse wild enthusiasm among English Christians.

Seen often as a polemical and divisive dogma, an ecumenical embarrassment, or arrogant assertion of papal claims in the pre-Vatican 2 atmosphere, the dogma is now widely seen as more than an irritant, at best a peripheral factor, at worst the most outrageous of the Marian heresies.

Yet in the Eastern churches this is Mary's feast *par excellence*, while Jung hailed the dogma as a sign of the restoration of the feminine dimension to the deity. Some feminist theologians such as Rosemary Reuther have pointed to the potentially liberating features of this and other Marian dogmas in an overwhelmingly male and cerebral Christian tradition. 'Liberation Mariology' is certainly on the North American agenda.

Undoubtedly much Marian devotion has been based on a distortion of the Mary of the Magnificat, the prophetic woman who according to the Anglican Consultative Council in 1973, 'praises the Lord for the radical changes in economic, political and social structures'.

The late Pope Paul VI in his encyclical *Marialis Cultus* (1974) also criticised the false Mary of corrupt piety, stressing that 'Mary of Nazareth ... was far from being a timidly submissive woman; on the contrary she was a woman who did not hesitate to proclaim that God vindicates the humble and oppressed, and removes the powerful people of the world from their privileged positions.'

In fact, the dogma of the Assumption is a development of that of the resurrection. As Christ is the first fruits of the harvest of the dead, so his Mother, the God-bearer, is raised up to share in the risen life of the glorified Body of Christ. As in the Resurrection of Christ, so in the Assumption of Mary, it is the whole personality, the *soma*, which is raised.

The Assumption rejects the dualism of body and soul which still affects the Christian world: it is the whole person which is raised, just as it is the whole material creation which is to be transformed and share the freedom of the children of God (Rom. 8).

Mary is thus the forerunner of the cosmic assumption of which Paul writes; she is the microcosm of the new and glorified creation. The dogma is in part an assertion of the materialistic base of the Christian hope.

But the raising up of Mary represents also the exaltation of the poor, the *anawim*, God's little people. Small is not only beautiful; small is Queen of Heaven. It is this reversal of power structures which Mary predicts in her 'hymn of the universal social revolution' (as Thomas Hancock called it).

God has looked lovingly on her humble state, her littleness, and as a result she will be *Makaria*, blessed. God puts down the *dunastas* and fills those in need. 'It would be easy to over-spiritualise the meaning of these verses and ignore that literal interpretation', notes the evangelical scholar Howard Marshall. 'The coming of the Kingdom of God should bring about a political and social revolution, bringing the ordinary life of mankind into line with the will of God.'

The Assumption is also a pointer towards the recognition of the feminine dimension in God. Not in the sense that Mary is exalted to the status of a fourth person of the Trinity: but rather that, through the raising of this woman to share the divine nature, we should face the necessary consequence that womanhood, as much as manhood, is involved in that nature.

God is not male, and the 'motherhood of God' needs to be taken seriously. Marian devotion can only too easily be used as a safety-valve, a way of transferring the feminine dimension away from God to an idyllic, virginal creature. So we relate to Mary, while retaining the essentially male-dominated symbolism of deity.

There is much to be wrestled with before we can assert positively that Mariology is a potentially liberating tradition. But the place of Mary alongside her Son can hardly be questioned. As the late Fr Raymond Raynes once said: 'If Our Lady is not in heaven, where the hell is she?' The truth of the resurrection demands that, whatever else we say, we must at least say that Christ is in heaven and his Mother with him.

Anglican Catholicism[10]

I recently discovered an article which I wrote in 1961, when I was 21, in *The Pilot*, the organ of the Society for Promotion of Catholic Unity, one of the papistical Anglo-Catholic groups in the UK. It was called 'Catholicism in Decay', and in it I deplored two developments in the 'Anglo-Catholic' scene at the time: the loss of any distinctive 'Catholic movement' in the sense of a dynamic tradition nurtured by theology and prayer and its replacement by a pietistic subculture; and the collapse of the radical social tradition. I compared the fate of Anglo-Catholicism to that of British socialism in the period of 'post-politics' and 'the end of ideology' and referred to the then Archbishop of Canterbury, Geoffrey Fisher, as 'an ecclesiastical Mr Gaitskell' (Hugh Gaitskell was the leader of the Labour Party and a revisionist who emphasised practical politics over against 'theology', his term for archaic, irrelevant theorising).

In 1961 I was an Anglo-Catholic of 'advanced' type, rigid and inflexible as was my politics. Politically I was a Trotskyist and had no time for revisionists and defaulters. In religion I looked to the 'catholic movement' for firm and intransigent positions on doctrine, for the defence of apostolic faith and order, and I deplored the vague and moderate centrism of establishment Anglicanism. Yet I found that the 'Anglo-Catholic' movement preferred pietism to politics, and I was appalled at its negative image. These were the years of controversy over reunion schemes and the threat to apostolicity. In East London, the church of St Mary, Cable Street, proudly and defiantly proclaimed in a large poster on its door: 'This church is not in communion with the Church of South India'.

Today things are a little different, and yet in many respects, much the same. The issue now is not CSI but women, though the same theological and ecclesial oddities flourish as in the earlier crisis. 'Anglo-Catholic' priests, although in far smaller numbers than the media claim, announce that they may become Roman Catholics at some unspecified date, though, as in the earlier period, most of them never seem to go! The spread of Catholic practices – the centrality of Eucharistic worship, sacramental confession, retreats, and so on – into the 'centre' has continued, along with the increased difficulty in identifying a distinct 'Catholic movement'. The ghetto subculture has become more gossipy, precious, and trivial, and its siege mentality has strengthened. So were I writing this article today, it would be different. And in fact I am writing it, and it is different. But much remains the same. I continue to lament the decline of an Anglo-Catholic movement and ethos which I believe has much to contribute to the renewal of Christian consciousness today, both inside and beyond Anglicanism. I continue to deplore the collapse of the radical social and political wing of the movement. However, I realise that now the preciousness, the 'gin and lace' dimensions of Anglo-Catholic identity, is not a post-1945 phenomenon but goes back to the early years of the movement. I realise too that to 'recall' many 'Anglo-Catholics' to the radical tradition is useless, for they were never part of it. It is rather like recalling John Major and his cabinet to the spirit of the 1960s.

And, of course, I too have changed. While I still prefer Trotsky to 'Anglo-Catholic' trivia, I am no longer happy with the 'vanguard' ideology either in politics or religion. When George Orwell described 'Anglo-Catholicism' as the ecclesiastic equivalent of Trotskyism, he was identifying something more profound than he realised. For in both traditions one sees the captivity to the past, meticulous devotion to the sacred text, the fetishism of correctness in all things, the utter conviction of one's own doctrinal purity, and the sectarian temptation to cultivate a world within a world. As Sheila Rowbotham wrote of her former Trotskyist comrades: 'They had all those certainties as if everything was known, the whole world and its history was sewn up and neatly categorized.'

Moreover, the ghetto subculture of 'Anglo-Catholicism' is not, on the whole, a healthy or positive force, and I think it is unlikely to produce anything creative, rather than to reinforce pathology. Much of it is nourished by what Franz Fanon termed 'the prelogical thought of the phobic'. The deep fear and dread of women is not, I believe, simply a theological difficulty but represents a profound sickness in the movement. Indeed, as the ordination of women drew closer, the more deranged and demonic features of the opposition became more pronounced: 'burn the bitches' and 'spiritual transvestites' were among the phrases used and widely quoted in the US media.

Now, of course, it is irritating (not least to the more restrained and more responsible critics of the ordination of women) to find that some of our odder clerical figures were cited in the American press as if they were taken seriously in Britain. But in a sense the opposition to the ordination of women as a whole, seems to have become more desperate: their voices have become higher and shriller, and their language more debased. The language of purity is now used, language reminiscent of the Nazi eugenics movement: we hear a need for bishops who have pure, clean, hands who are uncontaminated. The dread of women at the altar and in the sanctuary has more to do with unresolved sexual confusion (particularly around homosexuality) than with fundamental theology, and attending to this will be more helpful than anything else to emerge from this phase. If the ordination of women does nothing else, it will help to bring these questions to the surface where they can be looked at. However, it is important in spite of what has been said above, to stress how wrong it is to see most Anglo-Catholics as opposed to the ordination of women. In fact, not only do most Anglo-Catholics, on a world scale and within England, support the ordination of women, but many of the women themselves come from this tradition. (This seems to me so clear statistically, that the only way to deny it is to write opposition to the ordination of women into the definition of an Anglo-Catholic.) Indeed, were it not for this tradition, most women would not have wanted to be Catholic priests at all! It can therefore be plausibly argued that the ordination of women is one of the fruits, albeit unintended, of the Oxford Movement.

I do not think that the future for a liberated and liberationist stream of Anglo-Catholicism is bleak, but it cannot build on the ghetto consciousness or the 'gin and lace' tradition. We need to create new networks of solidarity and creativity within the tradition, building on its strengths and neglected potential. In this task the Catholic Fellowship could play a most important role.

Part Three

Ministry on the Margins

5
Inclusive Ministry

... since theology is not a purely cerebral activity,
it is important to try to live out a practical
theology of inclusion which is not idealist but
rooted in specific struggles, engagements and
alliances.[1]

The ministry of Jesus[2]

The ministry of Jesus, as described in the Synoptic Gospels, begins with the marginal people of Galilee and from there moves to Jerusalem, the seat of the mighty and powerful. He starts with the peasants, and only then, in their company, moves to the centre of power. The destitute, the unclean and ritually impure, the hopeless, the frustrated zealot militants, as well as the feverish, the blind, the paralysed and the lepers, are gathered together to form the core of the new messianic community. Jesus in fact creates a community of riffraff, and he who was himself born in the outhouse of an inn offers grace to those who had no hope of participation in the eschatological banquet.

It is these people, the excluded and the dispossessed, whom Jesus calls, and with whom he shares a common meal. This sharing of a meal was at the very heart of his ministry, his *diakonia*. So central is the meal in Jesus' ministerial style and method that it is astonishing how neglected it has been in pastoral reflection. There is no chapter of St Luke, for example, in which food is not mentioned, and the shared meal to which they were all invited plays a central part not only in the actual ministry of Jesus but in his parables of the Kingdom. Thus in Luke 14:1–24 we have the parable of the great banquet. Here Jesus teaches his disciples:

> When you give a dinner or a banquet, do not invite your friends or your brothers or your kinsmen or rich neighbours, lest they also invite you in return, and you be repaid.

But when you give a feast, invite the poor, the maimed, the lame, the blind, and you will be blessed, because they cannot repay you. You will be repaid at the resurrection of the just.

The significance of this invitation is easily missed by the modern reader. In the Levitical code, those forbidden access to the sacred food were the blind, the lame, those with mutilated faces, those with limbs too long, those with injured feet or hands, hunchbacks, dwarfs, those with sight defects, itching diseases, scabs, crushed testicles, or any blemish (Lev. 21:17–23). Similarly, in the rite of Qumran, those afflicted in the flesh, the crushed, the lame, blind, deaf and dumb, those with defective eyesight, and the senile might not attend the messianic banquet (1 Q. Sa. 2:5–22). It is this bias against those with handicaps and disabilities which Jesus reverses, and this becomes a cause of scandal. Indeed it is fair to say that Jesus was killed because of the way he ate and the company he kept. His enforced isolation in Calvary was the climax and conclusion of a ministry of subversive closeness.

The struggle on the cross was the outcome of a life of struggle and conflict. The crucifixion outside the gate in the company of criminals was the culmination of a life lived on the edge, as a friend of the rejected, and, as the outcast leper was forced to love outside the camp (Lev. 13:46), so Jesus died outside the camp. And it is there that we must follow him and serve him. 'Therefore let us go forth to him outside the camp, and bear the abuse he endured' (Heb. 13:13). In Christian discipleship there is a constant need to 'turn back to the condemned and rejected'. Indeed conversion itself is a case of 'always turning to the victim'. It is there that God is found.

In all that I have written, there are two central Christological truths. The first is the truth that Christ is found, now as then, among the poor and lowly, on the edge, at the margins. The second truth is that to be *en Christo*, to be icons of Christ, we need to follow his way of lowly servanthood, and because Christ is found among the poor, our response to the poor becomes both a diagnostic test of our Christological orthodoxy, and a sign of judgment.

What I have been putting forward is, in Latin American theology, endorsed by Pope John Paul II and the Roman Catholic Bishops. Termed the 'preferential option for the poor'. The American Roman

Catholic Bishops, in their Pastoral Letter on the economy of the US refer to it as 'the social and ecclesiological counterpart of the emptying (*kenosis*) of Jesus in the incarnation'. The option for the poor has nothing to do with any supposed innate moral goodness of poor people, or any innate sinfulness of rich people. Nor has it to do with a paternalistic and condescending idealising of poverty. It has to do with recognising that the Kingdom of God of the gospels only comes by a reversal of relationships, and therefore of structures, a putting down of the might and an exaltation of the lowly. In this sense God is one-sidedly the God of the poor and lowly. It has to do with recognising that the real values and priorities of any society are exposed and manifested in its victims. As R. H. Tawney pointed out, there is no criterion which reveals the character of any social philosophy more clearly than the way in which it treats those who fall by the wayside.

Christ is found among the poor and lowly. He is squeezed out of the mainstream onto the edge of society, and can only be found there alongside its other victims. Ministry to those whom society has rejected and marginalised must begin with a recognition and an exploration of our own marginal status as Christ's disciples.

Any authentic theology which is truly incarnational and passionate (passion-centred) must begin with a conscious act of solidarity with, learning from and standing by the people in one's neighbourhood who are at the bottom, the really helpless, the crushed and broken people. There is nothing romantic or dramatic about this. There is much pain, much personal upheaval, but a tremendous joy, liberation and release. More than that: there is a unique insight into the workings of the social order as seen from the underside of history.

Priestly ministry[3]

In my book *A Practical Guide to the Drug Scene* I suggested that there were five qualities which were particularly necessary in the priest who ministers among alienated young people, and they bear repetition here. None of them are qualities which I feel I possess adequately, and indeed I tend to view much of my failure as a pastor as the result of a failure to cultivate them. First, naturalness. There is an old Catholic maxim that grace perfects nature and does not destroy it: the Spirit of God works through human personalities with all their peculiarities, inhibitions, eccentricities and weaknesses. I find it very sad to see priests attempting to assume a role in order to gain effect, an assumed 'with-it-ness'. Certainly there is a desperate need for more beat priests, more hippy priests, more gay priests, more revolutionary priests, and one of our major problems in the Church is that so often we draw our ordinands from a fairly monochrome section of the population. The reason why ordinands are often out of touch with the growing youth culture is that they come from sections of the community which are least representative of the community as a whole – though this pattern is changing. But the answer is not for ordinands or priests to assume a facade, a way-out cover-up for a straight, conventional individual. We must never pretend to be what we are not for the sake of our image, for the sake of 'relevance', or for any other reason.

Secondly, a non-condescending approach. There is still too much paternalism around, the soup-kitchen approach, which treats people as objects of our pity: they are there to be done good to. We need to grow in humility and to care about people for their own sakes. 'If there's one thing I hate', said one young man, 'it's being worked amongst.'

Thirdly, the absence of the 'parsonic voice' and image. I really believe that the 'parsonic voice' has done a tremendous amount of damage. It is not just the dull monotony and the false impression of insincerity which it gives. It is more the cultivated style of talking *at* people, not *to* them. It is a corrupting thing which spreads like a virus: you can watch young clergy acquiring the voice, the intonation, the silly mannerisms, the precious affected air. With the voice and mannerisms goes the image of the nice, refined clergy, very fragile and easily shocked, insulated from the real world of conflict and suffering, protected by collar and dark suit from real human contact. So many youngsters feel that the priest is not really human, and that to talk about sex, for instance, would shock and shake. Too often I am afraid they are right. Certainly the natural, spontaneous way in which many young people talk about their sex hang-ups as well as their sexual pleasure would embarrass and shock a good number of inhibited clergy. So the discussion takes place when they are not there, either because the people are too kind to offend, or too scared to approach. So it is that the priest often misses out on the central areas of human life.

One result of this, sadly, is that clergy conversations tend to become pathetically trivial. One can see this at two levels. Because many people find clergy difficult, if not impossible, to talk to in a relaxed way, they restrict their conversations to superficialities. But also the clergy themselves, through an excessive cultivation of clerical gatherings, tend to talk about ecclesiastical affairs as if the whole world depended on them. The late Canon Stanley Evans once commented of one clergyman: 'Only surrounded by clergymen can he be happy: the superficial *bonhomie* of the common-room or the gossip of the sacristy appears to be necessary to his salvation.' I think that an excess of clergy meetings is as bad for the soul as an excess of alcohol is for the body. They encourage so much of the clerical image which alienates us from ordinary people.

Fourthly, a sense of humour. One of the authentic signs of freedom is laughter. I think that it is very important for priests to be laughed at. A ridiculously well-developed sense of the irrational and absurd is really important in contemporary youth culture. If all the clergy started to take *Private Eye* instead of some of the dreadful church papers, it would be a help.

Finally, confidentiality and trustworthiness. The priest needs to be seen as a reliable person whose confidence can be taken for granted. The issue of confidentiality is of the greatest importance. One's whole reputation as a priest may be damaged by a breakdown at this point. If one is not trusted, one cannot hope to be heard.

But, in the end, any recital of qualities and virtues must sound artificial and unreal. One cannot learn to be a true pastor from any book. I cannot hope to convey much more than a glimmering of how one approaches pastoral work simply by writing about it: so much depends on the kind of person we become. We can only show the fruits of the Spirit if we are filled with the Spirit.

Drugs and theology[+]

The Christian involvement in the drug scene has not always been an entirely happy one, and it is never free from certain dangers. These have been principally related to a false sectarianism or to a false spirituality. The sectarian mentality encourages some Christian groups to work in isolation from both the non-Christian groups and from Christians of different traditions. Thus one frequently finds exclusive and somewhat narrow groups functioning on the fringe of the drug scene, refusing to co-operate or to liaise with medical, psychiatric, and social agencies, for reasons which appear to themselves to be sound. Some of these groups put little faith in therapeutics, or, if their literature is a good guide, in accurate knowledge. Through their lack of co-operation and their apparent unconcern for strict factual accuracy, these fringe groups have often brought the Christian witness into disrepute.

Associated with this danger is that of a false spirituality which sees 'drugs' as one facet of a revolt against the established order and as being almost evil in themselves. Thus one finds Christians tending to adopt two disastrous positions. The first is to see the attack on drug misuse, sexual promiscuity, and the so-called 'permissive society' as a desperate last-ditch defence of the *status quo*. So one finds only too often Christians who take a 'hard line' on this limited field of morality adopting the most reactionary attitudes on race, housing, capital punishment, homosexuality, and nuclear weapons. The second position in fact is the theological basis of the first, for much of Christian thinking here has been tainted with the Manichean heresy, with its view that the flesh is evil in itself. Thus these Christians are led to a vicious type of 'puritanism' in which the attack on drugs goes hand in hand with a hatred of much in the secular world.

Against this Christians need to assert the goodness of creation, the need to see drugs as gifts of God to be used rightly within the order of redemption, and the fact that the church is by no means associated with the established order against which so many young people are rightly in revolt. The experience of the East Harlem Protestant Parish has shown how the body of Christ can become a revolutionary unit and exercise a disruptive and transforming influence within a disturbed and diseased society. In this country too, no task is more urgent than the recovery of the Church's role as an instrument of change.

But it must be change from within. In Soho we see our position to be four-square *within* the drug-scene, to care for it, to learn from it, perhaps to change it, but from the inside. This is the pattern of incarnation: within the subcultural groups, within the loneliness and disintegration, within the heartbreak and hopelessness, the Word becomes flesh.

Drugs and ministry[5]

The Christian ministry in the field of drug use and addiction raises many of the key theological ideas about sin, grace, human will, the world, and the Kingdom of God, which divide Christians, and it also offers a possible creative site for working through them ecumenically in co-operative action and praxis-based reflection. There is not space here to engage in a detailed theological examination of all these themes, but several of them are worth noting.

First, there is the concept of addiction and its relationship with humanity and human sin. Although addiction is conventionally seen in terms of sickness, there has been a trend recently in some circles to see addiction as a form of manifestation of original sin. 'Everyone is an addict of something' has become a fashionable concept, not only among Christians. The words 'addiction' and 'addictive' have become clichés and thought-substitutes in much writing. The context in which addiction arises is often ignored, so that the focus comes to be exclusively on personal sin, and on the addict as one trapped within the addictive prison. There is a tendency to equate victim and perpetrator. But, leaving aside whether sin and addiction can be equated, sin cannot be reduced to a single cause. There is a need to distinguish sin from victimisation. There is a self-surrender which is due to coercion or convention, as well as self-surrender willingly to a drug, or, under different circumstances, to the will of God. Here the Catholic stress on context, on the process of sanctification, and on detail and particularity can help us to avoid harmful generalities.

Secondly, what kind of God do we believe in? The view of God which is found in some religious groups working with addiction issues is often that of a dictator and controller. God can easily be portrayed as an alternative, albeit better, form of addiction. Christians need to be careful that we do not offer a diminished and trivialised understanding of God as a response to drugs. When Marx called religion an opiate, he was making an important observation – and a warning.

Thirdly, it is important to stress that there is no specific 'ministry to drug users'. The use of drugs raises specific questions and problems, but Christian ministry is to all people. The modern habit of labelling people (client, addict, alcoholic, and so on) does not fit well with the Christian view of what it is to be human or with the doctrine of the

Body of Christ in which all are equal. Nevertheless, the field of drugs can help to illuminate neglected areas of ministry and help us towards a clearer understanding.

Finally, there is a central place for silence, darkness and the way of 'unknowing'. Pastoral ministry in the drug field calls for a profound spiritual rootedness in God, and for those essentially priestly tasks of eucharistic sacrifice and adoration, intercession, and solidarity in Christ through the sharing of silence and darkness. I emphatically do not mean that these are tasks only for ordained priests, but rather that it is here that the priestly character of the whole Church, in which, of course, ordained priests and ministers have an important role, is most clearly revealed. This largely hidden dimension of the Body of Christ is of particularly central significance in a field such as drug addiction where it is not possible, much of the time, to see the prospect of immediate change, and it is important to stay with the pain, the wounds, the brokenness, the repeated crises and the darkness, in faith and trust.

Sacramental ministry, including the ministry of anointing and deliverance, is important in this area, and both laying on of hands and anointing should be exercised, with due care and preparation, but frequently and repeatedly. Often sacramental ministry, which relies on symbolic objectivity rather than on personal feeling, or intellectual argument will be of greater value than anything else.

The experience of work in the field of drug use can help to illuminate the nature of priesthood and sacrifice. It can help to bring out more deeply the inner reality of life in Christ. For the roots of priesthood, of the sacrificial ministry of the Church, lie in the redemptive work of Christ. Much ministry in the drug scene is marked by darkness, silence and uncertainty. It calls us to an apophatic style of pastoral care in which clarity and method give way to waiting and 'unknowing'. It calls us to recover some very traditional themes – the spirit of sacrifice, the theme of priesthood as an interior life not simply a job, the emphasis on ascetical discipline and on the practice of the Christian life. The priestly ministry is concerned with the work of intercession, of healing, of reconciliation, and this calls for a profound inner *ascesis*, a dark night of the soul, a sharing in Christ's dying and rising. In a world where many die alone and abandoned, the central task of the Church is to share that darkness and be a powerful witness to life beyond the tombs.

The experience of pastoral care in the drug scene is one which illuminates and reinforces the importance of stability and persistence through times which seem hopeless and bleak. It is not an experience of quick fixes or of band-aid ministry though it certainly includes this as an important element in the total picture. But it is an experience of sharing in the revolutionary patience of the God who transcends time, and who will heal and transform in strange and unexpected ways. Our task is to be faithful and attentive.

Homelessness[6]

From the beginning of our work with young people, the phenomenon of homelessness loomed very large. On 22 April 1968, I gave a talk to the Westminster Christian Council, an ecumenical group of Christians in the area, on accommodation needs for young people within the City. A Social Responsibility Working Party set up by the Council in 1976 had reported, not surprisingly, that the most pressing need in the City was for accommodation for the large and increasing numbers of homeless youth. On 3 April 1968, the Medical Officer of Health for the City of Westminster called a conference of all those concerned with the care of drug addicts in the City. One reason for calling the conference was a concern that 'unless a unified policy is agreed by all the parties concerned there may well be some overlapping of effort and perhaps over-provision of services and this, of course, should be avoided'. Nothing resulted from the conference although a number of people stressed the extreme urgency of the situation. In fact, we have found over the years that, in the field of accommodation for the homeless, the statutory bodies are often extremely unhelpful, and tend to leave most of the difficult problems to voluntary workers.

In November 1969 a group of us, including the Rink Project workers and a number of members of the Simon Community house in Camden Town, became very conscious of a major gap in our West End work. All of the agencies in Soho appeared to be spending most of their time in helping the same individuals, the 'West End regulars' who were known to us all. But at the same time, thousands of new youngsters were pouring into and through the West End, more new kids were getting involved with prostitution, new faces were appearing on the drug scene, and very little preventive work was being attempted. We felt that a new emphasis was needed in trying to avert the casualties and crises whose consequences we saw daily. As we discussed this, we realised that beneath us the basement of St Anne's stood derelict, unused for years, a virtual rubbish dump. So the idea of 'Centrepoint' was born.

We called our new project 'Centrepoint' because it was geographically at the centre point of Soho, and also as an ironic contrast to the other Centrepoint, the luxury office block which stood empty and useless a few hundred yards away. On 16 December we opened the converted basement as an overnight crisis centre where young people who were new to the West End could be accommodated and given immediate advice and help. The people we had in mind were new arrivals, youngsters who had come to London in search of work, or who had run away from difficult home situations and who were at risk of becoming homeless and destitute. We worked out a system of staffing with the Simon Community, a body which for six years had been involved with homeless, isolated people, and it was through Simon helpers that the project got off the ground. Neil McGhee, a little Scotsman, and Bill Rice from Limerick, were our first project leaders, and did a fantastic job. In the first two months we took in 600 youngsters, and the figure had risen to 1,000 by the end of three months. Of these, 670 were newcomers, of whom eighty-nine were from Glasgow, forty-five from Manchester, and thirty-five from Dublin. Fifteen per cent of the newcomers were Scottish.

In the first year of its existence, Centrepoint was taking in an average of twenty people each night, about 5,000 over the whole year. Our clients came from three main sources: Euston Station; voluntary agencies such as BIT, Samaritans or St Martin-in-the-Fields; and the local 'grapevine'. The contact with Euston Station proved immensely useful, for here the newcomers from the north arrived. Our workers found the British Transport police enthusiastic and helpful, and we soon established a practice of having a Centrepoint car at Euston each morning about 1.00 a.m. Other organisations were a main source of referral. In particular 'Benburg Base', a centre for the care of Irish youth, was tremendously cooperative. They provided us on three nights each week with several sisters, a priest, and other workers, and we referred new Irish youngsters to them for extensive counselling, accommodation or employment. During 1970, as a result of the troubles in Northern Ireland, we found an increasing number of

Belfast youngsters arriving. But it was Glasgow and Scotland generally which provided the largest single minority groups, and it is
important that a Scottish equivalent to Benburb Base should be
established in London as soon as possible.

In November 1970 Centrepoint and the Simon Community separated. A new committee was set up and we were fortunate in obtaining a number of large donations from individuals, and later given
several sizeable grants, so were able to employ a full-time director in
February 1970 who had previously been in charge of a rehabilitation
unit for alcoholics, and was closely involved with research activity. He
provided exactly the right help we needed at the consolidation stage of
Centrepoint: a strong, experienced worker, with a deep knowledge of
human problems, and a wide range of contacts. Our hope for Centrepoint is that it will expand into a twenty-four-hour service, providing extensive referral and counselling where necessary, but its primary
role remains that of an emergency all-night service for newcomers.

The Simon Community had been active in the field of homelessness long before the establishment of Centrepoint. I think that they
have been leaders in two directions in particular. First, in helping to
eliminate the 'we–they' syndrome in social work, and to emphasise
the unity of helpers and helped. Secondly, in rejecting the dividing
and labelling of human beings into 'problem' categories – alcoholics,
psychopaths, drug addicts, and so on – and treating them as human
beings with a wide range of needs and difficulties. The early Simon
houses refused to categorise people and did not attempt to be an
amateur social work department. Their houses of hospitality were
pointers towards what the Christian Church as a whole ought to be: a
non-judgmental, caring, loving community, accepting people as they
are in Christ's name. It is worth remembering that Simon, although it
has accepted workers of all faiths and none, has persistently maintained that its ideals and inspiration are Christian, and Anton
Wallich-Clifford, its founder, at least, seems to view it as a new-style
religious order. In Ireland, where Simon houses are more closely allied
with the Roman Catholic Church, this vision may be realised earlier
than in England.

Another body with which we have worked in the field of homelessness is Christian Action. David Brandon, who has acted as a social
work consultant to both Christian Action and Centrepoint, was a
friend of mine from Hoxton days, when he ran the London County

Council's Welfare Office for the Homeless at Charing Cross. His publications *The Treadmill* (1970) and *Homeless in London* (1971) have been major contributions to the fight for better housing and care of homeless people. With David's help, Centrepoint was involved in 1971 in a protest to the Registrar-General about the Population Census. We pointed out that while protests were being made, rightly in my view, about the questions on the birthplace of parents, there were a large number of homeless people who would not have a chance of answering the questions at all! A few weeks after the official Census, Christian Action conducted its own Census of the Homeless, using Centrepoint as its headquarters. In November 1971, Christian Action itself moved into Soho, and opened a shelter for homeless women in Greek Street, very near to St Anne's House.

Marginality and Mammon[7]

On the 26th June 2004 the *New York Times* ran an article entitled 'When faith and duty collide'. Police Officer Eduardo Delacruz had refused to arrest a homeless man in November 2002, and, as a result, had been suspended from duty. The story took me back to an earlier one, also in the USA, the story of Keith McHenry of the Food Not Bombs organisation in San Francisco, who had, between 1988 and 1994, been arrested 92 times for giving food to homeless people, contrary to local legislation.

I read the *New York Times* article as I was wading through thousands of papers, preparing to leave East London, trying to decide what to throw out. One of the papers I found was the Report to the City Deanery Synod on the proceedings of the General Synod meeting in February 2004, written by a person entirely unknown to me who took exception to one of the new collects of the Church of England, that for the 2nd Sunday of Christmas, in which Christians pray that God 'would lead us to seek Jesus among the outcasts and to find him in those in need'. This 'undermined the gospel by encouraging the idea of salvation by good works'. It is interesting to see the illogical jump, for the collect says nothing about 'works', but about seeking and finding, about presence. (Though Matthew 25:40, presumably the source of the offending collect, does focus on works: 'just as you did it to one of the least of these who are members of my family, you did it to me.')

Here we have two conflicting visions of the church, of the gospel, and, I suspect, of God. And what is shown in these two snaps is a microcosm of the Christian world.

So I want to reflect on ministry, marginality and Mammon, and on the church's preferential option for the rich. I must confess that the phrase is not original. It was my friend John Atherton, recently retired as Canon Theologian of Manchester Cathedral, who used it after a month in Chicago over 20 years ago. As he left the diocesan offices, he commented that the work of the Anglican church there was a manifestation of the church's 'preferential option for the rich'.

Chicago is an interesting case study for we see there the most extreme examples of 'polarisation' between rich and poor, white and black, of any city in the western world. The 'mainstream' churches have followed the wealth. In many of the very poor areas, Anglicanism has virtually disappeared, though Roman Catholics, Baptists and black-led churches such as the Church of God in Christ are often still present. (The Roman churches are closing as a result of lack of priests, sexual abuse claims, etc.)

The churches in Britain have a different history, not least in relation to social and political critique of governments, and to local social action. Yet as I leave as chair of UNLEASH, I think we have some cause for concern about the church's priorities. I don't say this to depress you, but to spur you to militancy. I want to make three claims and submit them to scrutiny and, if possible, refutation. But, if they turn out to be right, to action.

1. The churches are in danger of neglecting real pastoral ministry in favour of the cultivation of financial support in the interests of survival.

2. The people who will suffer most from this neglect are those on the margins who can provide no financial or direct support for the institution.

3. What matters most to the churches as institutions is adaptation to, and acceptance by, the power structures. They have taken seriously the words of Jesus 'You cannot serve God and Mammon' and they have opted for Mammon.

I want to draw on the thinking of two people who influenced my own thought greatly in the 1950s and 1960s, and in the second case until the late 1980s: Stanley Evans and Ruth Glass. Much of what they predicted has come true, many of their insights have been lost, most of what they said is more relevant today than when they said it. So in tribute to them I want to use their work as a way of looking at ministry, marginality and Mammon.

Evans, an Anglican priest, spent most of his ministry in East and South London. He wrote a good deal but the book which is most relevant to our concerns is very small: *The Church in the Back Streets* (Mowbray, 1962), only 50 pages long. It is a classic, rooted in his experience in the inner city. He coined the term 'the Church Condescending' as a way of describing how good, dedicated people moved into poor areas to minister to (rather than with) those whom they saw as belonging to a lower culture. These people were there to 'be done good to'. Evans went on to point out that at a certain stage, when 'these stupid, ungrateful people don't come', the Church Condescending turns into the Church Indignant. That syndrome is still alive and well. In his book he stressed the central place of argument, debate and local theological engagement. Every local church needed to be a thinking church, constantly grappling with issues 'from street crossings to hydrogen bombs'. Is this still happening, or have we fobbed it off to Boards for Social Responsibility (which the Archbishops' Council seems keen to abolish)? And he stressed the danger of substituting respectability for militancy. 'The Church respectable can do many things but it cannot convert.' How right he was. As I re-read Evans over 40 years on, I wonder how much progress we have made.

Ruth Glass was an atheist, a Marxist, a refugee from Nazi Germany, and the pioneer of urban sociology in Europe. She taught urban studies at University College, London, for many years, and is famous for having coined the word 'gentrification'. Most sociologists refer to her first use of the word in 1964, but I have an unpublished study by her of North Kensington housing in 1959 where she uses the word 'gentrified'. It took some thirty years for people to realise what she was saying: that there was a real danger that poor people and people in middle-income groups would be squeezed out of parts of Inner London which would become ghettoes of the wealthy or of the intelligentsia. This has now happened.

She also warned, in the early 1960s, of the likelihood that there would be a growth in the numbers of 'marginal people', including homeless people, in inner London, and that social polarisation would increase. This has also now happened.

In an essay on 'Conflict in Cities', dated 1966, she predicted that there would be riots or uprisings in many cities before 1984, and warned people who were concerned with justice that 'aloofness from conflicts does not lead to their comprehension'. Ruth was, in Gramsci's terms, an 'organic intellectual', one who put her intellectual work at the service of the local communities in their struggles for justice and equality. Her refusal to stay aloof from conflicts is now not common among academics who are looking over their shoulders for funding and for 'tenure'. Again, how much progress have we made?

As far as the churches are concerned, my sense is that they want to avoid conflict as much as possible, to be 'well thought of' (maybe this is the flip side of 'done good to', those two phrases ending, ungrammatically, with a preposition which sums up so much of our lives), in fact, to cause no offence. Mammon is powerful, and churches are happier as chaplains to Mammon than as prophets against it. We all want a quiet life. But the decline, and financial instability, of the church could be a trigger for a resurgence of the radical prophetic tradition. The fall of Babylon is often, though not inevitably, the impetus to the new Jerusalem. When you have nothing left to lose, you can stick to your principles. It would not be the first time that a crisis of the church would 'UNLEASH' the resources of the gospel.

Managerial ministry[8]

Nearly ten years ago, an article by the then Bishop of Chichester, Dr Eric Kemp, 'Following the example of Mammon', appeared in the *Church Times* (17 November 1995). It warned about the centralisation of power in the Church of England, and the danger that archbishops would come to be seen as managing directors.

The following day, Professor Richard Roberts, writing in The *Independent*, described Archbishop Carey as 'the John Birt of the Church of England', and the Church as a managed product-driven organisation.

These words still haunt me. They seem to confirm my worst fears about the Church. I am not attacking central institutions, or even bureaucrats as such, but questioning where our priorities should lie.

The retirement of the Ven. Gordon Kuhrt as head of the Ministry Division (previously ABM, previously ACCM, previously CACTM), and the advertisement for this highly paid post must bring up the question what Anglicans think ministry, and the Church, is about.

Bureaucratic centralisation has increased my worries about the Church's ideology – and its lack of theology.

Do I want to encourage yet more highly paid officials, some of whom may be priests, but who are basically managers, based at Westminster? Do I want to encourage the view of ministry expressed in Dr Kuhrt's book *An Introduction to Christian Ministry* (Church House Publishing, 2000) – a kind of 1950s managerial Evangelicalism, with little attention to priesthood, diaconate, sacraments, or the world? Of course not. I want to begin with the theology of Church and ministry.

The theology of baptism is crucial. Though it hardly figures in recent English writing on ministry, it is central in much that comes from the United States, and from the early Christian centuries. Experience in the remarkable, poor, but immensely creative diocese of Northern Michigan in ECUSA has shown how harmful has been the substitution of ordination for baptism, and the debasement of the laity.

The former Bishop of Northern Michigan, the Rt Revd Tom Ray, wrote in 1996: 'In terms of authority, dignity and expectation, there is a greater distance perceived between the baptised and the ordained than the distance between the baptised and the unbaptised. To the degree that there is any truth in this observation, to that degree we are in deep trouble.'

That diocese has abolished the word 'laity' because of its associations with 'untrained', 'second-class', and so on. It speaks simply of 'the people of God'.

From CACTM to the Ministry Division, as far as I can tell, the chief executives have always been white, ordained males. None seems to have been appointed for his theological expertise, though many have had considerable pastoral experience.

In spite of the increasing stress on diversity of ministry, none has been a lay person. In spite of the stress in reports on participation, formation, and 'life-long learning', my sense is that none of this has been reflected in appointments to this post.

There is also the problem of Church House itself, where I worked from 1981 to 1987. Its ethos owes more to the Civil Service than to the Christian tradition. The central Church has never had an institutional form that is related to the gospel.

So much of recent writing on ministry has been functionalist.

What about the Christian minister as a person of prayer? 'Prayer' does not even appear in the index of Dr Kuhrt's book. Yet, surely, if sacramental diaconate, priesthood, and episcopate can be justified at all, they can be defended and strengthened only by an emphasis on the character of ministry.

Themes such as silence, prayerfulness, and inner maturity are surely more important than most of the issues with which the ecclesiastical institution seems concerned. Dr Kuhrt's book hardly spoke of the laity, except to say that 'The Church needs to mobilise lay people'. Some of us thought the Church *was* lay people.

By contrast with Northern Michigan, the Church of England, in its national persona, seems excessively managerial, lacking in creative imagination, and untraditional. (Nothing is so central to the great tradition as the doctrine of the Body of Christ, while clericalism and bureaucracy are relatively modern phenomena.) I wonder whether this is where our focus should be, not to mention our money.

The Church has moved on, and centralised bureaucracies such as Church House are increasingly archaic. The future of ministry lies more among the majority of the Church, who are not ordained or deacons, priests or bishops. This is where the energy lies, and where the Holy Spirit is most active.

We ought to be reconfiguring ministry at the local level, and trusting that the national Church will catch up in due time. Speaking to colleagues in Cornwall, another poor but creative diocese where ministry is thriving, I was told that Church House seemed utterly irrelevant. Frances Ward's recent study *Lifelong Learning* (SCM Press, 2005) could help us move forward.

In case this is seen as sectarian, let me draw attention to the focus in the Second Vatican Council on the importance of the *ecclesia particularis*. And to the fact that most of the progress within Anglicanism in England and in other places has occurred because movements of renewal have developed at the local level.

There have been enduring examples of the renewal of ministry all over the Church. After 46 years in London, I moved last month back to my birthplace in Manchester. In both cities, I have been impressed by the holistic understanding of ministry in place after place. The local church is flourishing in many areas.

Perhaps the future of ministry depends less and less on the bishops and the bureaucrats. But, the future of the bishops and the bureaucrats depends very much on the nurturing of the grass roots. What is the point of bureaucrats and the episcopate if the rest of the Church has withered? In the world of *episcopi vagantes*, where almost all are bishops and there are few laity, this is fine – but is this what we want in the Church of England?

Local theology[9]

'Doing Theology in the Community' was the theme of a Consultation held by the Christendom Trust at the end of June 1992, in which a number of people involved in CAP and ACTS participated. The aim of this consultation was to bring together people who, in different contexts, were committed to the pursuit of theology from a community base outside of academia. It was clear that there is now a growing network of people throughout Britain, and in other countries, for whom the liberation of theology from its academic captivity, and the relocating of theology within the local community, is a vital concern. One of the papers which was circulated at the Consultation was Robert Schreiter's 'The Community as Theologian' which originally appeared in the French journal *Spiritus*. Schreiter's earlier book *Constructing Local Theologies* has been an influential text in this field, and Schreiter himself has played a major role from his base in Chicago in helping to earth theological concerns in both a local and a global context. Yet this has been in stark contrast to most western theology, which has lacked any corporate or collective dimension.

So, in the work of ACTS, we are, in a small way, involved in a revolution: rescuing theology from its elitist ghetto, restoring it to the people, reclaiming it as the people's work. Ordinary people do not stop asking extraordinary questions just because academics have hijacked the idea of serious thought. Such thought goes on in pubs, laundrettes, at street corners: theology as a struggle with the meaning of life and of God is a back-street task. ACTS and similar groups have not created this: they have recognised it, affirmed it, taken it seriously.

What then is the theological task to which groups such as ACTS are committed? I suggest that three elements are important. The first is the work of excavation. F. D. Maurice, in the 19th century, said that his main task as a theologian was to dig. If, as Julian of Norwich held, God is 'the ground in which we stand', this must be seen to embrace personal and inward and also corporate and social dimensions. God is not encountered in the abstract, or directly, but in the midst of concrete, highly personalised and politicised struggles. And these struggles call for understanding, for a kind of rigorous engagement which is analogous to the effort of digging. Such work is exhausting, slow, and never completed. The theologian, and the theologising community, must keep its ear to the ground, for there are hidden voices, neglected voices, to be heard, obscure truths to be uncovered, weeds to be dragged out into the light, much dirt to be handled. Digging is messy. It demands deep involvement in concrete issues.

A second task to which local theology is committed is that of articulation. *Theologia* means a word about God, and so the issue of language is crucial. A major problem here is the class character of institutional theology, itself an aspect of the class role of the academy. The theologian who seeks both to learn from and to serve communities of people needs to resist the pressure of the academic world to distance himself or herself from their roots. This is a persistent theme of the American black feminist writer Bell Hooks.

Theology is about articulation, about a community which seeks to express as clearly as possible its faith and hope in such a way that the widest possible range of people can respond to it. This process has to begin by a deliberate act of identification with the struggles of people at a specific point. Only from such direct involvement can we speak with integrity and true significance. Much of the work of ACTS is to do with struggles – struggles around housing, health care, employment, and so on. But there is a deeper struggle – the struggle to be taken seriously. For we are in a period when poor people, working-class people, people who do not conform to the spurious norms of the enterprise culture, are easily marginalised and written off as being of no significance.

Church-based communities may be, and in fact often are, extremely important here. For such communities are often radically different from many groups which operate at the level of education, many of which have only the most tenuous ties to the neighbourhood in which they are located. Although there is worrying evidence that the church has swallowed uncritically much of recent bureaucratic and 'professional' thinking, there is still in many places a rootedness in local communities which makes critical theological work a real and exciting possibility.

Finally, theology has to embrace the nurturing and nourishing of vision. The American theologian Walter Brueggemann has written extensively on the theme of the church as a community which offers an alternative reality, a subversive presence in any community. In seeking to express an alternative reality, theologians must work closely with others who engage in 'abnormal discourse'. Mainstream discourse, in political and cultural life, operates on the basis of certain accepted conventions. 'Abnormal discourse is what happens when someone joins in the discourse who is ignorant of these conventions or who sets them aside' (Rorty). I think that ACTS contains people in both categories. So, in order to make sense of ACTS, we need to understand something of this background. This activity is part of a wider movement, the world-wide quest for a theology of liberation. Such movements always begin on a small scale, with what seem to be trivial and localised issues. But they are of massive significance. Theology as a discipline is by its nature both local and global, concrete and eternal, in its origins and perspective.

May I add a final and personal word. As a Mancunian who has greatly valued the chance to spend more time in Manchester through this and related projects, I wonder whether there is perhaps something of importance for ecclesial communities in terms of breaking the hegemony of London over so much of what goes on in action and thought. The 19th-century novelists saw Manchester as the touchstone of a new industrial order, and my impression is that there is a good deal of digging, of articulation and of alternative vision among communities, including, but not restricted to, the churches, in Manchester and the north-west, much of it in sharp contrast to the exhausted and dated approaches of many London groups and movements. If theology is about breaking moulds, about new contexts, about dreaming dreams, and seeing visions of what could be, maybe Manchester – and, by extension, a whole range of places – needs to recognise its potential.

6
Faith and Race

... the role of religion will continue to be important, and no engagement with race and racism will be adequate which does not take this role into account.[1]

The God of the Jews[2]

The history of Israel is in a sense the history of God. That is the crude and startling fact of Old Testament revelation. In the progress from Haran to Babylon and beyond is to be found the earthly progress of God himself, a progress which culminates in the incarnation of the Word, and the raising of humanity to share the divine life. In the Old Testament, God enters into human history through a covenantal relationship with a particular people, the Jews. And, so Jesus tells us, it is from this people that salvation comes (John 4:22). It was to the Hebrew people that God said 'You only have I known of all the families of the earth' (Amos 3:2); upon Israel God had 'set his heart in love' (Deut. 10:15; cf. 23:5).

Jewish experience of God, from Abraham to the present, has been the experience of people in solidarity with each other, responsible for each other. 'Where is your brother?' (Gen. 4:9) has remained, across the centuries, a fundamental test of discipleship. 'Unless your ... brother comes down with you, you shall see my face no more' (Gen. 44:23) might be seen as God's own words to his people. For it is in community that God makes his presence known. The experience and vision of God is inseparable from the experience and vision of the brother/sister: to see our brothers and sisters in true perspective is to see something of the divine. In their desert experience of struggle, and in their attempt to embody both holiness and justice in the Law, the Jewish people came to know God not on the fringes, but in the midst of human society. Jewish theology can therefore be seen as a 'theology of recital', a proclamation of the acts of God. For the Jews, Word is inseparable from Act. It is in social history that God is revealed and that redemption occurs.

It is vital that we see the Christian understanding of God against the Old Testament background. The neglect of the Old Testament and of the essential 'Jewishness' of Christian theology and spirituality has led to the most appalling distortions of the gospel. The contempt for the material world and relapse into pagan approaches to matter, nature, and history; the 'privatising' of God and the false interiority which reduces spiritual life to an inner experience of the individual; the loss of the link which joins social justice to spiritual insight: these and many other evils are connected with the neglect of the Old Testament roots of Christian faith. The Christian God is first of all a Jewish God.

The contrast with pagan notions of God's relationship with the world is striking. In pagan religion, the life of the individual was an integral part of the sacred, rhythmical pattern of nature, a divine state of order and harmony, in which both humans and non-humans had their appointed place. Paganism was essentially a religion of hierarchy, order, and preservation of the *status quo*. However, the biblical God was revealed as Lord of nature, transcending the natural order. While his revelation is associated with thunder and lightning, wind and sea, the stress is on his use of these natural forces. Yet he remains beyond them all, and the unique relationship with Israel, involving an absolute demand and even jealousy, undermined and destroyed the whole basis of pagan religion. The doctrine of Yahweh's jealousy is of particular importance, for it introduces a tension at the heart of the spurious harmony of the pagan order, destroying human integration into the structure of nature.

The Jewish God therefore enjoyed a unique relationship with matter. He was also the Lord of history. Again, the contrast with paganism is very clear, for pagan religion had no doctrine of God in history, no doctrine of election, no covenant relation. Jewish theology sees knowledge of God as historical knowledge, but history means not simply general history, but salvation history, the history of God's dealings with Israel in specific acts and events. It has been said that history is the lengthened shadow of a man, and Israel, before it denoted a people, was an actual person, Jacob, the cheat (Gen. 27:36), who deceived his father, robbed his brother, and wrestled with God in a conflict from which he emerged wounded. The community of Israel, the community of salvation, received its name from this rather dubious character. And in a sense one can portray the entire history of the people as the lengthened shadow of Jacob, a prolonged wrestling with God until the light dawns, a process of perpetual interrogation and struggle. It is this history of persons and communities in conflict which provides the content of revelation. To neglect the Old Testament and the historical revelation is thus to fall prey to an idealist notion of God as pure spirit, a reversal to paganism. Today's 'Christian paganism', abandoning its Jewish insights of materialism and historicity, offers religion as an integrating process, a civic cement, a protection against disturbance. In so doing, it protects itself against the disruptive, disturbing God of Jewish and Christian history.

The sense of disturbance and conflict is central to Jewish spirituality. Jewish religion could therefore never be merely the private spiritual experience of those who fit, uncritically and complacently, into secular society. It is perhaps this sense of wrestling with God and of struggling for the divine justice on earth which has made the Jews a stumbling block to those who seek a religion which sanctifies the *status quo* in the classic pagan mode. Such a religion offers no threat to the powers of evil. In fidelity to their understanding of God, Jewish people today are deeply involved in the affairs of the material world and in the political sphere in a way which can be deeply shocking to those with a 'purely spiritual' idea of religion.

The God of the Jews is Lord of creation and of history. But his relationship with the people of Israel finds its central focus in the idea of the covenant (*berith*). It is the theme of covenant which is the key to the unity of the Old Testament and to the uniqueness of the faith of Israel. There was a disagreement about the nature of the covenant which is reflected in the Old Testament, between those who saw the covenant as established between God and the entire people of Israel (Exod. 19:3–6), and those who saw it as a covenant with Moses (34:27) and later with the royal house of David (2 Sam. 23:5). In Numbers 16 there is a record of conflict in the wilderness period about the authority of Moses and Aaron. Here the people complained to them, 'You have gone too far! For all the congregation are holy, every one of them, and the Lord is among them; why then do you exalt yourselves above the assembly of the Lord?' (Num. 16:3). The details of the differing understandings are not our concern here.

In Old Testament times, covenants were established between individuals, between husbands and wives, between tribes, between monarchs, or between a ruler and his people. When such a covenant was established, there were rights and duties on both sides, and covenants were sealed by gifts, by a kiss or a handshake, or by the sharing of a common meal. The origins of the covenant between Yahweh and Israel are not clear. It is possible that there is a link with the Shechem deity Baal-berith ('Baal of the covenant') whose sanctuary was taken over for the worship of Yahweh (Judg. 8:33; 9:4, 36; cf. Josh. 24). But it was the covenant at Sinai which was the central event in placing Israel in a relationship with God. This relationship depended upon the earlier redemptive work of God in the Exodus, and it was the combination of these events of deliverance and covenant which led to Israel's existence as the people of Yahweh. Exodus and covenant belong together, for the covenant was introduced by the proclamation of the Exodus event (Exod. 20:1–2). Like the Exodus, the covenant was an actual historical occurrence, not simply an idea. The biblical view of the relationship between God and Israel is rooted in the specificity of time and place: at Sinai in the thirteenth century BC the relationship was established in covenant form. Moreover, the covenant was initiated by God himself, who called for obedience and fidelity as a response to the Exodus (Exod. 19:4–5). And yet the covenant also looked forward to the mighty acts of Yahweh in the future.

> And he said, 'Behold, I make a covenant. Before all your people I will do marvels, such as have not been wrought in all the earth or in any nation; and all the people among whom you are shall see the work of the Lord; for it is a terrible thing that I will do with you.'
>
> EXODUS 34:10

Yet it was the present reality of Yahweh's presence on Mount Sinai which gave to the covenant the character of revelation as well as response to past events. The Exodus account makes it clear that God was really present, and that his presence was manifested to the people (Exod. 19:16–20) and, more intimately and uniquely, to Moses (20:18–21; 33:18–23; 34:5–6). Finally, the covenant was not between equals, for Yahweh was the Lord of the covenant. So there was a call for obedience (19:5–6). In the covenant relationship, Israel was to be a kingdom of priests and a holy nation.

It was to the Sinai covenant that the prophets looked back. Thus in Ezekiel, Yahweh addresses Jerusalem, using explicitly sexual language:

Your origin and your birth are of the land of the Canaanites; your father was an Amorite and your mother a Hittite. And as for your birth, on the day you were born, your navel string was not cut, nor were you washed with water to cleanse you, nor rubbed with salt, nor swathed with bands. No eye pitied you, to do any of these things to you out of compassion; but you were cast out on the open field, for you were abhorred, on the day that you were born. And when I passed by you, and saw you weltering in your blood, I said to you in your blood, 'Live, and grow up like a plant of the field.' And you grew up and became tall and arrived at full maidenhood; your breasts were formed, and your hair had grown; yet you were naked and bare. When I passed by you again and looked upon you, behold you were at the age for love; and I spread my skirt over you and covered your nakedness; yea, I plighted my troth to you, and entered into a covenant with you, says the Lord God, and you became mine.

EZEKIEL 16:33–8

However, there is also the hope of the new covenant, a hope which is expressed most clearly in Jeremiah:

Behold, the days are coming, says the Lord, when I will make a new covenant with the house of Israel and the house of Judah, not like the covenant which I made with their fathers when I took them by the hand to bring them out of the land of Egypt, my covenant which they broke, though I was their husband, says the Lord. But this is the covenant which I will make with the house of Israel after those days, says the Lord: I will put my law within them, and I will write it upon their hearts; and I will be their God, and they shall be my people. And no longer shall each man teach his neighbour and each his brother, saying 'Know the Lord', for they shall all know me, from the least of them to the greatest, says the Lord; for I will forgive their iniquity, and I will remember their sin no more.

JEREMIAH 31:31–4

Only Jeremiah, and he only in this one passage, speaks so explicitly of Yahweh's future relationship as a *new* covenant. However, Ezekiel also speaks of a future 'covenant of peace' and he also echoes Jeremiah's theme of a new age of the Spirit (Ezek. 37:26; 36:26f).

The Jews are the covenant people: 'to them belong … the covenants' (Rom. 9:4). Yet throughout the 'Christian' centuries, it has been the Jews, the heirs of God's promises, recipients of the revelation, who have been of all people the most despised and rejected, often deprived even of human dignity. Christian believers cannot escape the fact that anti-Semitism finds much of its theological support within the Christian tradition itself. Viewing the Jews as the murderers of the Son of God, and therefore as a people rejected by God, Christian spirituality prepared the ground for the Nazi atrocities. Even during the Nazi period, most German Christians failed to see any theological problem in the attack on the Jews, a failure which Karl Barth attributed in part to the neglect of the Old Testament prophetic tradition.

It is essential that Christian spirituality should recover from its false Gentile consciousness and rediscover the Jewish roots of its faith in, and following of, God. Much Christian theology, including much biblical study, has helped to sever the links between the Old and New Testaments, thus disconnecting the history of Israel from that of the Christian Church. This severance has formed the basis for a whole pathology in which materialism and spirituality, politics and prayer, are seen as opposites. To turn from such a deranged spiritual tradition to the faith of Israel, the faith of *our* fathers, is to begin the painful process of unlearning, and relearning what religion is about. We need to rediscover the Old Testament as *Christian* Scripture, and the Christian God as a *Jewish* God. And this rediscovery is of the greatest urgency.

'O my people'[3]

However, anyone who preaches the cross today must be aware of the danger of an approach which is triumphalist in a bigoted and intolerant way. This is not a new danger. From the earliest years of the Christian era the anti-Jewish polemic has been present in the proclamation of the cross. The removal of anti-semitic elements from the Christian liturgy is an ethical and theological imperative of our generation who have witnessed, and to a large extent colluded with, the horror of Auschwitz and of the Holocaust. For it is clear that the Holocaust emerged out of the very heart of Christian Europe and was the culmination of trends in European culture and in Christian thought going back hundreds of years. After Auschwitz the preaching of the cross can only take place – as it always should – with deep penitence and humility.

The potentially (and often actually) anti-Jewish elements in the liturgy of Good Friday focus mainly on two areas. One is the reading of John's Gospel in which 'the Jews' can be seen to mean the Jewish people as a whole rather than a particular group of enemies of Jesus. The second is the use of the Reproaches, a traditional anthem which begins with the words 'O my people …' The Reproaches originated in the Mozarbic Rite and entered the Roman Rite in the eleventh or twelfth century, assuming their final form in the *Missale Romanum* of 1474. Because they can be seen as anti-Jewish, the American Book of Common Prayer omits them altogether. The Book of Alternative Services of the Anglican Church of Canada, however, has adapted them in a sensitive and thoughtful way which makes it clear that the accusation of infidelity and sin belongs to the whole of humanity. In this version the Reproaches begin: 'O my people, O my church …' They include the following section:

> I grafted you into the tree of my chosen Israel:
> And you turned on them with persecutions and mass murder.
> I made you joint heirs with them of my covenants:
> But you made them scapegoats for your own guilt.

Today, as Islam grows in the west, and as many people in inner areas of British cities are Muslim, it is of the greatest importance that Christians preach the good news of Christ crucified with humility, gentleness and love, not using the cross as a weapon, but bearing witness to our belief that there was God's love and compassion most clearly shown. Churches need to spend much time in thought and prayer in looking at how their witness, in word and in liturgical celebration, can be set forth so that the 'offence' of the cross is not confused with offensiveness against particular groups of people or faith traditions.

Antisemitism[4]

Judaism, Christianity and Islam belong within a common religious tradition. While they differ about fundamental matters, they have a common origin and a common faith in one God. Much of the ancient history of Israel is common to all three faiths and to their sacred texts. They are often referred to as 'Abrahamic' faiths because the figure of Abraham is central to each of them. In principle, therefore, one might have expected that there would be a broad area of dialogue and engagement between them, and to some extent this has been the case. On a global scale, however, conflict has been more obvious than positive and creative relationship. If racism and religious bigotry are to be overcome and transcended, the improvement of relationships between these three faith traditions must be of central importance.

I want here to begin to look, I hope, in a way which will lead others to action, at the relationships, historically, spiritually and in contemporary life, between these three 'Abrahamic' faith traditions. I do not think it is my duty or my right to speak on behalf of Jews and Muslims, nor do I have the expertise to do so. But I do feel, as a Christian believer, a duty to call my sisters and brothers within Christianity to critical thought, self-examination and repentance – as well as to genuine and informed respect for our own tradition. In relation to racism, however, repentance is of critical importance. It can only come as a result of honestly facing our own history, and it is essential to do this if we are to understand one another and work together against the evil of racism. So let me say clearly that, in relation to Jewish and Muslim faiths, the record of Christians is not good, is at times appalling, and that it calls for serious reflection and for a systemic shift in attitude and approach.

Anti-Judaism goes back to ancient times. In the Christian tradition, anti-Judaism has a religious basis, and it is important to distinguish this from the modern antisemitism that derived more from notions of biological inferiority and conspiracy theories. Anti-Judaism is deeply rooted in the Christian tradition, and many writers, such as Rosemary Reuther (1974), have argued that it is present within the New Testament documents. The history of Christianity in relation to the Jewish people is marked and marred by bigotry, violence, and, at its most extreme moment, genocide. Christians are not in a strong position to oppose racism if they do not face the horror of this history.

The idea that the Jews as a people were responsible for the death of Jesus is deeply rooted in Christian history, if not in the New Testament itself. Certainly there is an anti-Jewish element in the New Testament documents. In the Gospel of John, the phrase 'the Jews' is used 70 times, and, while this refers to specific groups who were opposed to Jesus, much later anti-Judaism drew on this Gospel. To this day the solemn reading of the Johannine account of the Passion is the heart of the liturgy of Good Friday in the Christian Church. There is important work to be done here since liturgy shapes, and distorts, the thought of the worshipping community.

Rosemary Reuther has described anti-Judaism as 'the left hand of Christology'. However, it should not be forgotten that conspiracy theories about the Jews can be traced to the third century BCE and to the Egyptian priest Manetho. St John Chrysostom saw the Jews as 'the most worthless of all people'. They were lecherous, greedy, rapacious, murderers of Christians, and they worshipped the devil! 'It is incumbent upon all Christians to hate the Jews.' Thus spoke the one of the 'golden tongue' whose writings on the Christian responsibility to the poor are rightly treasured.

Fear of the Jews was an important aspect of Christianity in the Middle Ages. In late medieval Spain, for example, pure Spanish descent was necessary for office in the Church, and legislation against *conversos* began in 1449. Some have seen this as the beginning of the history that culminated in the Aryan Laws of the Third Reich. The word 'antisemitism' seems to have been invented by Wilhelm Marr in the 1870s, and is a very western term. It must have made little sense to Muslims at the time since both Jews and Muslims are of Semitic origin.

Today the Jewish population of Europe lives in the aftermath of Nazi extermination, and in a reduced form because of that history. In 1939 25 per cent of all Jews in the world were in Poland, Hungary and Czechoslovakia. By 1945 there were only 50,000 Jews in Poland, and only 10,000 Czech Jews had survived. All the old centres of Jewish culture had been destroyed. Today Poland is seen as one of the most Christian nations in the world, the birthplace of Pope John Paul II. Yet in 1991, 26 per cent of Poles thought that there was too much Jewish influence there, and 40 per cent did not want any Jews living near them. It seems that antisemitism is alive and well in Christian Europe. Few Christian traditions can claim immunity from this terrible legacy. German antisemitism certainly bears the mark of its Lutheran background. As Marc Ellis has said, 'the land of the reformation bore the seeds of the death camp'.

In recent years attention has been directed to the record of the Roman Church in relation to Nazism as well as Italian, Spanish and Portuguese fascism, and Pope Pius XII has come in for particular criticism. While the controversy around Pius will continue, certain facts are clear. It is known, for example, that there was a draft encyclical on racism, written by the Jesuit John Lafarge and presented to Pope Pius XI shortly before his death. This 'hidden encyclical' was never issued by his successor, Pius XII.

More generally, support for fascism among Roman Catholics is well documented. Beyond Germany, fascism received much Christian support. Most Roman Catholics supported Franco, and many were openly fascist. Cardinal Hinsley had a photograph of Franco on his desk, while the Roman Catholic journal *The Tablet* on 11 February 1939 urged Catholics not to support the anti-fascist cause. Of course, fascism, antisemitism and Nazism are not the same, but Christian history is ambivalent in relation to each of them. *The Tablet*, in an editorial on 3 April 1937, saw Nazism as anti-Christian but argued that it differed fundamentally from fascism. In this it reflected the views of Pope Pius XI, who saw cooperation with fascists as the way to restore the Christian confessional state to Italy. The encyclical *Quadragesimo Anno* had links with fascist thought, and Mussolini claimed that he was putting that encyclical into practice; many Roman Catholics in Britain saw fascism as its practical working out. Indeed Roman Catholics were over-represented in membership of the British Union of Fascists, while elsewhere they figured prominently in anti-Jewish polemic. In the US, Fr Charles Coughlin, the father of 'hate radio' in the 1930s, week by week identified Jews with Communism from his radio station in Michigan.

The collusion of Christians with the persecution of the Jews was widespread, and was not peculiar to any one form of Christian tradition. An issue which continually demands our attention, concern and repentance is the degree to which fascism, in this case its Nazi mutant, appealed to large numbers of ordinary 'decent' Christians. Most of the Christians in Germany supported Hitler. A famous telegram was sent in 1934 from the Ecclesiastical Council of the German Evangelical Church to Hitler. It committed the church to unshakeable loyalty to Hitler, who, it said, had 'staved off the Bolshevik peril', and it prayed that, under his rule, a new order would emerge in Europe.

It is, of course, sometimes claimed that ordinary Germans did not support the Nazi regime, and that surrender to the appeal of antisemitism was an aberration. The historical data, however, seem to suggest a different picture. Goldhagen's detailed study concludes that Hitler was 'adored by the vast majority of the German people', and that a 'demonological racial antisemitism' was deeply rooted in the national consciousness. The idea of exterminating the Jews was not new, and had been discussed in the nineteenth century. It was ordinary not extraordinary, normal not eccentric, integral to German culture, rooted in racist ideology. So, Goldhagen argues, most Germans were not very concerned about the attack on Jews at Kristallnacht on 9 November 1938.

Nor was this support for fascism, or sympathy towards it, peculiar to Germany. In the UK Cyril Garbett, later Archbishop of York, saw Hitler as a bulwark against Communism. Bishop Headlam of Gloucester was a strong supporter of Hitler, and saw the Jews as 'not altogether a pleasant element in German, and in particular, Berlin life'. He said that National Socialism was compatible with Christianity and denied that there was persecution at a time when it was already occurring.

This is an essential part of the background to any discussion of inter-religious engagement. Christian churches played an extremely ambiguous role in the build-up to the 'Final Solution', while sections of the press used language abut Jewish refugees similar to that used today, often by the same papers. The *Daily Mail* warned that the 'floodgates would be opened', a reference to the prospect of Jewish refugees coming to Britain.

By the end of the twentieth century, more had been written about the 'Holocaust' than about any other historical subject. There are differing views abut the uniqueness of the 'Holocaust', even about the term itself. Many prefer 'Shoah', others prefer the term used by the Nazis themselves, the 'Final Solution'. A holocaust is a sacred term, a way of describing a sacrificial offering. There was nothing sacred about the mass murder of a whole branch of the People of God. For what we are talking about is a deliberate programme of extermination, and it was, for much of the time, accompanied by the 'dead silence of unconcern'. Zygmunt Bauman saw the extermination as a paradigm of bureaucratic rationality. In similar vein, Victor Frankl, writing almost thirty years earlier, claimed that 'the gas chambers of Auschwitz ... were ultimately prepared, not in some ministry or other in Berlin, but rather at the desks and in the lecture halls of nihilistic scientists and philosophers'.

In spite of this upsurge in study, in recent years there has been a growing movement in various parts of the world to deny the seriousness of the Nazi attack on the Jews. It has come to be known as 'Holocaust denial' although not all the writers deny that Jews were exterminated; some hold a 'revisionist' view that the degree of the extermination has been exaggerated. Since a recent libel action in the British courts, the Holocaust denial movement has come to be associated in the popular media with the historian David Irving. However, many of its ideas go back to earlier work by the scientist Arthur Butz, an academic at Northwestern University, and author of *The Hoax of the Twentieth Century* and *The Myth of the Six Million.* Some years ago fascist groups in East London circulated a pamphlet by 'Richard Harwood', *Did Six Million Really Die?*, to all schools in the area. ('Richard Harwood' has never been identified and appears to be fictitious, though the author is believed to be a former member of the National Front.)

Denial of the extermination of the Jews has become an important part of neo-Nazi mythology. The spread of what has been, rather pretentiously, termed 'historical revisionism', and of the 'Holocaust denial' movement, has led to a range of attempts to rehabilitate Hitler and to deny, or downplay, the Holocaust. The movement has spread in many places, not least in the Arab world, where *Mein Kampf* has been reissued in Beirut and many copies distributed to Lebanese bookshops. In Germany itself, *Der Spiegel* in 1989 claimed that 6.4 million people (14 per cent of the adult population) held a positive view of Hitler. Of course, it is easy to oversimplify and over-dramatise these developments but it is still easier and far more dangerous to ignore them. The pendulum of political orthodoxy has been swinging to the right, not least in the UK, since the 1970s, and positions on all kinds of issues have hardened in a markedly authoritarian direction.

In the US, where racist and antisemitic groups flourish, the World

Church of the Creator has been linked to synagogue fires and other attacks. The Christian Identity movement has been in the forefront of antisemitic rhetoric. The UK and other parts of Europe certainly witnessed an increase in antisemitic attacks on buildings and people during and after 2002. In spite of all this horror, Jews and Christians have continued to work together, and movements such as the Council of Christians and Jews have played a crucial role in inter-faith dialogue and action in Britain.

One of the most sensitive, and often inflammatory, questions at present concerns attitudes to the state of Israel and to Zionism. It is often assumed that attacks on Israel are *per se* antisemitic. But is Israel to be free from moral and political critique? The radical traditions within Judaism respond with a resounding no. The prophetic movement, which has never completely died out in Jewish history, is rooted in the need for continual moral scrutiny. However, my feeling is that there are questions here which are more to do with credibility than with 'objective' truth. I remember once asking Ruth Glass for her opinion of another academic who was well known as an advisor to British governments. She replied, 'He often says things which are right, but they don't sound right, coming from him.' A cynical comment, no doubt, but one that has to be taken seriously, coming from her, a refugee from Nazi Germany. The man, in her view, lacked credibility. What right have Christians and Muslims, people outside all faith traditions, secular socialists in the west, or any other group, to attack the behaviour of Israel in the light of their own highly dubious role in relation to the historic persecution of the Jews? I can see no way out of this impasse except by the building of alliances between Jews, Muslims, Christians and others which are based on mutual respect and mutual honesty. People only take criticisms seriously if they respect the credibility of those who are criticizing. This is a slow and painful process, but the peace of the world may depend on it. The peace of Jerusalem may determine whether there can be a peaceable future for us all.

Demonising Muslims[5]

That there has been a rise of Islam in the west is obvious. Most of it is due to immigration, but there are also significant numbers of converts to Islam in the UK, and this is no doubt also true in other countries. The statistical data are not clear. In 1990 the geographer Ceri Peach called the conventional figure of 1–2 million Muslims in Britain into question. He argued that if all Pakistanis, Bangladeshis and maybe one-third of Indians were Muslim, this would lead to a figure of 762,000 Muslims of South Asian origin in the UK. The largest groups of Muslims in the UK originated in Pakistan and Bangladesh. If we were to add to this figure the African and Arab Muslims and British converts, the figure would reach one million or less. The largest Muslim settlements in the UK are in Birmingham. In Europe as a whole, the number of Muslims is perhaps 30 million. In France there are more Muslims than Protestant Christians. There has also been a significant growth of Islam in the US, through conversion as well as immigration, perhaps reaching three million in 1988. Since the various wars in the Middle East, based on the need for oil and on the fear of 'terrorism', and particularly since the attacks on sites in the US, a kind of demonology of Muslims has developed, mainly among people with no knowledge of Islam. But the term 'Islamophobia' (fear of Islam) antedates the very recent atrocities. It demands thoughtful and committed responses from people of faith and goodwill.

One of the terms currently used in relation to Islam is 'fundamentalism', a term which originated within evangelical Christianity in the US. It is not a term that was known within Muslim countries until it was exported to them from the western media. However, what many of the writers have in mind, without knowing it, is the revivalist movement known as Wahhabism, founded by Muhammad ibn Abd al-Wahhab in Saudi Arabia. Wahhab called for a return to the purity of the Koran, and his movement has been compared to the Reformation within western Christianity. But in Britain most of what is called 'Islamic fundamentalism' occurs in London and in universities. The majority of Muslims in most British towns have no contact with these movements, and tend to belong to more devotional, revivalist and politically conservative streams of Islam.

Moreover, it is wrong to see Islamic 'fundamentalism' – as it is wrong to see Christian fundamentalism – as synonymous with 'traditionalism' or 'orthodoxy'. These movements are quite modern, and indeed are a product of, and a reaction to, modernity. Khomeinism, for example, developed from the work of Rubollah Khomeini in the 1960s, and grew among the Shia Muslims in Iran after 1979. This and similar movements represent a major break with both orthodox Islam and the earlier reformist, secularised streams. Islam is, like all religious traditions, in flux. There is discussion of an 'Islamic theology of liberation', and one British student of Islam has spoken of a 'fragmented Islamic tradition'.

Attacks on Islam can be most harmful in local contexts. An interesting, but depressing, example of local anti-Muslim rhetoric came recently from a fairly obscure political figure, a professed Christian, in East London who stood as a candidate in local elections on the basis of an attempt to create a rift between Jews and Muslims of a fairly standard populist kind. Muslims, in his view, are seen as a threat to the social order. He ended his election statement with the words: 'I give you a commitment that I would do all I could to support and protect the Jewish community in Tower Hamlets.' His grammar is interesting, even if not intentional, and his switch to the subjunctive might even suggest that he realises that his is a lost cause – 'I would' rather than 'I will' – for the Jewish community in the East End of London is now smaller than it has been for many years. This is a classic example of an attempt to play one 'ethnic' group off against another. However, while we should not over-react to this ignorant stuff, it is important to consider some of his claims. 'The Jews learnt to speak English ...' in contrast to the Muslims, he argued. In fact, this is exactly what critics of the Jews, including Sir Oswald Mosley, said about Jews in the 1930s. The history of anti-Jewish polemic is full of this kind of claim that they 'do not use English'.

The claim that Muslims in East London – and almost certainly elsewhere – 'do not use English' is contradicted by all the educational data. Certainly there are older Bengali women who do not speak English, but progress in literacy in English among Bengali youth has been remarkable. Kobi Nazrul Primary School, where I was a governor for five years, is a fascinating example. In a borough with very low literacy rates, the Bengali children at Kobi Nazrul were proficient in English, Bengali, Arabic and, in some cases, French. Statistics from Tower Hamlets College confirm that this is also true of older students. Bengalis have a higher level of linguistic ability than most indigenous white people, and the pattern is repeated from town to town.

Local populists, exploiting ignorance and prejudice, will be with us for some time. Unfortunately, anti-Islamic rhetoric also comes from more significant figures in the churches. In April 2004, both former

Archbishop George Carey and Cardinal Cormac Murphy-O'Connor, Roman Catholic Archbishop of Westminster, criticised Muslim leaders for their failure to condemn violence – a strange comment from two Christian churches whose record on violence is ambiguous, to say the least. When questioned, O'Connor condemned world poverty and violence, but said that his role was to promote reconciliation and peace, and that political issues, for example about Iraq, should be 'left to the political leaders'. Leaving aside the content of the rhetoric, it does raise the question, Do these people have any credibility? There may be parallels in other traditions, but my impression is that Christian leaders have done great harm by ill-informed and ill-timed utterances on matters about which they know very little. (Rowan Williams is a welcome exception.)

The Bengali writer Tazeen Murshid has pointed out that 'Islam has never been a monolith nor can it be explained away with a few generalizations.' In fact, Islam in Britain – and no doubt elsewhere – is complex and constantly changing. I have been particularly struck in East London by the intelligence, creativity and willingness to interrogate and critique the tradition shown by young Muslim women. For many young women, particularly those of Bengali origin, life in the East End of London has been their first experience of Islam in an urban context, and in an area where Islam is a minority faith (though in the ward where I lived for many years, it was the majority faith). It was mainly the young women who were raising major issues, calling the tradition to account, suggesting new ways forward, yet doing so within the framework of an evolving and developing Islamic tradition. However, since the rise of the Asian youth movements in the 1970s and 1980s, as an element in the resistance to racism, there has been a shift among many young Muslims towards membership of more religious, ethnic and sectarian groups. It should be stressed that, while the crucial role of the 'community mosque' in many areas has been evident for years, recent political and spiritual developments have made it more important. Indeed in some British towns and cities, the mosque has taken over the social role once played by the Anglican parish church.

Of course, Christian–Muslim dialogue must go on. But I am wary of the term 'inter-faith dialogue'. It often suggests a disconnected, middle-class, rather intellectual activity which is cut off from the mass of the people, both inside and outside the faith communities. To be of practical value, dialogue must be localised, honest and courageous. It must explore common ground while recognising that there are important differences between faith traditions. It must also be very practical. For example, it is often of critical importance that faith communities get together quickly, and the mechanisms that enable this to happen must be put in place. Sadly, the history of inter-faith dialogue suggests that the situation is often the opposite. Often the dialogue is not rooted locally but is vaguely national. It is kind and charitable but tends to blur or avoid areas of controversy. It explores common ground but only at an intellectual level. It avoids differences, and creates no ability to act together when such action becomes really important. Fortunately there are many examples to the contrary.

I intend no disrespect to Hinduism, Buddhism and other faiths in what I say here, but my main experience has been with Judaism, Christianity and Islam. These three faith traditions have a common belief in communion with God. As I have said, I believe that, in the context of inter-faith work, Christians need to develop a new and extended idea of catholicity. This involves the transcendence of birth, ethnicity, race and nationality, and the commitment to the struggle for a common humanity.

Other faith traditions[6]

Out of our experience here, some insights have emerged which we should share. First, it is essential to recognise and learn from the spiritual strengths of other traditions. For example, within Islam there are areas of what we would call 'spirituality' from which we could learn a great deal. There is a sense of belonging to a strong community, the *umma*. The mosque is a crucial centre and source of new life. There is the stress on fasting, prayer, almsgiving (as an obligation of justice), and pilgrimage – all of these neglected by western Christians. There is a concern with the physical dimensions of prayer – bows and prostrations – which puts incarnational Christianity to shame.

Take, for example, the issue of fasting. A central element in Islamic spirituality is the practice of the Ramadan fast. It was once said of Bengali Muslims that 'they never give up fasting as long as they have life in them'. The close proximity, in 1999 and 2000, of Ramadan to the secular preparation for Christmas made the commitment of the Ramadan fast more startling than usual in London. In Sainsbury's in Whitechapel, the contrast between the immense sales of food to the 'Christian' customers and the dedicated fast of the (mainly Bengali) assistants was immensely moving and dramatic. As with the Orthodox Christians of the East, Muslims know both how to fast and how to feast, and Ramadan ends with the feast of Id al-Fitr, a celebration in which sweets are shared and new clothes are worn. This is a spirituality which is essentially corporate, physical, homely and rooted in hospitality and comradeship.

Inter-faith dialogue must be a spiritual activity, and, for Christians, this must include penitence, and a recognition of the evil in our own history. (Of course, Muslims and others have much to confess, but that is their responsibility.) St Bernard of Clairvaux, for example, claimed that Christ was glorified in the death of Muslims. It is important too to approach people of other faiths with reverence, awe and immense respect. The late Max Warren said that the first step in inter-faith conversation was to take off one's shoes.

We must build on the traditions of justice in the faith traditions. The Koran condemns the neglect of the orphan and the poor (89:18–21) and insists that the just share their resources with beggars (51:17–19). It attacks the amassing of wealth (92:5–11). The issue of money and the just use of money is crucial to our future work together. The work of the Grameen Bank in Bangladesh and its system of microcredit is one from which Christians could learn. The bank lends to around 2.4 million in the 93,000 villages in Bangladesh, and 94 per cent of its borrowers are women. Through its work, there has been a strong emphasis on the place of health and nutrition as well as on the fundamental question of monetary justice. Christians, according to the Koran, are the 'closest in friendship' or 'nearest in affection' to Islam (Koran 5:82; 9:29). We need to work together in the cause of justice.

Second, it is essential to see that things are changing. Cultures are not unified or static. In the diaspora situation of religions and cultures, many elements are changing, things are going into solution, things which were once thought solid are melting into air. Of course, the theme of journey is central to Islam, but it now appears in a form not anticipated by earlier generations. Akbar Ahmed has referred to the Muslim intellectual as existing in 'a state of despair, torn between an ideal world he cannot order, and a reality he cannot master' – a state of exile.

For most Muslims, life in Britain is their first experience of life in a society where Islam is a minority religion, while, in the 'Christian' West, we are seeing a residual Christianity, with a collapse of the symbolic framework, but also with new forms of Christian presence emerging.

On the whole, Islam has not coped easily with dissent and diversity, although there are hints in the Koran that diversity of faith may be God's will, and that there must be no compulsion in religion. But now in East London, everything is coming under scrutiny. Bangladeshi Islam is having to rethink the position of women as feminism has made its impact. For example, surveys have shown that most Bengali girls see sex education as an important part of their life. Then there is the issue of homosexuality. In some Muslim areas, there is a demand for gays over the age of ten to be executed, and for lesbians to receive life imprisonment. Yet there are now organisations for gay Muslims, such as Al-Fatiha, founded in the USA in 1977, and Homan, a gay group for Iranian Muslims in Britain. It has been claimed that 75,000 of Britain's 1.5 million Muslims are gay.

In this situation of flux, positions which people take can be surprising. Thus in 1992 many apparently conservative Muslims in the East End supported – and sold – Taslima Nasreem's novel *Lajja* ('Shame') in spite of the hostility to her in Bangladesh. The novel was written after the destruction of the Babri Mosque at Ayodha. There is discussion of an Islamic theology of liberation. And, of course, many key issues are being raised by children in our multi-faith society. A colleague has looked at the questions raised by children in one district, and no doubt in thousands. They include:

Is Jesus stronger than Allah?

Are we Christians or are we English?

Will Parmesh go to heaven?

Aleisha's a Hindu. So do we have to get her a Christmas present?

Third, we need to take care in our use of the word 'fundamentalism', a term not known in Islam. Yet the most publicised aspect of Islam in the western media concerns the growth of 'fundamentalism' with its implication of warfare, and there is an assumption that the warfare model might be reproduced locally. Actually, while 'holy war' ideas arise from time to time, this is not a key influence in Britain, nor are most Muslims here 'fundamentalists', though there are spin-offs from the media coverage.

Fourth, our experience is that co-operation and mutual learning often start with immensely practical issues, whereas 'inter-faith dialogue' which is not concretely based in local action tends to be a rather disconnected middle-class activity without roots in the communities. A real and growing dialogue is more likely to grow from local co-operative action. Thus the issue of female circumcision (or, as it is better called, female genital mutilation) has become a major issue among Somali women and others. The Black Women's Health Action Project, based in the East End, has been the pioneering group in this field, and Shamis Dirir one of the key figures, and it has brought together numerous groups and individuals.

Then there is the question of drug abuse. In the early 1990s the Maze Drugs Project, which I chaired, worked closely with the Young Muslim Organisation (YMO) over this issue. We based some of the work on a very successful anti-smoking campaign, run during Ramadan by the YMO, and developed it into an educational project on the use of other drugs, based on the Ramadan calendar. Combined with this we held the first of a series of conferences on drug abuse in the Bengali community, attended by 350 people. The day was run bilingually, in English and Bengali, and was aimed at Bengali parents. It was held in the mosque, with breaks for the 1.00 p.m. and 3.30 p.m. prayers. Out of this has grown a good deal of co-operative work involving Muslims, Christians and others.

A movement which has also taken root around practical issues is Community Organising, a movement committed to broad-based solidarity between organisations and communities. The movement began with the work of Saul Alinksy (1909–72), and much of the early work focused on churches. The Nehemiah Project in Brooklyn emerged from the local churches. In Britain the Citizens Organising Foundation was formed in 1988. Communities Organised for a Greater Bristol appeared in 1990, and Merseyside Broad Based Organising in 1992. In the 1990s also came TELCO, The East London Community Organisation.

Fifth, it is best to begin with issues on our own doorstep. In a survey in 1995 92 per cent of people in Newham believed that people of different faiths should work together on issues of human need, and we need to build on this goodwill. The work of John Webber, inter-faith advisor in the Stepney Episcopal Area, has been important in getting local work off the ground. Work by the chaplaincy team at the London Hospital has led to increased inter-faith dialogue and common action around the approach to dying and death. The work of the Servite priest Joe Collela and the 'One for Life' project has focused attention on the importance of silence, for sharing pastoral concerns and work together on common problems and needs. For several years a small group at St Botolph's looked at approaches to dying and death in a multi-faith context.

In fact much progress has actually been made in the East End. There is, after all, a wealth of accumulated wisdom and expertise here, going back over a hundred years. As in so many fields, I suspect more theological exploration and inter-faith encounter may be going on in primary schools (or some of them) than in churches, synods and groups of adult Christians. I hope we can make some quiet progress in looking, as all good theology must, at what is actually happening among communities.

Sixth, networking across continents can be immensely useful. In rural Wiltshire there has been a link for over eighteen years with a Muslim fishing community in Gunjur in the Gambia. The educational resources which have been developed from this link are now used in 1,600 primary schools in Britain, and have led to greater understanding of the place of older people in communities, the centrality of water, and many other areas.

Finally, there is much theological work to be done. There are evangelical Christians who hold that there is 'one way' to salvation, through conscious allegiance to Jesus Christ. This conviction is often narrowed down even further to exclude forms of Christianity, particularly Roman Catholicism, which do not fit within the thought-forms of evangelical orthodoxy. However, this position also has its Roman Catholic equivalent which can at times exclude most other types of Christian. There is also an aggressive 'end of dialogue', militant and crusading stance, often dressed up in the language of postmodernity and even radicalism. However sophisticated it may seem, this position is at heart a regression to an earlier phase of Christian imperialism, 'a kind of exploitation, a new religious imperialism, a theological form of racial harassment' against which Hooker and Lamb warned in 1986.

At the opposite pole there are Christians who have opted for an 'inclusive' approach, characterised by the idea that God leads people to truth by a variety of routes, an approach which sometimes avoids critique of alternative positions. One tendency has been to see different faiths as approaches to the same reality. It is perfectly true that 'God has many names', but it does not follow from this that all religions are equally valid paths, and this approach can be an excuse for intellectual laziness.

Is there a *via media*? (I avoid the English version 'middle way', with all its strange modern associations!) Yes. It is a way of affirmation (*via positiva*) combined with a way of negation (*via negativa*), a combination central to the Christian mystical tradition and to Eastern Orthodox theology. It is important that we affirm our own experience of, and commitment to, the revelation of God in Christ, and share it, lovingly, passionately and humbly, with others. It is equally important to recognise that our ignorance of God is more central to our life than our knowledge of God. We forget this at our peril, for to forget this is to jeopardise our whole relationship with the God who is always beyond our reach and range. We need a rich, deeply rooted and humble approach to our faith tradition if we are to counter the intolerant and damaging tendencies of much in the contemporary Church.

David Tracy of the University of Chicago has called for the central place of conversation. As Tracy recognises, conversation will involve dispute and challenge, elements which can be forgotten in the use of the word 'dialogue'. But dialogue has its origins in the theme of argument. Thus Paul in the Ephesus synagogue both spoke out boldly and argued persuasively (*dialegomenos kai peithon*, Acts 19:80). The idea of dialogue is ancient and its practice is not without its conflictual edge. But it is always rooted in equality, respect and genuine conversation. It is not inherently confrontational and polemical, though these aspects are part of the dialogue.

Christian testimony within a context of plurality of faiths should be marked by reality, not fantasy; by humility, not aggressiveness and arrogance; fidelity, not embarrassment; and openness, not inflexibility. Our context is similar to that of the ancient world, the world out of which Christianity grew, but to which we cannot return as if the Constantinian/Christendom epoch had not occurred. We need to learn from the early Christians but also learn the lessons of Christendom. Neither epoch can be recreated.

Black Christians[7]

Some years ago a well-meaning white liberal English bishop wrote a letter to churchwardens in each parish in his diocese about the importance of making ethnic minorities welcome in the churches. The letter had taken account of recent debates within the Church about racial justice, and it contained all the right sentiments. It had only one fatal flaw. It was quite obvious from the way in which the letter was written that he took for granted that all the individuals to whom he was writing were white. In fact, a good number of the wardens, and many members – in some areas the majority – of the congregations were black. It was a classic example of the assumed leadership of the dominant white community, a community which has often taken its role for granted. The whole edifice of 'whiteness', with its history of domination, needs to be confronted and set free from its constructed and sustained invisibility.

Most Christians today are black, or at least not of Anglo-Saxon origin. (It is perhaps even worth reminding white readers that the Christian movement itself began in the Middle East, only spreading to 'white' areas later.) This is true not only within urban areas of the UK – 50 per cent of churchgoers in London are black, for example – but globally. The typical Anglican in the world is probably a young black woman in Africa. When we look beyond Anglicanism, which is, after all, a minority tradition among Christian movements, black Christianity is an enormous, powerful and growing force throughout the world (as indeed is Hispanic Christianity, both in Central and South America and the US). It is valuable to begin with the black Christian tradition, not simply because it is historically extremely important, but also because, as a matter of statistical fact, a high proportion – if not the majority – of practising Christians globally are black. White Christians in the UK tend to forget this if they ever knew it, although the fantastic growth of the black-led churches within the UK itself may even have helped to change their minds.

But it is not just a matter of changing minds. A change in personal and social consciousness, in orientation, in perspective is needed, and for white Christians this must surely mean liberation from the tyranny and captivity of 'whiteness'. By this I do not, of course, mean the abandonment of the fact that many Christians are 'white', or, more accurately, pinko-grey, in their physical complexion. I do mean the abandonment of the myth that 'whiteness' is normative, dominant, central to Christian reality. Yet this process of abandonment is not simple, for the structures of domination within the world's major churches are inextricably bound up with 'whiteness'. The Roman communion is dominated politically by white male Italians, and culturally by the Irish – though the odd Pole manages to intrude, and survive for a long time to be replaced by a German! Anglicanism is still dominated by Canterbury, a city in the very white English county of Kent. Eastern Orthodoxy is overwhelmingly organised from within the Greek, Slavic and Russian communities (although the Ethiopian Orthodox have attracted many black Christians with no geographical link to North Africa). So most Christians are black – what does this mean in terms of global politics, and of Christian praxis? The issue is a complex one, but it cannot be evaded.

The allegiance of black people to Christianity is rooted in specific histories. In the US, for example, many slaves became Baptist, and the Baptist churches are still a major force within American black Christianity. They represent a major public sphere for survival and for the nourishing of alternative vision. This is significant and worth noting, not least because the Southern Baptist church (one of many politically and socially diverse 'Baptist' churches in America) is a reactionary political group in the US, was a major bulwark in electing President Bush and, with some exceptions, is deeply racist. Yet black Christians have found in the Baptist tradition a source of resistance, manifested most powerfully in recent decades in the witness of Martin Luther King, Jr.

Other black Christians are identified with the Pentecostal tradition, which grew from the Holiness movements of the late nineteenth century and from the Azusa Street revival in Los Angeles in the early twentieth century. Cornel West in the US and Robert Beckford in the UK, who both belong to this tradition, are among a number of recent black Christian theologians who have stressed the need for a prophetic voice from within the black churches. In recent years, in both the US and the UK, urban black-led churches have played a greater role in economic development and in community action. (Those churches where there is direct influence from Africa will be aware that a key word in Swahili is *ujumaa*, cooperative economics.)

In Britain, the Aladura churches, Christ Apostolic, and the Cherubim and Seraphim flourish among Nigerian Christians. There are other African churches, and churches of African-Caribbean origin, as well as those which grew out of the US and spread via Jamaica to Britain. Of the latter, the most significant are the New Testament Church of God and the Church of God of Prophecy, both of which have a large presence in inner-city areas of England. Originating in Tennessee, the Church of God and its offshoots are, in the US, mainly white and rural: only in Jamaica and England are they mainly black and urban. Theologically, these churches grew out of the Southern plantocracy and inherited the pietistic theology of revivalism. It is this otherworldly theology which is now being called into question within the British context.

Jawanza Kunjufu has divided black-led churches into three groups: entertainment churches ('sing, shout and holler'); containment churches, essentially churches of the status quo; and liberation churches which seek transformation. White Christians may find nothing new here, for the same divisions exist in the white-led churches. However, it is important to pay attention to what is happening within some of the black-led churches. Many observers, black and white, write of the black Pentecostal churches as hopelessly apolitical and otherworldly. Certainly, as Robert Beckford has said, 'many black Pentecostals are simply unaware of the socio-political motivations that produced their Christian tradition'. But a process of radicalisation and deeper prophetic understanding about the whole-ness of the gospel message has been taking place, much of it influ-enced by black Christians such as Cornel West, James Cone, Desmond Tutu, Patrick Kalilombe, Robert Beckford, Jacquelyn Grant, Katie Cannon and many others. Alongside this has been a grass-roots movement which has led many black Christians in the inner cities of Britain to reject as unbiblical and wrong the 'other-worldliness' of the white revivalist traditions which gave them birth. Black Christian thinkers in Britain such as Io Smith, Joel Edwards, Robert Beckford and Ron Nathan have been important in aiding and influencing this shift, while in the Church of England the testimony of John Sentamu, Rose Hudson-Wilkin, Eve Pitts, Lorraine Dixon, Eileen Lake and others has been crucial. But it would be wrong simply to list well-known names. The black-led churches, and black Christian communities in all the UK churches, are changing dramati-cally, and we will see in the coming years a real grass-roots ecumenism which will be evangelical, Pentecostal, deeply worship-centred, but also incarnational, redemptive and political in its resistance to injustice and oppression.

New critical voices are continually appearing within the black communities, calling much conventional ministry to account. A black student in the University of London has written: 'Some of the vicars go into the streets of Brixton to preach, but the youth are not interested. Have they got a message that is attractive to the youth? I think not.'

Yet, as Bob Dylan memorably sang, 'the times they are a changin'', and we are in the midst of powerful transformations in the field of responses to racism and in the Christian witness to the righteousness of God.

This resurgence of black Christianity is, of course, a global phenomenon. But my sense is that to call it the 'next Christendom', as Philip Jenkins does, is a serious oversimplification, indeed a distortion of what is taking place. Rather than invoke the old language of Christendom, it is probably better to speak of a 'new Pentecost'.

Black Anglicanism[8]

I am too fond of Wilfred Wood as a person, and too aware of his contribution as a fighter against racism from the days of Shepherd's Bush and the Institute of Race Relations, not to be pleased at his consecration as a bishop. There is no way that this consecration can be seen as incidental to the issues of race and colour. Wilfred is not only the first black bishop in the Church of England. He is, as far as I can recall, the first bishop to be consecrated in Britain (rather than appointed after experience elsewhere) whose anti-racist credentials were clearly established prior to his consecration. Now how far those facts were in the minds of those who appointed him we do not know. The appointment of bishops, white or black, in the Church of England is a highly secretive affair, and we are not supposed to know what is in the minds of those responsible – whoever they are! It is to be hoped that now that there is a solid phalanx of bishops in Southwark who are committed to equality, democracy and social as well as racial justice, they will help to bring the present system by which they themselves were appointed to an end. We shall see.

For there are warning bells to be rung in the midst of the rejoicing, and there are some real dangers which must be recognised. The first is the danger that, now that Wilfred has been made a bishop, the question of black people in the corridors of power in the Church will be forgotten for a while. After all, we are now a multi-racial hierarchy: we have one black bishop. And perhaps, after ACUPA has reported, a black clergyman will be found to occupy a senior position in Church House. But the underlying issues about equal opportunities and affirmative action (to which the Archbishop of Canterbury has at least committed himself in print) will be shelved. There is no real evidence that anti-racism has taken root within the institutional structures of the Church, whatever Boards for Social Responsibility may say.

The second danger is that attention will be focused on the promotion of black candidates to positions of authority (not questioning the methods by which they will be appointed) instead of looking at the communities from which black leadership must be drawn. Black bishops do not descend from heaven. Wilfred came from Codrington College, Barbados. But over 50 per cent of black people in Britain were born here and perhaps 70 per cent of black Christians belong to independent black-led churches. (Many black-led churches contain a percentage of white people. But when a black-led church has 10 per cent white members, it is still termed a 'black church'; when a white Anglican church has 10 per cent black members it is called multi-racial!) Only three black clergy in the Church of England were born here and there have been few black ordinands in theological colleges in the last decade, all of them from overseas, almost all going back. There are at present, to my knowledge, two British-born black people in training, both female. Who is taking this situation seriously? The recent publications from Heather Walton for Ethnic Minorities in Methodism and from the (now defunct) Catholic Commission for Racial Justice show a similar situation. The Methodists seem to have made more progress in tackling it, while the position in the Roman Church seems (as it is in the United States) rather worse than ours: there was, at the time of the report, no black person in training for the priesthood in any diocese in England and Wales.

So attention needs to be focused on black Anglicanism at the grass-roots level. And this raises the third danger.

The question of black people in the Church of England, whether as bishops and leaders, or as members of parishes, highlights the historic situation of the white working class in relation to Anglicanism. It is, of

course, appalling that while in some urban parishes, the majority of
practising Anglicans are black, the leadership, power and decision-
making are all in white hands; and it is equally appalling that the
black majority are often not consulted about these matters. But when
have white working-class people ever been consulted about their
bishops, their parish priests, or the future of their churches? Even
well-known anti-racist bishops have been known to act in very
authoritarian ways in relation to working-class people. Will the entry
of black Anglicans into power begin to change the class contours of
Anglicanism? The USA experience suggests that this is not necessarily
so. Anglicanism attracts the black bourgeoisie as it attracts their white
counterparts.

So it is no disrespect to Wilfred Wood to say: two cheers for this
event. But do not think the battle is now over. On the contrary it has
only just begun.

Anti-racism and social justice[9]

In recent months there has been a good deal of oversimplification and distortion of aspects of racism and anti-racism, not
least in the tabloid press. Many people who have for long ignored or
rejected the concept of racism as inapplicable to Britain have now
discovered that there are genuine racists in our midst: they are the
'anti-racists', most of them black, all of them left-wing, who practise a
simple and unified form of brainwashing – 'anti-racism'. A minor
industry has grown up among the intellectuals and quasi-intellectual
pamphleteers of the right to attack this phenomenon.

The attack on 'anti-racism' has run parallel with an increasing
tendency to ignore, downplay or even reject the need for strategies
against racism and disadvantage, an area where so little progress has
been made. Yet now 'anti-racism' is portrayed as the real danger.

It is perfectly true that many groups and individuals, including
some local authorities, have interpreted 'anti-racism' in a simplistic,
bureaucratic and absurd way. In so doing they have given ammuni-
tion to the right-wing media who never showed any interest in
combating racism in the first place, and to a whole new galaxy of
writers whose concerns about racism have never been evident until
now. As anti-anti-racists, they have suddenly acquired an identity. In a
sense, it was almost irrelevant that these groups played into the hands

of the new breed of anti-anti-racists, for they would have attacked them anyway. We are in a climate where it is increasingly difficult for the facts to be heard, a climate of untruth and of propaganda.

There is, in fact, no single phenomenon called anti-racism any more than there is a homogeneous entity called the 'race relations industry'. There is a whole cluster of positions and groups. The view, often ascribed to all anti-racists, that to be white is to be racist, is probably held by some people – though one rarely meets them – but it is strongly rejected by most. The only unifying factor in the 'anti-racist movement' is a commitment to attack and undermine racism within institutions and individuals.

Undoubtedly, one of the weaknesses of much of this activity has been the separation of race issues from those of class and of justice in general. One reaction against this separation, which has long been a feature of some Marxist groups and has recently appeared in a different form among writers of the right and centre, is to play down racial disadvantage in favour of class and poverty. Britain is said to be a country whose society has been formed by the fissures of class rather than race. Again, one has to check carefully who is saying this. Many of the new protagonists of the evils of class division are people who showed no interest in the issue until race divisions were mentioned. Yet it is as mistaken to reduce class to race, or race to class, as it is to make a sharp contrast between them. Race and class are not the same, but they are intimately connected. The lesson to be drawn from their interconnectedness is that all anti-racist activity must be set within the context of the attack on class division and class oppression. Colour has added new and specific divisions which cannot be ignored.

A central feature of much of the current polemic is an attack on positive discrimination or affirmative action. This is interesting, because the attack has taken place at the very point at which such action is just beginning to make slight progress in Britain. The work of Professor Julius Wilson in Chicago has shown conclusively that positive action policies in the United States have benefited mainly the aspiring black middle class, while the conditions of the black poor have deteriorated markedly during the very years in which positive action has been most successful.

Wilson does not support free-market principles nor does he argue *against* positive action: rather does he stress the need to widen and strengthen the attack on social deprivation and on the social isolation of the inner city. In British cities there are no equivalents of the American urban ghettoes: what we have are areas of acute deprivation and poverty involving people of all colours. The limits of positive action on race to deal with this situation must not be distorted into an attack on the limited yet significant achievements of such policies. It is, however, necessary to reiterate that the ideology and practice of immigration control undermines attempts to combat racism within Britain. Racism is indivisible. Racial discrimination at the doors of Britain is no basis for combating racial discrimination within Britain. As long as 'good race relations' is linked with tight, race-specific controls on entry, the seriousness of government rhetoric, and Labour Party policy, against discrimination will remain in question.

Eight practical steps[10]

(1) An anti-racist spirituality demands corporate support and discipline, and the recovery of that vital word solidarity. This is not a time for lonely wilderness crusaders. Rather we need to shape 'a community of comrades who are seeking to deepen our spiritual experience and our political solidarity.' MacIntyre stresses the need for a network of small groups of friends who can sustain and nourish spiritual and moral values through the coming ages of barbarism and darkness. We have tried to do this in the Jubilee Group network in Britain. It is vital if we are to overcome loneliness and fragmentation.

(2) We need to take seriously the issues of anger and pain, and not to seek to diffuse or sanitise them. There is much glib talk in the church about reconciliation is the aim of the Gospel and of Christian ministry, but it is rarely the immediate result. The ministry of Jesus did not, in the short term, lead to reconciliation, but to division, hostility and crucifixion. The only people who were described as being reconciled as a result of the ministry of Jesus are Herod and Pilate.

In the field of 'race relations' there is much talk of the need for harmony. But the rhetoric of 'good race relations' and 'racial harmony' can obscure the nature of racism. For, while good relations are better than bad relations, it is injustice and righteousness which is central. And the impetus to the attainment of righteousness is historically linked to violence. We need a spirituality which can make sense of what is often termed 'meaningless violence' or 'mindless violence'. Such violence is neither meaningless nor mindless, but is rooted in a recognition that violence does achieve what many years of research and documentation may not. When, in 1981, urban rebellions occurred in Liverpool 8, one of the best documented and over researched districts in Britain, government minister Michael Heseltine told some community leaders including local priest Austin Smith: 'Violence will get you nowhere.' 'It got you up here' was Smith's response. If Christian spirituality is to be a spirituality of nonviolence, it must be a nonviolence which understands and, in the literal sense, sympathises with the violent urge to change, not the violence of those who wish to remain pure and aloof.

An anti-racist spirituality will be a spirituality which recognises the centrality of conflict and struggle. And here we come into collision with the assumption within the liberal tradition that improvements and reforms can occur without any fundamental threat to, or break with, the existing system of power relations. If we adopt the 'coat of paint' theory of racism, that is perfectly possible. But if racism is not simply a pathological growth on an otherwise healthy and just society, but is deeply rooted in that society, then to attack racism is to threaten the whole fabric. And it is the prospect of so fundamental and painful an upheaval that many liberal Christians cannot face. Anglicans in particular are prone to a theology and a spirituality which has no place for conflict. As Conrad Noel once commented, 'they imagine that the mighty will be put down from their seats so gently that they will not feel the bump when they hit the ground.'

(3) An anti-racist spirituality must include the dimension of self-scrutiny and confrontation with our own illusion of falsehood. It was Nietzsche who said that those who fight with monsters are in danger of becoming monstrous. There is a real danger that in the course of struggle we will become bitter, permanently angry, broken and unattractive people. We will need purity of heart, intense love and persistence, as well as the guidance and watchfulness of others.

The British feminist Sheila Rowbotham writes of the phenomenon of the lonely militant, hard, erect, self-contained, controlled, without the time or the ability to express loving passion, who cannot pause to nurture, and for whom friendship is a diversion from the struggle. The lonely militant can so easily become a caricature, living on illusion, with a single transferable speech and correct line on everything.

(4) So an anti-racist spirituality needs to be contemplative and reflective, for we are working for deep healing. As we seek to be more intensely active, so we will need prayer, silence and solitude more and more. Martin Luther King saw clearly that if he did not practise such prayer in solitude, the movement would suffer.

(5) One of the problems of the left in secular politics and in the church, is that of institutionalisation. There has been a great deal of exaggerated talk in recent years about 'tenured radicals' usually in the context of so-called 'political correctness'. I am not addressing this large and confused issue, but there is an aspect which has profound spiritual consequences: the tendency in managerial radicalism towards a distant elitism which has ceased to listen to the voices from the back streets. Much professional anti-racism has become very managerial, operating in effect on policies of 'trickle down' and influencing the 'policy villages', often fighting racism from above the battle. We need constantly to return to the streets and hear the forgotten voices.

(6) The struggle against racism within the church must recognise that many of those who, in their rhetoric, agree with us, are not in fact on our side, and that our allies will be found in surprising places. So we need to be working well beyond the boundaries of the church, and this raises the question of making connections.

I believe that anti-racist spirituality must avoid two mistaken ways of looking at racial oppression. One is to see racism as so fundamentally different from other forms of oppression that it must be understood and combated in its own right, as an issue, separate from other issues. To this it must be replied that, while there are indeed unique dimensions to racism, it is important to see the connections and parallels with other levels of oppression, injustice and discrimination, and to build alliances with those involved. If this is not possible, the outlook for any significant attack on these evils is very bleak.

The second approach, however, links oppressions in such a way as to dissolve them into one another, losing the specific and concrete character of each, and producing a kind of imprecision and conceptual and practical flabbiness which impedes action and induces paralysis. Such an approach refers airily to 'human liberation' though I have noticed that many of those who speak of 'human liberation' never showed much concern for anybody's liberation until women and blacks started to raise questions. It is in fact a way of saying we have no intention of addressing your concrete demands.

Racism must be combated at the level of the concrete and the specific, but connections must be made. Racism is in fact a litmus test or a barium meal which reveals other injustices and other levels of oppression within the body politic.

(7) I believe that much Christian opposition to racism has been sidelined to the sphere of 'social responsibility' or 'social justice ministry' so that it is seen as an area of interest for certain people, but is not central to the proclamation of the gospel and to the liturgical life of the church. Yet history shapes consciousness and inspires activity. And anti-racist spirituality must place the struggle against racism right at the heart of the baptismal covenant and of the Eucharistic celebration.

(8) And this leads me to my final point: that an anti-racist spirituality needs to include the dimension of celebration. In recent years South African Christians have shown us how necessary it is to sing and dance, to celebrate the dragon's downfall even though we ourselves were bleeding. Babylon is falling, and we need to prefigure the victory of the Kingdom of God in our prayer and praise.

Part Four

Spiritual Theology

7
Time and Eternity

Prayer and theology are concerned with the experience of God, with the point at which time and eternity meet.[1]

'All shall be well' [2]

In a highly activistic, work-dominated culture such as ours, in which people are defined by what they do rather than who they are, the very existence of solitaries and hermits presents a fundamental test of our belief in the life of prayer. Judged by the managerial professional model, that is, in terms of function and efficiency, the solitary is absurd. Julian of Norwich was a solitary of the fourteenth century. It is clear that her life of solitude was not a selfish, egocentric withdrawal, a flight of the alone to the alone, but a life of love, warmth, and care toward her 'even Christians', a life of solidarity with Christ's passion that overflowed in compassion for humanity and the world. Like Saint Anthony, the first hermit, Julian would have insisted that her life and her death was with her neighbour, and that only those committed to the common life could risk the commitment to life in solitude. No one who is enclosed within the false self, the self-absorbed self, can be a true solitary. The Christian solitary lives and has meaning only within the context of Christian solidarity, within the living organism of the Body of Christ. Julian the solitary mystic is part of this common life.

Both Julian and her context speak to me in my London context of the late twentieth century. For the fourteenth century in England, like our own time, was a period of great social upheaval and intense interior striving, an age of militancy and mysticism, of upheaval in soil and soul. Externally it was a time of distress among agricultural labourers, of exploitation of the rural peasants and the urban poor, of sickness, disease, and social violence. It was the age of the Black Death and the Peasants' Revolt. Among the peasants and others who rose up in 1381, there was a thirst for social justice and for equality, a desire to see the end of serfdom and bondage. Though many commentators blamed the rising on those heretics and 'outside agitators' who were loosely lumped together as 'Lollards' – a term used in a similar way to the current use of the terms *Marxists* and *anarchists* (as used, for example, by Margaret Thatcher in relation to the poll tax revolts of 1990) – historians suggest that the social radicalism of the period drew its impetus more from the orthodox Christian tradition and from patristic writers like Saint Basil, Saint Ambrose, and Saint John Chrysostom, whose works had been rediscovered with enthusiasm.

With the revival of interest in the English mystics at the end of the 1960s, Julian has attracted much attention. Since Thomas Merton described her as one of the greatest English theologians, there has been increasing attention also to the theological direction in which Julian can guide us. Some have looked to her as a prophetic figure, 'the dawn star of the truly Catholic reformation which is now only emerging over the whole world.' Her cell at Norwich has become a place of pilgrimage for people from all over the world, not all of them Christians, in search of mysticism and a contemplative approach that is rooted in simplicity, optimism, and earthiness. Simplicity, optimism, earthiness: these are positive, creative, and abiding contributions that Julian can make to our theological understanding and to our discipleship, and they have been a continual source of strength in my ministry. They are brought together in her powerful and unifying symbol of the 'small thing the size of a hazelnut'. I believe that the popularity of Julian and what we might term 'hazelnut theology' is soundly based. She is a wise guide for those who seek a spirituality grounded in the common life.

The simplicity of Julian is central to her life and theology. To a large extent the attraction of Julian is linked to the need for a corrective to centuries of cerebral, head-dominated religion. Historically Julian came at the end of a period in which a major cleavage between heart and head had damaged Western religion. A wedge had been driven between theology (in the head) and mysticism (in the heart). Julian is a mystical theologian, however. In her understanding of God, she returns to the older tradition of seeing God as the Ground of all reality and as intimate and knowable. God, she claims, is courteous and homely. Her dominant theme is the closeness of God. God is closer to us than we are to ourselves. 'It is very greatly pleasing to him that a simple soul should come naked, openly and familiarly.' Linked with this is the sense of the ordinariness of prayer and contemplation. Prayer is natural. It is sin that is unnatural. The way of prayer involves us in a return to simplicity, a return to the reality of what we in essence are.

This sense of contemplative prayer as ordinary and available to all is one of the most important insights of our era. It was of crucial significance to me in Soho. Julian saw it clearly, but the centuries have obscured it and 'ladder' notions of the spiritual life gained ground. During the 1960s Archbishop Michael Ramsey emphasised that 'the contemplation of God with the ground of the soul, is, as those old writers insisted, accessible to any man, woman or child who is ready to try to be obedient and to want God very much.' Julian is important for teaching that prayer is natural: it is what we are made for, and it is open to everyone.

A second feature of Julian that has been important to me is her optimism. Julian is optimistic, hopeful, and joyful. She stands as an abiding corrective to that cosmic theological pessimism that is often associated with a high doctrine of the Fall combined with a low view of human potential and of the power of grace. This combination has done great damage to Christian discipleship, eroding hope and vision, reinforcing gloom and acquiescence in evil. There are still Christians who talk and write as if the Fall and original sin were the only Christian doctrine. But Christians do not believe in the Fall in the same way as we believe in God, in the cross, or in the power of the Holy Spirit. Christians accept the Fall but believe in the power of grace to transform and transcend it. Against the tradition of pessimism, Julian asserts that sin is unnatural. It is 'in opposition to our fair nature'. Indeed 'it belongs to our nature to hate sin'. She goes further, insisting that 'in every soul that shall be saved, there is a godly will that never consented to sin, nor ever shall'.

This approach to sin is at the heart of Julian's optimism. She held that we are more truly theomorphic, God-shaped, than fallen, that we are more truly in heaven than on earth. So her theology is marked by confidence and joy. In contemplating the victory of the Cross she 'laughed greatly'. The Christian response to the Passion of Christ, she claims, is one of cheerfulness, and she speaks of the 'joy and bliss of the Passion'. Though she does not deny the reality and power of sin, she asserts that all shall be well, and this is repeated with emphasis.

I may make all things well, and I can make all things well,
and I shall make all things well, and I will make all things
well, and you will see yourself that every kind of thing shall
be well.

This theological optimism is in sharp contrast to the immense sadness
that marked the waning of the Middle Ages, a pessimism brought on
by war, sickness, plague, and economic depression. Julian offers a
necessary corrective to the pessimism of her age, and to that of ours.
Her theology is rooted in a belief in the image of God in humanity.
She teaches that the image of God in us, that central point that does
not consent to sin, is of far greater theological significance than the
Fall. Sin is, in the strict sense, accidental; it is not part of what makes a
human being. This is not shallow, superficial, naive optimism, but
optimism it certainly is. The confidence of Julian's 'All shall be well
…' comes as a result of that encounter with the Passion which is so
central to the book. It is a confidence that is rooted in the experience
of transfiguration through suffering. Julian's cheerfulness and laughter is not superficial heartiness: it is passionate because it is Passion-
based.

And there is an earthiness about this spirituality that has spoken to
me in my ministry in London. Julian stresses the solidarity of all
people in God. In the sight of God, all people constitute one humanity. Very deliberately – and in line with the Eastern Christian tradition
– she insists that 'our nature is joined to God in its creation'. And this
solidarity includes both the physical and nonphysical aspects of our
nature, our substance, and our sensuality. The whole of us, all of our
nature, is God. Wherever I am, in Cable Street, Hoxton, Soho,
Bethnal Green, or Aldgate, or anywhere in the world, I am in God,
the Ground in which I stand.

St John of the Cross[3]

Saint John of the Cross (1543–91), the Spanish mystic, has
been a major influence on my life and understanding. On the surface
this may seem very odd. What can a Carmelite friar living four
hundred years ago have to contribute to life and work in the inner city
at the end of the twentieth century? At a superficial level there would
seem to be no connection.

Saint John of the Cross was a poet, and his writings include both poems and more systematic texts on the inner life as a journey toward, and within, the reality of God. His best-known works are *The Ascent of Mount Carmel* (of which *The Dark Night of the Soul* is a section) and *The Living Flame of Love*. The phrase 'the dark night of the soul' is the sum total of most people's knowledge of John's work, and the phrase is usually misunderstood. It is often believed to be a pathological condition of the religious life, an illness, a kind of spiritual depression. But to see it this way is to misunderstand John of the Cross very seriously, for, in writing about the dark night, he is writing of the very nature of faith itself.

It was in Soho that the writings of John of the Cross began to make sense to me and to express much of what I was feeling and seeing. Here I was encountering people who were entering a kind of darkness in which they seemed to be lost, but through which in fact they would find themselves, a darkness that was a way of progress. People who had found no nourishment in conventional religion were encountering, sometimes with the aid of drugs, levels of reality of which they had been unaware. They were coming into contact with experiences that traditionally had been seen as 'mystical'.

Here too I was finding that my own life was undergoing a shift from the pseudo-certainties of youth to a more obscure and interior way, a way of faith that was at home with darkness, uncertainty, and humility in the face of mystery. And this is essentially what John of the Cross is writing about. His concern is with the transition from intellectual understanding (or failure to understand), to a deeper and more obscure level of knowing that, following early Eastern theologians, he calls 'unknowing' (*agnosia*). He claims that in order to make progress in knowing and loving God, and in attaining full humanity, we need to come to the end of our conventional 'certainties' and move beyond it to a new level of knowing. This new level is the way of faith, a way of knowledge through darkness. The purpose of the Christian life, and the aim of spiritual direction, is to help people enter the dark night of faith. Yet much conventional religion simply helps people to find a refuge from this darkness. It offers protection rather than encounter. Thus the mystical teaching of John of the Cross undermines, and challenges, forms of conventional religion that rely for their success on false certainties and rigid forms.

The way of faith, John insists, is necessarily obscure. We drive by night, only seeing a little of the way ahead. We make progress precisely by not understanding, by darkness. In Soho I was coming to see how important this truth is in pastoral work and in political struggle. We need to act on the basis of faith, on an insight that is nourished by darkness, a conviction that has its roots in silence, a vision that is not clear but is firmly based in that mysterious reality which is the darkness of God. If social and political action is not to decay into fanaticism, it needs those deep roots.

For John of the Cross, the dark night is not a negative and destructive experience: it is the experience of fire and light, of the living flame of the love of God, as experienced by finite beings. Faith blinds and dazzles the intellect; the sheer intensity of faith over-whelms it. And the darkness grows always deeper. For the dark night is not a phase, it is a symbol by which John speaks of the whole of reality. All our life and all our activity takes place in the context of this darkness.

The night comes upon us. We are never prepared for it, for the essence of the night is the sense of being out of control, of being bound and controlled by the mysterious working of the Spirit of God. Only later do we identify what has been going on and are able to express it. I believe that the effectiveness of our work for justice in the world is directly related to our encounter with this central core of darkness, For truthful and just action can grow only out of deep roots in truth and justice.

As I read the words of this Spanish mystic, so distant from my present life and experience, I am led into the darkness of which he speaks. I am helped to understand something of the mystery of God and of the way of faith and through this to help others who are beginning, or continuing, their own spiritual journey. For Christians who are seeking to enter into their own inner darkness and to work for justice in the light of faith, Saint John of the Cross remains a wise and perceptive guide.

Prayer as conflict[+]

The Christian Gospel arose in the context of conflict and struggle. Galilee was the seedbed of popular revolt, and it was out of the Galilean turmoil that Jesus came with his proclamation of the Kingdom of God, of the year of jubilee, of deliverance to captives and freedom from oppression. His ministry was surrounded by conflict, his message was seen as subversive and seditious, bringing not peace but a sword, dividing families, and undermining both religious and political establishments. The only people apparently who were reconciled by his message were Herod and Pilate, and he was sentenced to death, in Conrad Noel's words, by 'a coalition of the worldlings and the next worldlings'.

In spite of this, Christianity in our society is assumed to be invariably a force for harmony, conflict being of the devil. The Church is valued as an instrument to achieve calm, pour oil on troubled water, a unifying force. Church people seem to find the expression of conflict peculiarly difficult, and church gatherings are often extremely polite, refined, and more sober than vigilant. Emotion and anger are suspect, and debates such as the recent 'Church and the Bomb' debate in General Synod will be praised for their 'high level' not because of the quality of their theology or the intensity of their convictions but because of their genteel and balanced character. The New Testament is neither genteel nor balanced, nor does Christian spirituality involve merely the search for interior peace or exterior harmony.

How does Christian prayer connect with the spiritual conflict which is central to the faith? At two levels. First, growth in prayer depends upon an ability to move out of illusory comfort into a conflict of soul: without such conflict, there can be no progress towards maturity. Prayer begins with self-knowledge, with the confrontation of the false self. The Way of Purgation is the necessary beginning of the spiritual journey, and involves stripping, purification of heart, and the unmasking of illusion. It is a painful process, and so many run from it preferring the safe convention and superficial religiosity which protect us from ourselves and from truth.

But self-knowledge is only the beginning of prayer. The aim of prayer is union with God, and this also involves a movement beyond the conscious self, a movement out of security, away from the comfort and safety of idols to the God who is consuming fire. This journey is expressed most powerfully in the Christian spiritual tradition by the symbols of Desert and Dark Night. From the time of Abraham's movement out of Ur to an unknown land, the desert has played a central role in the Judaeo-Christian movement. It was crucial to the spiritual formation of Israel and it has been of great importance in the

Christian Church from the fourth-century desert movement to Charles de Foucauld in the twentieth century. The desert is the place of spiritual conflict, of encounter with evil, a place which holds the possibilities of spiritual progress and of ultimate betrayal.

The symbol of the Dark Night, as used by St John of the Cross, develops at the personal interior level the theology of 'Unknowing' (*agnosia*) in the early Greek Fathers. The Dark Night is a symbol of the way of faith, involving a movement away from false lights, and experience of inner conflict, of purification, enlightenment and healing through darkness.

Prayer then involves an interior conflict, the battle for the human heart. But, there is a second sense in which prayer can lead to conflict. Marx saw religious belief as an analgesic, painkiller. But is this the only role it can play? The experience of reflection and prayer may lead to a clarifying awareness, an enriching of vision, and intensifying of sensitivity to the anguish of the world and of people. In so doing, it may well increase, rather than reduce, conflict by pushing many people, through their heightened spiritual awareness, into open criticism of, and hostility to, the anti-spiritual forces in our society.

Prayer may equally help to provide the inner resources necessary for the maintenance of such criticism and hostility and, by its vision of an alternative reality, symbolised in the social character of the Eucharist, may encourage discontent and dissatisfaction with the way we live now. Prayer may thus be an important way of undermining the structures of evil, and if religious and political establishments saw this, they would increase their efforts to discourage it, and urge people to return to the safety of conventional religion which opts for comfort rather than transformation.

Obstacles to prayer[5]

Prayer is the fundamental relationship of humanity to God, a state of attention to God, involving the whole personality. 'In prayer', wrote the nineteenth-century Bishop Theophan, 'the principal thing is to stand before God with the mind in the heart, and to go on standing before him unceasingly day and night until the end of life.' This expression 'the mind in the heart' is a favourite one of the Eastern fathers, and is their way of insisting that prayer must involve the unifying of the personality, the integration of mind and heart into one centre. They also insist that prayer is primarily the action of God. 'Prayer is God', wrote St Gregory of Sinai in the fourteenth century, 'who works for all things in men.' In another place he defines prayer as 'the manifestation of baptism'. Prayer then is not essentially a work but the manifesting and flowering of God's grace in us. All prayer then is charismatic, all prayer is a gift. There is an Eastern story of a person who came to a monk and asked, 'Father, what is prayer?' The monk held out his hands and flames shot up from his fingers. 'That is prayer', he said. He was a soul on fire, and where necessary he could manifest the fact. To pray then is to be aflame with God. The purpose of human effort, and of spiritual direction, is simply to clear away obstacles to this manifestation of the divine flame.

The most fundamental of these obstacles is, of course, sin. That may seem a rather obvious point, but it is easily forgotten that ethics and spirituality are one. Today when we tend to have moralistic notions of sin, we need to recover the theological understanding of the Scriptures, and to remember that 'sin for Jews was seen as a quenching of the Spirit'. It was thus the very negation and opposite of the path of prayer. Scripture is emphatic that it is human sin which separates from God. 'The Lord's arm is not so short that he cannot save, nor his ear too dull to hear. It is your iniquities that raise a barrier between you and your God. Because of your sins, he has hidden his face so that he does not hear you' (Isa. 59:1–2). Throughout the Bible, there are a number of specific aspects of human sinfulness which are named as definite obstacles to prayer.

First, refusal to forgive. Forgiveness in prayer is not possible if there is a refusal to forgive others (Matt. 6:15). Secondly, anger and quarrelsome thoughts. Thus St Paul urges prayers to be said in the congregation by people who 'shall lift up their hands with a pure intention, excluding angry or quarrelsome thoughts' (1 Tim. 2:8). The implication is that such thoughts hinder or prevent prayer. Certainly the experience of Christians is that angry thoughts are among the commonest forms of distraction, and they may in fact become a form of 'anti-prayer', the shaping of a consciousness which is of the flesh, not of God. Thirdly, refusal to be reconciled. The existence of disharmony, linked with injustice in social relationships, is seen in the prophets as a barrier to prayer. 'When you lift your hands outspread in prayer, I will hide my face from you. Though you offer countless prayers I will not listen. There is blood on your hands' (Isa. 1:15). The context makes clear that what is actually preventing the prayer from being heard is the sickness of the nation (1:5–6), and the refusal to seek justice and mercy (1:17). Similarly Jesus warns that if one is bringing a gift and suddenly remembers a grievance, it is necessary to sort this out. 'First go and make peace with your brother and only then come back and offer your gift' (Matt. 5:23–4).

A fourth area in which prayer can be hindered is that of distorted sexuality and lust. There is no hint in the Bible of the Manichean view that sexuality and physical relationships are the enemy of spirituality. But there is certainly the sense that disorder in sexuality is related to disorder in the spiritual life. St Peter urges couples to conduct their married lives with understanding, and tells husbands to honour the woman's body, because they share together in the grace of God. 'Then your prayers will not be hindered' (1 Pet. 3:7). Self-control, self-discipline and sobriety are linked to prayer and are its essential prerequisites. The same epistle speaks of 'an ordered and sober life given to prayer' (4:7). St James blames the fact that prayer requests are not answered on the fact that people pray from wrong motives, in particular the quest for pleasure (Jas. 4:2–3).

Fifthly, involvement in the occult and in magical rites is seen in the Old Testament as an impediment to spirituality. The Mosaic Law calls dabbling with wizards, spirits and soothsayers an 'abomination' (Deut. 18:10–12). Disobedience to God's will is a sixth way in which prayer can be frustrated. God listens to those who obey his will (John 9:31). Seventhly, refusal to confess one's sins in the community seems to be suggested as an obstacle by St James, who urges such confession combined with mutual prayer in order that healing may result (Jas. 5:16). The implication is that it may fail to occur if confession and prayer are absent. Finally, greed and avarice are listed in Luke 6:38 where it is pointed out that it is the person who gives generously who will receive from God.

Sin is therefore the first type of hindrance to the life of prayer that must be recognised, and the examination of one's motives and one's life is essential if prayer is to flourish. There can be no spiritual life if ethical demands are bypassed or sins ignored. So all Christian liturgies begin with recollection, confession and the cry for mercy '*Kyrie Elesion*'. Similarly, at the heart of all spiritual discipline is the search for self-knowledge. This introversion, this turning inwards must not stop. We must go beyond the self to God, the deepest centre of consciousness. Yet without self-discovery there can be no further progress. Without such self-knowledge our love remains superficial. But the self which we seek to know is not the fleeting ego which provides one's normal focus of awareness. The movement which the tradition calls the Purgative Way is essentially concerned with stripping away the false self, the removal of illusions.

The acquaintance with one's inner depths is intimately connected with the encounter with God. The process of self-discovery is inseparable from personal relationships. It is through the encounter with others that we grow in self-knowledge. Growth cannot occur in a vacuum, and so the establishment of sound relationships within a family is of the utmost importance to the future health of the spirit. Out of the experience of *lack of love* can come a spirituality of self-centredness, the fruit of bitter resentment. The sense of interdependence of relationship with God and relationship with human beings is very biblical. 'He judged the cause of the poor and needy: then it was well. Is this not to know me? Says the Lord' (Jer. 22:16, RSV). 'If anyone says, "I love God" and hates his brother, he is a liar: for he who does not love his brother whom he has seen cannot love God whom he has not seen' (1 John 4:20). So there is a horizontal dimension in spiritual growth. How can a person be a friend of God if they are incapable of friendships with people? Inability to relate at the human level is an impossible basis for the building up of spiritual relationships.

So the best preparation for the life of prayer is to become more intensely human. Sin diminishes and distorts one's humanity. Lack of self-knowledge and inability to relate to people are both signs that one is far from mature humanity. Both require a degree of depth, and so one of the factors which will always work against growth in prayer is shallowness and lack of inner discipline. The word which most accurately conveys the condition is the word *promiscuity*. Today we tend to restrict the word to the narrow sexual area, and even there it is used imprecisely. We seem in fact to believe in and accept promiscuity in every sphere except the sexual! For the *Shorter Oxford English Dictionary* defines 'promiscuous' as follows:

1. Consisting of members or elements of different kinds pressed together without order; or mixed and disorderly composition or character.

2.That is without discrimination or method, confusedly mingled, indiscriminate.

3.Casual, careless, irregular.

To apply this definition to the life of prayer and to spirituality is to see how dangerous is promiscuity of the spirit. It does not allow prayer to progress. In Jesus' parable of the sower, the seed which falls into good soil is that which bears fruit, while that which falls along the wayside comes to nothing. St Gregory of Sinai put the same point when he said, 'Trees which are repeatedly transplanted do not grow roots.' So in the life of the spirit, there is a vital place for disciplined rule. Without this inner *askesis*, the life will wither for lack of roots. The deeper the degree of self-knowledge, the greater the need for this *askesis* of spirit. For the encounter with the depths of one's consciousness is an encounter with the shadow, the dark side of oneself. In particular one meets the forces of pride and egocentricity, as well as the temptation to despair. The latter may well intensify as the insight into the dark side of one's nature deepens. Spiritual pride, however, is the hazard of all religious people, and it is a major obstacle to spiritual growth. The disciplines of self-examination and confession, of humble service to others, of learning to receive as well as to give, are valuable correctives. Without constant vigilance, they are always likely to occur. Without purity of heart and continuous *metanoia*, spirituality becomes demonic.

Confession and penance[6]

To go to confession is an ancient Christian practice. The early church, however, was much more rigorous over the matter of sins committed after Baptism than we are today. The person was admitted into an order of penitents, clothed in a penitential robe, and joined other penitents in a special part of the church. Periods of penance might last from the forty days of Lent to several years, and during this period strict continence, long periods of prayer and almsgiving were obligatory. But one was only admitted to do penance once. If afterwards one then fell into grave sin, it was too bad: there was no further remedy. The practice of repeated acts of confession and absolution did not arise for some centuries, and when it did, was frowned on by the official church and regarded as a sign of permissiveness and laxity! While public penance was still referred to by Thomas Aquinas, the practice of private confession at frequent intervals quickly established itself, and in 1215 the Fourth Lateran Council established the practice of a minimum annual confession and communion at Easter ('the Paschal Precept') as normative in the western church.

What is the point of going to confession? The practice has been condemned as 'priestcraft', as introducing 'a priest between my soul and God', as destroying the free access of sinner to Christ without others as intermediaries, as encouragement to further sin, as 'Popish', and so on. However, the pioneers of the Catholic revival in the Church of England in the nineteenth century were correct to see the revival of sacramental confession as absolutely central to their work. Thus John Keble could say, 'We go on working in the dark, and in the dark it will be, until the rule of systematic confession is revived in our church.' In other words, confession is not a drastic remedy for the desperate or the grave sinner, or an extra devotion for the super-pious or fastidious: it is a necessary element in every Christian growth in prayer and life.

When we make a confession within the framework of the Sacrament of Reconciliation, we are participating in the mystery of Christ's reconciling work. This is the sacrament of reconciliation and peace: here Christ who won for us forgiveness of sins specifically mediates the forgiveness to a specific sinner in a specific place. Christ's forgiveness is here made real to the individual. There is nothing essentially different in the way confession works from the way the other sacraments work. The claim that a priest 'stands between the soul and God' could perfectly well be used as an objection to Baptism, to the Eucharist, to anointing, to any and every sacramental ministration. The priest in confession acts in the same capacity as in any other sacrament. Here, as elsewhere, God uses the human relationship to communicate divine grace and power. In this ministry, there is a renewal of Baptism. The grace of the baptismal event is restored to us, and we are again received into Christ's Body. As sin is social, so this essentially social sacrament restores to us communion with the Body.

Confession is a way of making systematic and effective the essential struggle against evil which is so central to the life in Christ. It is not an abnormal, crisis activity, but is part of the day-by-day, domestic ministry of the church. Of course, there are crisis points in our lives when it is urgent and essential that we make our confession, 'make a clean breast of it', and nothing but such open acknowledgement of sin will suffice. And, of course, there are people for whom sacramental confession and the assurance of forgiveness is more necessary than others. Yet the ministry of reconciliation, communicated to an individual human being by another individual human being within the Body of Christ, is a necessary and normal part of the life of grace. Every priest at ordination is told 'Whose sins you forgive, they are forgiven; whose sins you retain, they are retained.' The forgiveness of sins is therefore central to the exercise of priesthood. It is hard to see how that ministry can be exercised in any meaningful way without the practice of self-examination and thorough, personal confession.

For it is to *me* that the gift of forgiveness is given. Penance is the most intimate and most personal of all sacraments. The Gospel demand, 'Repent!' comes to me, and only I can decide to respond. This is not a contradiction of the essentially social character of sin. But repentance must begin with me. Its consequences are social, and there is a solidarity in salvation as in sin. But the confrontation with the sin in me, the opening up of myself to the Light – this is only done in the solitude of my own being. I come alone into the Light. There are no general absolutions in the Gospel: every human being comes alone face to face with God. Here Jesus Christ confronts me with the choice between death and life, between selfishness and discipleship. There is no way of reaching the Kingdom by somehow being swept along with a crowd. Similarly there can be no comfortable dodging of the demand to repent by a muffled, embarrassed general confession which evades the self-scrutiny and the confrontation with sin. In the sacrament we are brought face to face with the demand of Gospel repentance. The ministry of reconciliation is delivered to me, for my own sins.

What then does it mean in practice to 'go to confession'? The mechanics are simple. The person wishing to make a confession goes to a priest, either by appointment or at a set time in church, and kneels down or sits facing the priest in the place appointed for this purpose. The priest will welcome the penitent and give him or her a blessing. The penitent then proceeds to confess their sins, mentioning how long it is since their last confession (unless, of course, this is their first confession, in which case they say so). After the confession, the priest may give advice if it has been sought, though it should be emphasised strongly that the giving of advice is not a necessary part of the sacrament, and in many cases is not called for and should not be given. The purpose of the sacrament is forgiveness, and so, after giving a penance, or simple act done out of gratitude (saying a prayer or reading a passage of the Bible, for example), the priest will give the absolution. Then he will bless the penitent who goes back to their place and says their penance before leaving.

That is the basic framework, but there are as many variations in the way in which a confession is made as there are Christian people confessing. The place and position, for example, may vary. In the past, confessions were often made in an anonymous atmosphere in a large structure called a confessional box. The priest was hidden from the penitent by a screen or grille. In many Anglican churches there was, and still is, a modification of this by which a kneeling desk is situated next to a chair, with or without a screen in between them, and so there is not the same degree of anonymity, through there is a formal structure for the relationship. However, since the revision of the rite in the Roman Church since 1974 the old structures have gone in many places. Priest and penitent face each other across a table in a 'reconciliation room'. There is more informality and warmth in both the setting and the way of making the confession. There will be Scripture readings, prayers said together, and an emphasis on the pastoral, rather than the judicial, role of the priest. It is important for each person making a confession to do it in the way which is right for them, and which enables them to confess their sins fully and honestly.

Frequency of confession too varies a good deal from one person to another. Once a month will be right for some people, while for others a quarterly confession is more valuable. It is helpful to discuss this with the priest who is to hear the confession. Choosing a confessor is important. Often the confessor and the spiritual director are the same person, and this is probably the best arrangement. Spiritual direction, however, is not necessarily given in the confessional, and the two activities may be separated in time and place, even though the people are the same. But sometimes there are circumstances which make it right that the confessor and director should be different. For instance, a spiritual director need not be a priest. The question of lay confession and absolution is an important one but cannot be gone into here. But the practice of moving from one priest to another for confession is thoroughly bad, and should only happen for the most extreme of reasons.

Regular confession should be seen as an important aspect of regular prayer. Its purpose is not only the removal of sin but the recovery of the Holy Spirit. St Jerome in the fourth century saw this clearly. Writing of the confessor, he said, 'He imposes his hand on the subject and invokes the return of the Holy Spirit.' In the recent revision of the rite, the stretching out of the hands over the head of the penitent has been restored at the absolution, thus linking absolution with the other sacraments of healing and strengthening, the sacraments of the Holy Spirit. The *Order of Penance* (1974) makes it clear that the absolution 'shows the connection between the reconciliation of the sinner and the paschal mystery of Christ, and the part that the Holy Spirit plays in the forgiveness of sins' (paragraph 19).

A confession, if it is to be full and thorough, needs to be preceded by a rigorous self-examination. The purpose of self-examination is self-knowledge leading to repentance, and we can only repent of what we know. So we try to look beneath and beyond the facades and pretences which we build around us, and to see the reality of our own sin. This involves facing the fact of projection, the process by which we disguise our real condition and our inner conflicts, and cast all the responsibility for our ills onto the behaviour of others. We face our lack of faith, our unwillingness to trust, our defences by which we protect ourselves against the reality of God. Repentance involves both self-acceptance and self-denial, and these two are not contradictory. To accept ourselves is to see ourselves as we really are. To deny ourselves is to renounce the ego or false self which surrounds us with false goals and facades: the stripping away of this false consciousness is a vital first step in repentance and in the process of inner prayer. Self-examination is not morbid introspection or self-condemnation, but the honest, fearless confrontation of the self, and its abandonment to God in trust.

Many old forms of self-examination consisted of 'sin lists', and even today many of the guides seem to be based on Old Testament methods, for example, following the pattern of the Ten Commandments. But a 'Ten Commandments moral theology' is not really adequate for examining oneself in the light of the Gospel. We need to go deeper than simply going through a list of personal violations of rules, looking more closely at the corruption of the will than at the particular external acts committed. Sin does not consist only in transgression of external laws, but in an inner alienation of the personality from God. So we need to find forms of self-examination which will help us to understand our own situation better in the light of God's revelation; and which will also help us to see our sin in its social context.

Self-knowledge, the spiritual writers tell us, is also God-knowledge, and theology is closely related to spirituality. So we are trying to see how the theology, the truth about God, becomes true *for me* and *within me*. In self-examination we face the conflict which is at the heart of our beings, the conflict which we seek to disguise by our bogus sense of assurance, blocking off doubt in the security of pseudo-conviction. Yet deep down we cannot hide from our ambivalence, and within us are the roots of holiness and of blasphemy. Camus said that every blasphemy is a participation in holiness: we can only really love God and other people at the expense of being able to hate them. In the same way, one makes more progress in wrestling with crises and with God than one does in living a life of respectability shielded from adversity. Respectability is usually a form of protection against conflict: it is also a protection against growth. For, as Rilke said once, 'If my devils are to leave me, I am afraid my angels will take flight as well.' One of the greatest enemies of the spiritual life is pseudo-innocence. In self-examination and confession we try to rid ourselves of it.

Our task then is not to eliminate conflict, struggle and doubt but to learn to live in the midst of them through the light of faith. Our aim is not inner security and spiritual ease, putting to death the difficult awkward side of us which persists in disturbing the tranquillity and order of the soul. Christian penitence always has something of the knife-edge about it. We may banish the doubting, troubled side of us to the unconscious, but it is still there and will cause more trouble if it is not recognised, or, as so often, hidden beneath a facade of triumphalist faith and certainty. Repressed doubt can lead to the worst kind of fanaticism: the zealot, the fascist, the spiritual rapist who assaults the souls of others and bombards the world with the noise of their own insecurity. Self-examination means honestly recognising our own insecurity and the reality of our doubt, without embarrassment, without guilt, trying to see how doubt and struggle are part of the life of faith. From spiritual smugness and the lifelessness of idols may the fiery troublesome God deliver us.

Prayer and silence[7]

Physical silence and stillness are not in themselves creative. Silence can be a destructive and disturbing force. The negative silence of solitary imprisonment can crush the human being. There is a silence of hatred, a silence filled with fear and terror, a silence of the unknown. There is a silence which is so threatening that we make sure that all the gaps are filled with synthetic noise. Silence, as in Paul Simon's song 'The Sounds of Silence', can grow like a cancer or, as in Ingmar Bergman's film *The Silence* (1962), can signify the death of God. Silence in Scripture can mean ruin – Isaiah saw Moab put to silence – or death – 'The dead praise not you, O Lord, nor all they that go down into silence.'

Coming to terms with silence is a necessary element in self-knowledge and in prayer. Throughout the writings of all the great spiritual guides, we find the call to inner silence. In the tradition of the desert, the early term for a monk was *hesuchastes*, one who lived in solitude and silence. *Hesuchia* was seen as the essential condition of prayerfulness. It is more than silence, it is a state of soul characterised by sobriety, inner vigilance, attention to God. One of the Desert fathers, Arsenius, was told, 'Flee, keep silent, be still, for these are the roots of sinlessness.' St John Climacus uses the same language about hesychia which Evagrius used about prayer itself. 'Hesychia is a laying aside of thought.' Closely linked with the idea of inner silence in the hesychast tradition is the stress on breathing. 'Let the remembrance of Jesus be united to your breathing, and then you will know the value of hesychia.' It is this conception which is the background to the Jesus Prayer. Before true prayer can begin, there must be a discipline of thought through the practice of silence and withdrawal, and a discipline of the body through the practice of some degree of physical solitude and stillness. Then, says St Basil, 'When the mind is no longer dissipated amidst external things, nor dispersed across the world through the senses, it returns to itself; and by means of itself it ascends to the thought of God.' It is in this context that silence can help us to grow by reducing the overcrowding of the mind, and enabling the heart to become centred in gentleness and peace.

The practice of silence is, of course, inseparable from the discovery of one's own inner depths. For when one descends into the depths of one's spirit, there is a realisation of the closeness of God, the ground of one's being, the depth in which our own soul stands. The eastern church has seen this process of introversion as a return to the heart (*kardia*), the centre of the personality. Through inner silence, one comes to see the inner face, the focal point of spirituality. In the Bible the heart is the seat of intelligence and of life. But it is also from the heart that the depths of wickedness issue forth. The human heart is desperately wicked according to Jeremiah (17:9), and Jesus tells his disciples that it is from the heart that murder, adultery and other evils proceed (Matt. 15:18–19). The heart therefore is in need of purification, and this is an important part of affective prayer. The purpose of silence is to allow the heart to be still and listen to God. 'When you pray, you yourself must be silent ... Let the prayer speak.'

To build up inner resources of silence and stillness is one of the central tasks of training in prayer. In a culture which has almost outlawed silence, it is a matter of urgency that Christians create oases, centres in which inner silence can be cultivated. At times, such a search for silence needs to be particularly concentrated, and this is the purpose of retreats. A retreat is a period of silence, lasting usually between one and five days, in which an individual will sever herself from her environment in order to give herself up more completely to the will of God. An annual retreat of some kind is probably an essential feature of serious Christian living, and the conducting of retreats is an important element within spiritual direction. Not all priests are good retreat conductors, but many are, and there is a need to draw more individuals into this growing sphere of work. A retreat is a time of awakening, of new vision and new zest. Another major part of a retreat is to allow an individual to relax and to expand at leisure, to give some creative space in which to grow.

Prayer and death[8]

Prayer and dying are clearly close if only because they accompany each other through life: all life is involved with the process of dying, and in Christian understanding all life is prayer. Throughout our lives there is dying and the birth of new life through death, and this is as true at the spiritual level as at the physical level of tissues and cells. And the facing of the reality of death in daily living is central to New Testament spirituality: the person who seeks to save their life will lose it. It has been said that the best way to live is to die every night, and that one of our chief dangers is that of clinging to our past and seeking to preserve it against the harsh spiritual facts of new life through death.

If this is so then it follows that to prepare ourselves for death by living lives of self-abandonment is the best preparation for our pastoral ministry to the dying. The Christian who has at least begun to face death in himself can begin to enter into the experience of the dying person with sensitivity. Dr Cicely Saunders, the pioneer of the hospice movement, wrote of a dying patient whom she asked what he looked for in those who were caring for him. He answered, 'For someone to look as if she is trying to understand me.' And understanding must involve the understanding of the person's need to prepare for death. The refusal, or inability, of many doctors to tell the truth to dying patients, a fact which emerges very clearly from a number of recent studies, is therefore worrying. For the onset of death is too important for the Christian to be deceived about it. Many dying people, of course, do know the truth, and need the opportunity to express it and have their insight confirmed. The Christian has a vital contribution to make here in trying to help people to face death and in holding them before God during their period of dying. But he or she must also recognise that to do this demands a real facing of that terrible reality in her or his own life, and that their own prayer will be deepened by the insights of the dying.

Prayer alongside the dying will usually be a silent kind of watching. 'Watch with me' is its most accurate slogan, for its principal marks should be respect for the dying person, and attention to their agony and distress. It is a deeply contemplative form of prayer. We need to listen to and learn from the prayer of the dying, as indeed from elderly people in general. Jung held that in the second half of life the unconscious spontaneously invades consciousness. The onset of middle age brings difficulties and opportunities in prayer life. We often make the mistake of seeing the ageing process in entirely negative terms, as decline and loss of function. Of course, growing old does involve the shrinking of the number of functional brain cells, and it has effects on intelligence, memory, and so on. But the positive contribution of the old to the praying life of the Body of Christ needs strong emphasis. In many parishes in fact it is the obscure prayer life of a few old people which is the spiritual mainstay and source of strength. And as death draws near this prayer may grow in silence, simplicity, and confidence.

So we are to share in the prayer of the dying. But prayer also is needed at the time of death, and after death as we continue to hold the departed in our prayer and in the pleading of the Sacrifice of the Mass. The liturgy of Christian burial needs to express the faith in the resurrection. For death is the last enemy to be destroyed, and Christian prayer is living prayer, prayer which is a sharing in the risen life of Christ. But that experience of being risen in Christ comes only through the experience of dying: light comes through the sharing of darkness. That is the meaning of dying daily: every day we do 'die a little' and so prepare for the final conflict. True prayer should help us face, and not evade, that conflict, by enabling us to live as we shall eventually die.

8

Human Transformation

*God is the searcher of minds and hearts (Rev.
1:23), and theology is an ascetical discipline
concerned with human transformation, with
personal holiness and with the transfiguration of
the self.*[1]

Spirituality and social justice[2]

In the Old Testament the prophets united spiritual religion
and the struggle for social justice. They were not two things: they were
one thing. And their attack on injustice in society was framed in the
language of oppression, fornication and rebellion. Grinding the faces
of the poor, playing the harlot, refusing to hear the word of the
Lord were all part of one syndrome which represented the direct
opposite of the monastic vows, and the whole syndrome was called
idolatry. And I want to suggest that our society, far from being a
secular society, is in fact an idolatrous society.

Our society is largely alienated from spiritual values, but at the
same tolerates and even encourages, and in parts of the United States
financially supports, pockets of spirituality, having reduced them to
the status of hobbies. And in this society we see the anti-type of the
Christian community with its anti-vows where poverty, chastity and
obedience have become demonic, the exact opposite of the monastic
vows, symbols of oppression and idolatry. The anti-vow of poverty, a
commitment to inequalities of wealth and power, concentrated financial power, growing areas of enforced poverty and deprivation in
society. And note, not simply pockets of incidental poverty, but
unfortunate blocks of poverty on the urban landscape: essential and
inevitable poverty, so long as the maldistribution of resources and the
imbalances in society remain. The prophets insist that spirituality
cannot co-exist with oppression and injustice.

Secondly, the anti-vow of chastity. A commitment to dehumanisation, to what Marcuse calls the 'one-dimensional Man': the denial of human sexuality, the denial of the physical. Surely not, say the critics. How can anyone seriously maintain that we live in a desexualised society? Over sexed maybe, but desexualised never! Yet in fact the apparent explosion of sexual licence, pornography and all the rest is statistically trivial compared with the prevalence of serious sexual and emotional repression and ignorance in our society, a prevalence to which any Samaritan, any marriage counsellor, anyone working at the personal level with individuals and couples would testify. The surface manifestations of apparently liberated sexuality are merely the pathetic admission of the lack of it. On the contrary there is a dulling of the feelings, sexuality is banished to the bedroom and to the genital area. And we can no longer say, as Julian of Norwich could say, that our substance and our sensuality together are in God. We suffer rather from what Thomas Aquinas called 'in-sensibilitas', and which he stigmatised as a vice. But without growth towards emotional maturity in human fulfilment, there can be no true spirituality. In Catholic spirituality grace perfects nature and does not destroy it.

And the anti-vow of obedience, for we have become an increasingly repressive and authoritarian society, the society of the corporate, strong state where the Yes-persons prosper and there are very few Christian voices raised against this most sinister development. In such a society, says Thomas Merton in his 'Meditation on the Death of Eichmann', the sane people are the ones who are not plagued by doubt, who obey orders without question. And the most sinister aspect of these anti-vows as I have called them, is that they are not even freely made. They are simply accepted as part of the way things are and will be. And so there is in our society a disease of anti-contemplation, a disease of partial perception or no perception at all. Now what is the relevance of this to spirituality? Simply this. That there is a direct link between what happens within the soul and what happens within the social order.

And so spirituality is not a private concern at the fringes of life, but is concerned with the unity between the interior life of human beings and the life of society.

Spiritual renewal[3]

First, *all spirituality is theological.* We must reject the unhealthy and heretical split between theology and spirituality. There will be no Catholic renewal unless there is a renewal of the concept of what theology is. Theology, claims Eric Mascall in his recent book, is in danger of becoming an extinct discipline. But theology is not an academic discipline which goes on in lecture halls. It is inseparable from prayer and contemplation and a quest for holiness. Theology is inseparable from contemplation and from transformation as the Eastern Church has always realised. It involves commitment, choice and discipleship and so one cannot be a theologian apart from the quest for holiness. It is not only undesirable, it is impossible. Theology involves of its nature purification and inner conflict. As Evagrius said, 'A theologian is one whose prayer is true.'

Secondly, *all spirituality is materialistic.* We have heard not too much in this conference, although we began to hear a bit in the last session, about the urgent problems of our country. In our search for renewal we are always in grave danger of seeking only ecclesiastical renewal. The ordination of women may be desperately important, but there is no point discussing the ordination of women if we have all become radioactive. You cannot confer holy orders on the dead. So perhaps we ought to think that an issue like the neutron bomb is at least as important as the ordination of women. Spirituality is concerned with finding the will of God in the midst of matter. It must be concerned with the issues of inner-city decay, with the evils of race and class oppression. But let us remember that there are forms of spirituality that oppress and enslave us, just as there are forms of spirituality which set us free. And Christian spirituality is rooted in the specific material physical crudity of Incarnation, resurrection and Eucharist. As Father Adrian Hastings says in his book *The Faces of God*: 'For all their devotion and all their sincerity, the spiritualisers and demythologisers hold to a different Christ and a different Gospel.' It is only the flesh of the risen Christ sacramentally present in the Eucharist which provides the link between spirituality and the transformation of the world. It seems to me to be a disastrous error to oppose spirituality to materialism. Today we use materialism as a pejorative expression. The choice is not between spirituality and materialism, but between true spirituality and false, between true materialism and false. Listen to the words of St John of Damascus which are highly relevant to our present situation. 'I do not worship matter', he said, in the iconoclastic controversy, 'but I do worship the Creator of matter, who for my sake became material, who vouchsafed to dwell in matter and through matter effected my salvation. I will not cease from reverencing matter, for it was through matter that my salvation came to pass.' So the renewal of Catholic materialism is an urgent necessity because, as one of the great fathers reminded us, 'What is not assumed cannot be healed.'

And thirdly, and lastly, *all spirituality is essentially social.* Let us bring to an end for ever the belief that social responsibility or that blessed Anglican expression 'social implications', is a by-product of the Gospel and somehow might lead us away from the spiritual life. Of course there is a danger, and Evelyn Underhill was pointing to it many years ago, of a shallow form of social reformist religion which exalts service at the expense of awe. That sort of religion, she said, 'does not wear well'. But Catholic theology is essentially social theology. In the words of de Lubac, 'It is social in the heart of its dogma.' 'The Holy Trinity as the basis of a new world order' was the title of the first chapter of a book by Conrad Noel. Catholic spirituality is rooted in the social teaching about the Trinity in whose social image we are made; about the taking of us into God, an essential part of the Incarnation which we frequently forget; about the social life of the new age which the Eucharist foreshadows. There is therefore no social Gospel, there is simply 'the Gospel' which is essentially social because God is social. And this is absolutely vital to spiritual theology because much conventional religion does not worship God at all but a different God, a God who is remoter from the structures of this world and dwells in an unapproachable isolation. This is not the God of Catholic orthodoxy, this is the God of the Arian heresy, remote, aloof, incapable of sharing his nature, and because he couldn't share it, he didn't share it. And don't think for one moment that Arianism is dead. It is in fact the conventional religion of England. And it is this remote, spiritual, uninvolved God who has recently resurfaced in current establishment theology. Thus it is that much current so-called radical theology cuts at the root of Christian social action and Christian social criticism. By accommodating theology to the world, it undermines any critique of the world by theology and ends up totally conformed to the world. Arian theology, whether it be in its crude

form or in its sophisticated Wilesian form, can have no social consequences for its God is especially impotent. Professor Alasdair MacIntyre was perhaps more correct, when he said, 'The Creed of the
English is that there is no God and that it is wise to pray to him from
time to time.' Bad theology leads to social autism. But equally social
autism distorts theology and spirituality. There is an essential connex-
ion between them.

Last of all, there will be no renewal of spirituality in my view unless
we discover the centrality of what Canon Percy Widdrington, 50 years
ago, called 'The Kingdom of God as the regulative principle of
theology.' In 1923 Widdrington in a book called *The Return of
Christendom* predicted that when the good news of the Kingdom of
God is rediscovered in the Church, it will bring about a Reformation
compared with which the Reformation of the 16th century will appear
a very small thing. It is that vision of the Kingdom of God, of a
restored universe, the home of justice, love, and peace which must
renew our hope. We look for new heavens and a new earth where
justice dwells. Without that hope, the future which lies before us as a
Catholic movement is stagnation and the future which lies before the
world is universal death.

Youth culture[+]

From its beginnings the Underground has emphasised the
idea of community, and the quest for alternative life-styles has been a
fundamental feature of its growth. The movement into communes
has been the particular facet of this quest which has attracted most
publicity, although individual communes have mostly escaped the
notice of the media. The idea of the commune goes back beyond the
hippy culture. Joseph Ledger had set up a vegetarian society, Ahimsa,
and a journal *Ahimsa Progress* appeared in 1964, followed in 1965 by
Ahimsa Communities, the organ of the breakaway Vegan Communities of Tony Kelly. In August 1996 the Sarvodaya Communities
Newsletter appeared. Meanwhile, in November 1965, the Selene
Community, the first actual commune, was formed; however, not
until August 1968 did the Commune Movement, with its journal
Communes, evolve from Selene. A little earlier, in 1967, the British
Diggers had emerged under the leadership of Sid Rawle, and soon
there were a number of Digger groups, the Hyde Park Diggers being

the largest one, with an inner group, the Tribe of the Sun. Later the London Street Commune, a beat solidarity group centred on Piccadilly Circus, made national news through occupying various premises in Central London. Other Digger groups appeared – the Hapt Diggers in 1967, the Coventry Diggers in 1968 – but the main group has now moved to an island off the west coast of Ireland.

The Commune Movement in Britain is strong and growing, as is the literature on making communes. The aim of the movement has been expressed as a wish 'to create a federal society of communities wherein everyone shall be free to do whatever he wishes provided only that he does not transgress the freedom of another'. Many communes in their revulsion from technology have moved in a rural direction. Some have a religious basis, while others are more 'therapeutic' in orientation, and many are inspired by social and political action. The Kingsway Community grew out of Christian ideals, and its members have mainly been addicts of various drugs. The Blackheath Commune too was Christian-based but more politically involved. The Findhorn Trust in Moray, Scotland, certainly the largest commune in Britain, has existed since 1962 and has a spiritual orientation, 'towards the Western occult tradition', though individuals in it may be drawn towards Christian, Buddhist or Vedantic Hindu ways of thinking.

The appearance of the commune movement, it has been suggested, is one answer to the common accusation that the counter-culture has emphasised liberation, expansion of consciousness and aesthetics, but neglected the creation of new institutions. Their 'revolutionary' potential lies in their example, in their refusal to wait for a future revolution. But there are certainly some problematic areas. It has been argued that the average life of a religious community is fifty years but that of a secular one, five years, and this has been attributed to the systems of discipline and control in the religious groups. In the secular communes in particular, the question of sexual relationships has been a thorny area, as indeed it was in the nineteenth-century Oneida Community, a Christian group which practised 'complex marriage'. Some of the religious, as well as the secular, communes are exploring ideas of 'group marriage', but the majority of them appear to follow the 'extended family' idea. Rejection of the nuclear family is almost universal: it is seen as leading to isolation and separateness, rather than to outgoing love and care. Yet sexual exploitation remains, as do difficulties about privacy and property.

In the United States, the movement into communes has been most marked in the post-hippy development of California. As a general rule, the communes there are strongly opposed to publicity. They know only too well that the cause of the psychedelic movement in America was largely determined by the public image of the hippy, an image created by the media. So the communes avoid drawing attention to themselves. They know that if they do so, Middle America will declare war on them, and large numbers of 'straight' young people will attempt to climb on to the commune bandwaggon. However, the media did discover them and declared 1969 'the year of the commune.' In fact, the type of commune which began to increase most rapidly in both urban and rural areas was the 'crash-pad' type. Unlike other kinds of commune, the crash-pad type has been devoid of any real goals, discipline or philosophy, and the health and drugs problems are more than normally severe. They are the most unstable type of commune and the most dangerous. Throughout the commune movement as a whole, the incidence of drug use is extremely low, and, indeed, the communes of California are among the most successful non-drug treatment modalities. One of the leading authorities on the communes in North California has suggested that the total consumption of psycho-active chemicals in the communes is substantially less than the average American norm.

In addition to the communes, there are now a large number of alternative styles of community. In the United States, the Synanon movement was an early growth out of, and response to, the drug scene. Synanon was founded in 1958 as an educational process, a 'counter epidemic force' within an increasingly disordered society. The Synanon structure is like a large family, with strict disciplines and an emphasis on group work, including the 'Synanon game' which has been called a verbal street fight, and on the re-creation of community. Out of the Synanon grew Phoenix, a therapeutic community using encounter group and confrontation methods in the cure of narcotic addiction. In Britain, the Philadelphia Association developed from the work on schizophrenia by Laing, Cooper and Esterson; similarly, Kingsley Hall, an experimental community for people with schizophrenia, grew up in East London in 1965. In Nottingham, the Craft Centre in St Ann's district became well known to a wide audience through an ITV film *A Completely Different Way of Life*. By 1973 we read that 'the life within the centre now revolves around the spiritual'.

A different but very important element in the alternative community movement has been the growth of Non-Violent Action Groups such as that in Manchester (MANVAG), groups which have derived inspiration and support from the Quaker and non-violent direct action tradition.

The experiments in co-operative living have been many and varied. The Free Universe Co-operative, created in 1971 in Brighton, was concerned with achieving cut prices for food and organising food and organising food distribution. Each Saturday members of the co-operative would pay a sum of money with their orders for the following week. During the week a group of volunteers collated the orders, bought the food from a fruit and vegetable market or 'cash and carry' store, and later separated it into individual orders. Prices were calculated to match wholesale prices as closely as possible. Similar ideas have been used in Nirvana Market in Nottingham, and in St George's Hall and CMPP Food Co-operatives in North London.

In 1972 in London a group called Community Music was set up as an attempt to introduce the co-operative idea into pop music. The group stated its underlying beliefs as follows:

(1) that societies based on materialistic values destroy man's/woman's sensitivity, creativity and individual uniqueness.
(2) that most societies today whether they be capitalistic/state capitalistic or socialistic are to varying degrees materialistic/exploitative in nature.
(3) that revolution is unfortunately not the answer to a change in 'human values'.
(4) that our only hope in changing our societies is to set up structures that will in theory and practice create values and relationships that are based on mutual respect, compassion and love.

This statement is an important and impressive example of the kind of values and beliefs which are helping to shape the search for an alternative society and which are motivating projects of various kinds.

The search for alternative forms of community has included alternative schools. There has been a revival of interest in those schools which already exist as alternatives – Froebel School in Roehampton, the Rudolf Steiner schools, St Christopher School in Letchworth, the Krishnamurti School near Alresford – but there have also been new developments, including the setting up of 'free schools'. In Britain, the Scotland Road Free School was opened in Liverpool in 1971 as a school which would be totally involved in its environment and would be 'in the vanguard of social change in the area'. The idea of a free school is to cause the state system to fragment into smaller, all-age, personalised democratic and locally controlled community schools. In 1970 an offshoot of the California Malcolm X Montessori School opened in Notting Hill, and a free school was opened in Islington in London in 1972.

As well as these kinds of experiments, we ought to include the spread of encounter groups, sensitivity or T-groups, and other forms of group work which emphasise closeness and physical intimacy. The T-group training phenomenon began in a small way in America in the 1940s and is now a major industry. It is based on the belief that human relationships can be improved by assembling groups of people who will talk freely about their relationships with each other. The T-group (training group) was first used in the context of training programmes, but in the 1960s there was a deepening of interest in personal growth and fulfilment rather than simple improvement in relationship skills. So out of T-groups grew encounter groups which emphasised non-verbal communication – touching, gestures, mimes, and so on. The encounter group aim is to enable individuals to experience their true self, to affirm their identity, to 'do their own thing'. So popular have these groups become that ready-made encounter group tapes are now available as well as a large number of books and therapeutic games.

Finally, a factor of tremendous importance in the whole area of alternative communities has been the search for alternatives to the conventional systems of psychiatry and penology. The People Not Psychiatry (PNP) is not an organisation but simply 'a scattered commune of friends', the idea being to encourage reliance on human contact and friendship rather than psychiatric medicine. In the field of penal policy, Radical Alternatives to Prison (RAP) has attacked the prison system and recommended alternatives.

The urban desert[5]

In his book *Unfinished Animal* Theodore Roszak draws attention to the need for 'a healthy ecology of the spirit'. For, he says, 'where fertility is not matched by careful cultivation, it yields no liveable human habitat, but instead the deadly luxuriance of swamp or jungle'.

He goes on to emphasise the paramount importance in the contemporary spiritual revival to develop criteria of discernment, to find our way through the maze of paths.

In the Christian tradition the desert is supremely the place of growth and spiritual discernment. 'The best fruit', St John of the Cross says, 'grows in land that is cold and dry'. The desert in Scripture is the place both of sterility and of the divine presence of demons and of the revelation of God. The road of faith goes through the desert, a road marked by risks; one is brought face to face with starvation, with deadly serpents, with hostile forces.

There is no gentle suburban route to God. But the desert also is the place of solitary communion and rest. That is the paradox of desert spirituality.

The wilderness liturgy is marked by adoration of the divine presence, and by the exorcism of demons; here is the place of slowing down, of simplifying, and yet also the place of temptation and of the sharpening of conflict and of perception. What then is this desert?

First, it is the place of encounter with God. Jewish history gives a special place to the desert generation. Yahweh is the God of desert, storm and sea.

Desert spirituality is rooted in the revelation on Mount Sinai: 'He found him in a desert land, and in the howling wastes of the desert'. Amos looked to the desert as the age of pure worship. From the desert era came the divine Name. It was there that Moses led the people to the west side of the wilderness to Horeb the mount of God.

So in the desert experience worship is purified and strengthened. So, too, Isaiah looks to the desert as the place of future renewal. 'The wilderness and the dry land shall be glad; the desert shall rejoice and blossom ... waters shall break forth in the wilderness and streams in the desert.'

Second, the desert is the place of confrontation with oneself. From the early centuries, monks and hermits went to the desert to discover their identity. Today Carlo Carretto writes of the Sahara as the place where he learnt to pray. He comes from the tradition of the Little Brothers and Sisters of Jesus, founded by Charles de Foucauld from his experiences in the desert.

Third, the desert is the place of conflict with the demons. So St Athanasius, in his Life of St Anthony, tells us that the devil, driven out of the city, sought refuge in the desert. There Anthony went to meet him with the weapons of prayer, fasting and solitude.

So desert prayer is the prayer of solitude. The desert is a place of aloneness, a place of discovering our own true selves, a place of stripping. Yet in this solitude one realises that solitude and communion are sisters, that only through discovering our own essential solitude can we truly become a communion.

Thus it was that Thomas Merton, through his solitude, became more aware of the forces that were shaping and distorting American life. Through his solitude he became more prophetic, more open to the world's need.

So today more and more people who are involved in the struggle for justice and for a new social order are seeing the importance of contemplation and of the solitude in which lie the roots of social change and of resistance to oppression. Gandhi many years ago saw the unity of inner and outer change.

Let us then look at the consequences of the symbol of the desert for our prayer today. First, we need to recover the need of the solitary dimension. Solitude is not a luxury, a form of spiritual escapism. It is a necessity if our action and our commitment to justice is to be pure and authentic.

Radical action follows from radical contemplation. Solitude is necessary to preserve us from superficial activism, from exhaustion, from fanaticism. To wait in adoration, to watch with the eyes of the Dove, to seek discernment, is a vital prerequisite of Christian action. We act only if we have seen, and the desert is the place of sharpened perception.

Secondly, we need to stress the need in our modern urban deserts for houses of prayer. Today the desert has come back to the city. It is in the city that we see the marks of sterility, of dryness, of desperate isolation. Never has the city more urgently needed its contemplatives.

Finally, the urban desert is a place of conflict and spiritual resistance. When the church became established, the early contemplatives sought the wastes of the desert in order to maintain the purity and revolutionary vision of the Gospel within a compromised Church. Now, as the Constantinian era draws towards its close the contemplatives are returning to the cities.

Thomas Merton saw the desert as the place of struggle and purification. It is in the desert that a person becomes fully awake, vision
enriched, perception deepened.

Nothing is more urgent today than the recovery of the desert
contemplative and prophetic tradition; for the desert is the place of
contemplative vision and of prophetic zeal for justice; and it is on the
unity of these two that the future of western Christianity to a great
extent depends.

Creation spirituality[6]

In the United States there has been for over ten years a
movement of 'creation-centred spirituality' associated with the writings of the Dominican Matthew Fox. Recently his works have
become popular in some circles in Britain. Fox's basic thesis is that the
Christian spiritual tradition has been too dominated by a Fall/
redemption spirituality.

Fox goes on to propose the abandonment of the Fall/redemption
tradition, and its replacement by the older but neglected tradition of
creation spirituality, a tradition which has been kept alive by artists,
poets, scientists, feminists and political prophets – but not by theologians. The tradition is thus 'utterly new to our culture'. It calls for a *via
positiva* towards the universe: it is a theology which stresses the senses,
human mirth and pleasure.

If Fox is a little unfair to theologians, it is possibly because of his
ignorance of the Catholic socialist tradition within Anglicanism, as
exemplified particularly in the writings of Conrad Noel, where creation spirituality was strongly emphasised.

Now undoubtedly Fox has a point, as Noel did, and there is much
truth in what they say. But the real danger here is two-fold. First, that
a romanticised theology of nature and of the senses can quickly
degenerate into a kind of spiritual romanticism of which we have seen
antecedents in the cult of Merrie England and in the eco-mysticism of
California. These are essentially forms of retreat, which can only
flourish in particular contexts. They are part of the anti-urban tradition, but they are also highly selective about the natural order. The
harsh and cruel side of 'nature red in tooth and claw' is ignored.

The second danger is that a theology which stresses creation and
incarnation but which ignores the dimensions of sin, redemption and

judgment, quickly becomes non-prophetic and can easily degenerate into culture religion of the kind that helped to prepare the way for fascism. It is a theology which finds God in the natural order, in the folk tradition of race and nature, in the rich culture of the *Volk*, but which has no criteria from which to challenge and judge the society in which it is set – and which therefore ends up as a spiritual reinforcement for the dominant order. Noel saw these dangers and laid equal stress on redemption and on the transformation of society. He saw that Christian theology and Christian spirituality must always be a theology of redemption, of transformation, and therefore of struggle for a new heaven and a new earth.

Spiritual direction[7]

It is over 15 years since I wrote a book called *Soul Friend*. At the time, and for some time afterwards, it was the only modern book available on the British and American markets about the ministry of spiritual direction. It still sells, to an audience quite different from the one I anticipated, and indeed has recently been reprinted in the original edition in the United States although it is urgently in need of revision. When I wrote this book I specifically rejected the idea that it should be seen as a guidebook, a 'how to do it', and I expressed grave doubts as to whether such a book was possible or desirable. I also strongly emphasised my belief that spiritual direction was part of the ordinary ministry of the Church, not a specialist field reserved for experts.

Now, in the 1990s, where are we? Spiritual direction is 'in' again with a vengeance. There are workshops, institutes, cassettes, courses, books galore. Everywhere, and in all traditions, there is a concern with the 'inner life' and with personal guidance. Popular books have been produced aimed at a much wider market than mine was. Institutes and networks have grown up to train people, mainly lay women and men, as spiritual directors. There has been considerable attention to the role of women. And, of course, there has been the remarkable revival of interest in and practice of Ignatian retreats. All this has been exciting, healthy, positive, hopeful. Why then am I worried?

I am worried, first, that spiritual direction is being seen as more important than it is. It is, after all, one ministry among others. Directors play an important but quite a lowly and limited function within a wider context of pastoral care and theological formation. I detect now a tendency in some quarters to make the spiritual director more important than he or she is, in a way which is at variance with the mainstream of Christian tradition.

I am worried that this ministry is being professionalised and seen as a specialist ministry in a way which is potentially extremely dangerous. There is now an international organisation of spiritual directors with headquarters in the United States. There – and here maybe – some spiritual directors charge fees for their services, something which would have horrified the saints in all ages. People are being 'accredited' with certificates, diplomas, and doctorates in spiritual direction by the many institutes and departments which have sprung up.

I stand by my insistence in 1977 that spiritual direction is not essentially a ministry for specialists and professionals, but part of the ordinary pastoral ministry of every parish and every Christian community. Even more so do I stand by my suggestion that the role of 'training' is extremely limited, and that this ministry is essentially a by-product of a life of prayer and growth in holiness. Part of our task is to discover, help, and affirm the work of direction which is already being done by unknown people who do not write books or run courses.

A whole chapter of *Soul Friend* was devoted to trying to clarify the differences between spiritual direction, counselling, and psychotherapy, recognising the significant areas of overlap. I am increasingly worried not only by the tendency in some quarters to blur these distinctions and to assimilate direction into a therapeutic model but also by the uncritical and simplistic adaptation of certain quasi-therapeutic tools. The most obvious example of this is the use of the Myers-Briggs Type Indicator. This grid of 16 personality types, based on a rather questionable theory of temperament, has rapidly become 'de fide' in part of the spirituality circuit.

There are other examples of the way in which methods and techniques, in themselves helpful, have become part of a cult. I am entirely in favour of people keeping journals, and have done so myself for many years, but the way in which Progoff's 'intensive journal' method has been taken up so that the whole of spiritual formation is reduced to it – when did 'journal' become a verb? – is alarming.

I am worried, finally, because much spiritual direction assumes a view of spirituality which is not wholesome and only tenuously Christian, and which reflects the individualism and privatisation of religion in the West rather than an embodiment in a corporate tradition. Within classical Christian understanding, spiritual direction is a personal ministry which takes place within a corporate framework of sacrament, discipleship, and social action. It takes place within a context of theological reflection and social struggle. Only within such a context can it make sense or make progress. It is because I see a loss of such a context that I remain, and become increasingly, worried.

The spiritual director[8]

Historically it was from the movement of desert monasticism that we received the idea of spiritual direction within the framework of Christian practice. As Thomas Merton says, 'spiritual direction is a monastic concept'. It was with the growth of the solitary life in particular that the need for intensive personal guidance was felt. So the *pneumatikos pater* emerges in the spirituality of the East, and later becomes the *staretz* of the Russian tradition. In the West, we meet spiritual direction in the modern sense, associated closely with the confessional, in the period of the mendicant friars, and a further growth during the Counter-Reformation of a movement of spiritual guides concerned particularly with the guidance of contemplatives. In the twentieth century we have seen a considerable amount of rethinking about the place of direction in the life of the church.

From the tradition, the spiritual director appears, first, as *a person possessed by the Spirit*. The director's role, says Merton, was not in any sense hierarchical, but 'was purely and simply charismatic. It was sanctioned by the father's own personal holiness.' The first and essential characteristic of the spiritual guide is holiness of life, closeness to God. It is this quality too which, in the thought of the eastern Christians, makes the theologian. So Callistus in the fourteenth century urges the seeker to choose 'a man bearing the Sprit within him'. So the Russian *startsy* help their disciples not so much by what they say as by their radiation of sanctity and inner peace.

Secondly, the spiritual director is *a person of experience*, a person who has struggled with the realities of prayer and life. There is no substitute for this experience. Guides who have not encountered their own passions, their own inner conflicts, who do not truly know their darkness and their light, will be of no value in the spiritual battle. The great helpers of humankind are not 'the ideal bearers of final truths' but rather 'the most extraordinarily human members of the community'.

Thirdly, the spiritual director is *a person of learning*, though learning without spiritual maturity can be dangerous. St Teresa, however, puts learning as a very high priority in spiritual guides. The guide must be one who is steeped in Scripture and in the wisdom of the Fathers.

Fourthly, the spiritual director is *a person of discernment*. *Diakrisis* is the word which recurs with tremendous frequency throughout the literature from the Desert Fathers onwards. The spiritual father, according to Cassian, is one from whom we receive *diakrisis*. So spiritual directors must be people of perception and insight, people of vision, who can read the signs of the times, the writing on the walls of the soul.

The spiritual director is, finally, *a person who gives way to the Holy Spirit*. For the relationship of direction is to be one in which the channels of grace are opened, and the Holy Spirit is able to move freely in the Christian person, drawing her to a closer union and a greater freedom as a child of God. Jean Grou in the eighteenth century was very insistent that the disciple must look beyond the director to God and be prepared to give the director up if God so required. Spiritual direction is therefore a means to an end. The end is God, whose service is perfect freedom.

The role of therapy[9]

It seems that there are close parallels between the spiritual tradition and therapy, but there are certain dangers in accepting too uncritically a clinical model for spirituality. Spiritual direction is not primarily concerned with states of emotional distress, or indeed with problem-solving. It is very easy to misrepresent St John of the Cross in his writing about the 'dark night of the soul' as if he were talking about a state of clinical depression. St John of the Cross's teaching is that the dark night is the *normal* path to God. There is nothing pathological about it. It is the usual path which all Christians must take. It seems that there is a danger of creating what Lambourne called a 'hang-up theology', of seeing the spiritual path in terms of the identification and solution of problems. There is also a danger for therapy of creating an unreal world in which all problems are internalised. Perhaps one of the main reasons why we have psychiatry on the National Health Service is that there are many thousands of people in this country who, because they are under very severe pressure of housing, unemployment and other social and economic problems, cannot cope with their lives. Very often psychiatry is one way of helping not to solve these problems but to evade them.

Further, spiritual direction is rooted in the Christian community. It is not primarily a professional clinical phenomenon. It is very noticeable that, from the Hindu guru through to the Christian spiritual guide, there is a great insistence that the spiritual guide does not charge for services. In fact, the authentic Hindu guru will most probably warn against the phoney gurus in the West who are distinguished by the fact that they charge fees! So, while it seems reasonable to speak of a clinical theology, it is a false conclusion to draw from this idea that theology is itself clinical. And here there is a real danger that the 'growth industry', so highly developed in the US, may actually cash in on human suffering and distress and create a profitable undertaking. Anthony Clare ended his review of one of Thomas Szasz's books with the words, 'Psychiatry is alive and well and living in Beverley Hills.' There may be close parallels here with religion, for, whatever we may say about secularisation, the human potential movement, growth groups, primal screams, and non-prophetic forms of contemplation and meditation are flourishing multi-million-dollar industries. In the US, and to a lesser extent here, they have come to be important parts of the culture of capitalism.

Spiritual direction is closely related to prophecy, and in this it has an essential social and critical dimension. It is not concerned with helping people to adjust, to adapt to the dubious value systems of society, but to question fundamentally those values. And this leads me to a final point: that, as well as learning from therapy, the Christian spiritual tradition must ask important questions of counselling, therapy, and the growth movement.

Christian spiritual theology needs to ask questions about the nature of consciousness and of personality, and to question some of the assumptions of physical-based psychiatry. It may well be true that religion has neglected the unconscious forces, but it would seem that a good deal of current health care and physical-based psychiatry is more or less determinist.

It seems that Christian theology needs to ask questions about the politics of therapy and counselling. What are therapy and counselling actually doing about the problems confronting human society? Are they in fact simply helping people to be well adjusted in a society whose fundamental values and interests remain unquestioned? Kathleen Heasman, in her *Introduction to Pastoral Counselling*, actually defines pastoral counselling as 'a relationship in which one person endeavours to help another to understand and to solve difficulties of adjustment to society'. This seems to me to be a highly dubious goal for the Christian, and though social work has been traditionally a conservative force, I am very pleased to see the rise of movements such as Radical Social Work and Red Therapy which are beginning to question the role of social work and counselling as instruments of social control.

It does seem, in fact, that therapy and counselling have one of the lowest levels of political awareness among the various disciplines. Thomas Szasz may be 'radical' in his theories of mental health, but he is certainly not radical in his conclusions which seem to be a psychiatric version of Milton Friedman's economics: therapy is simply available on the free-enterprise market for those who can pay for it. There seems to be a growing danger of the misuse of therapy and counselling in order to dodge and evade fundamental social and political issues, and this danger is not restricted to the Soviet Union. It is at this point that the Christian prophetic tradition of asking fundamental questions about justice in society is extremely important.

The real turning point in our dialogue will come when the search for inner wholeness and inner liberation comes into collision with the search for external wholeness and external liberation – when we see, in fact, that, in Roszak's words, 'the fate of the soul is the fate of the social order'.

Subversive contemplation[10]

Increasingly the choice for Christians in the West is between established religion and biblical faith. Established religion makes its peace with the prevailing socio-political order; it is a religion of appeasement, of accommodation and conformity, a religion from which struggle, conflict, and crisis have been removed. But once this has happened, the essentially prophetic stance of the Church is undermined. For prophecy and contemplative vision, of which prophecy is a by-product, depend upon the positioning of the Church at the overlap of the ages (cf. 1 Cor. 10:11). As Charles Péguy wrote: 'Everything depends upon that dovetailing of the temporal and the eternal. Everything collapses once that adjustment is unsettled, or out of true, or taken to pieces.' The sun then goes down on the prophets; vision fades; the eyes close, or become glazed over.

Christian spirituality is rooted in the experience of the incarnation and passion of Christ. It is a Christ-ening, a putting on of Christ, so that our consciousness is changed. But this transforming process in Christ, this new creation, is distorted in established religion into conformity with the *status quo*. The troubled and troubling vision gives way to the cosy security of the glazed eye.

Prayer and contemplation, in established religion, become purely private practices within a social order which they neither question nor threaten. That order is simply a neutral backcloth for the practice of religion. Religion has become privatised, a phenomenon which some Christians actually welcome. Not only that, the private religions have become a multi-million-dollar industry. They are part of capitalism's success story – religions as commodities, religions which in no way threaten or disturb social stability. In this situation, the most urgent need for the Christian Church is for the recovery of the unity between contemplative vision and political struggle, the mystical and the prophetic, between the inner and the outer worlds. If the eye is sound, the whole body is full of light (Matt. 6:22), and the contemplatives are the eyes of the Church.

Now one of the central features of established religion is the removal of conflict and of spiritual warfare. For this religion is one of comfort, security, and safety. But the subversive character of Christian spirituality derives from the subversive character of Christ himself. The Christ of the New Testament was not a universally popular figure. He broke conventions, accepted the despised and rejected, and was condemned for political subversion. Simeon's prophecy that he would divide the hearts of many was a true one. He was a threat to the established order of his day, to the *status quo* in Church and state, to established religion. The Kingdom of God dislocated the stable order and it does so still.

The recovery of vision and the recovery of prophecy are indivisible, for prophecy is a by-product of vision. So it was with Amos and with 'the *word* ... which he *saw*' (Amos 1:1). It was out of his vision of the divine justice that he raged against the Bethel sanctuary and warned of a time of famine for the Word of the Lord (8:11). In 1967 R. D. Laing took up this prophecy of Amos and saw the spiritual famine and loss of vision to be an essential feature of our western society. Five years later the same theme of loss of vision was taken up by Theodore Roszak. Our society, he argued, suffers from, indeed is based upon, a diminished mode of consciousness. The eye is no longer sound, and so our society has become a wasteland of the spirit, an idolatrous culture. Idolatry is closely linked with loss of vision. In the Old Testament, the God of Israel is the living God who is known only within the process of life and obedience. The idols, on the other hand, can be known in themselves, for they are objects, and they are recognisable. They are the gods of established religion, from which the living God comes to set men and women free.

The Old Testament prophets moreover saw that idolatry is not simply a grave sin, but that it is the source from which other evils flow: and this is still true in our society. It is at this point that the terrible failure of established religion is exposed as a failure of *vision*. For established religion cannot *see*, and therefore cannot act, for action follows from vision. Contemplation therefore is concerned with clear perception, and this includes the perception of evil and oppression. The idolatry in our society leads to gross evils. To name only three: enforced poverty, the defacing of humanity, and sinful obedience. The enforcement of poverty through the unjust accumulation of wealth. In western societies, the existence of gross inequalities of wealth and power, the concentration of economic power, and the growth of areas of poverty and deprivation, are not simply accidental and unfortunate blots on the urban landscape. They are inevitable elements in a society based upon organised injustice. They therefore constitute a spiritual problem for they are part of a false consciousness. The defacing of image by reducing human beings to mere mechanisms vandalises the soul and spiritual values are undermined.

The encouragement of wrongful obedience, one of the aspects of idolatry of which the early Church was most aware, and which was portrayed under the symbol of the worship of the Beast. Like pagan Rome, we too have become an increasingly authoritarian and repressive society, the society of the strong state. In such a society, the sane ones are those who are not plagued by doubt, those who obey orders without question.

The Christian pursuit of contemplation does not take place in space, but within this broken and fallen world-order. Contemplation has a context: it does not occur in a vacuum. Today's context is that of the multinational corporations, the arms race, the strong state, the economic crisis, urban decay, the growing racism, and human loneliness. It is within this highly deranged culture that contemplatives explore the wastes of their own being. It is in the midst of chaos and crisis that they pursue the vision of God and experience the conflict which is at the core of the contemplative search. They become part of that conflict and begin to see into the heart of things. The contemplative shares in the passion of Christ which is both an identification with the pain of the world and also the despoiling of the principalities and powers of the fallen world-order.

For the contemplative confronts the world of false consciousness and of systems rooted in false consciousness with the living Word of truth which pierces through the falsehood. It is an essential characteristic of contemplation that it unmasks illusion. Thomas Merton saw this unmasking of illusion to be the special work of the monk who must always assume a critical attitude to the world in which he is set. Through the monk's searching and questioning, his solitude and inner struggle, his exploration of the wastes of his own being, he listens more deeply to the hidden voices of the world. So it is that solitude and communion with God lead to a greater and deeper awareness of the needs of humanity. This is true, not only of the monk, but of anyone who practises contemplative prayer.

Christian contemplation therefore is not a smug search for interior peace, for the resolution or reduction of conflicts and tensions. On the contrary, faith is a principle of struggle and purification before it comes one of peace. The Christian mind is one that risks intolerable purifications. The need for radical purification is expressed in the symbol of the desert, the symbol, above all, of contemplative prayer. The desert is the place of conflict in which God appears often to be absent or to assume terrifying forms. It is the place of spiritual resistance, of the encounter with evil, and of the purifying of our spirits. It is expressed too in St John of the Cross's symbol of the Dark Night through which all human souls in search of God must pass if they are to mature: a process of seeing by not seeing, of *agnosia*, the way of ignorance.

The solitude and inwardness which the symbols of the desert and the Dark Night express are essential to the common good, for without solitude, human society cannot become a communion but only a collection of separated individuals. It is in solitude, in the depths of aloneness, that there lie the resources for resistance to oppression. As Roszak says, 'We can now understand that the fate of the soul is the fate of the social order, that if the spirit within us withers, so too will all the world we build about us.'

Thus Christian contemplation is rooted in the crudity and squalor, the despair and cosmic struggle, of the incarnation and passion. The vision of God is glimpsed within the world of matter. Contemplation is not a search for consolation or comfort or inner peace, however much these may at times follow. But, as Simone Weil wrote, 'love is not consolation it is light', and she went on to point out that 'religion, insofar as it is a source of consolation, is a hindrance to true faith. In this sense, atheism is a purification.' So much Christian preaching today makes Christ's teaching innocuous and tame by removing its central concern with spiritual blindness, truth, and wisdom, and concentrating exclusively on such areas as compassion, kindness, and sincerity.

Today, when there is a major resurgence of false spiritualities, it is worth noting that the dangers of pseudo-contemplation were familiar to, and condemned by, all the great mystics. *The Cloud of Unknowing* noted that 'the devil has his contemplatives', while St John of the Cross warned of the harm done by an immature religiosity which acted as a positive impediment to spiritual growth. One of the strongest attacks on bogus contemplation comes in the writings of the fourteenth-century Flemish mystic John of Ruysbroeck. In *The Book of Supreme Truth* he wrote of 'the men who practise a false vacancy', who are 'turned in upon the bareness of their own being' but who mistake this state for God. They neglect the sacraments and the common life because they believe that they have 'passed beyond all these things' and have become super-spiritual. In fact, says Ruysbroeck, they are 'the most coarse and crude of all men living'.

False contemplation does not only isolate the seeker in a spiritual cocoon, and removes him from the anguish and struggle of common humanity: it also dulls the consciousness and produces a spiritual blindness, an inability to see what is really happening. Whereas true contemplation awakens consciousness and heightens awareness, the false contemplation and false religion become, as Charles Kingsley, saw, opium for the people. Kingsley was thinking of opium as a drug of escape from reality, whereas Marx, who later used a similar expression, used it quite differently, to refer to the analgesic (pain-killing) properties of the opiates. Religion might not be a way of escape, as Kingsley, Maurice, and most Christian Socialists had criticised it for being, but, so long as the causes of human suffering remain, religion may serve a useful role as a pain-killer. Such an analgesic view of spirituality is far removed from a cross-centred spirituality and from true contemplation which heightens, rather than reduces, one's sensitivity to the pain of the world.

> Evil and good stand thick around
> In the fields of charity and sin
> Where we shall lead our harvest in.

It is in the 'fields of charity and sin', of wheat and tares, of vision and compromise, the world of politics, in fact, that Christian contemplation takes place. The familiar picture of the Buddha sitting on the earth, with one hand pointing to the sky, and the other pointing to the earth, symbolises our situation well. Vision and the daily round must be held together if we are to avoid the false polarities of utopianism and reformism. Contemplative prayer is, at its best, a state of seeing, a deepening of vision, so that the will of God is more clearly seen, and the signs of the times more accurately discerned. It is this clarity of vision which makes Christian contemplation a truly subversive activity.

Prophecy and spiritual direction[11]

I want to suggest that prophetic dimension relates to, and is indeed central to, the full exercise of the ministry of spiritual direction in today's church.

First, the spiritual director is concerned with the attainment of spiritual discernment. Discernment of spirits is a vital element in the New Testament discussion of false spirituality, and it remains central to the understanding of direction from the Desert Fathers to St Ignatius Loyola. *Diakrisis* is in many ways the key word in the whole tradition, and it is a task which is closely akin to that of the prophet, for it is concerned with the attainment of a clear vision, of the insight which can discern between true spirituality and false, between reality and illusion, between paths which lead to maturity and wholeness, and those which lead only to destruction and death. We could say therefore that the central aim of spiritual direction is the achievement of such discernment. The enriching of consciousness, the enhancement of vision, the sharpening of awareness: these are the essence of spirituality. If the eye is sound, the whole body is full of light. The spiritual director calls into question the concern of the religious mind with morality apart from vision.

Secondly, spiritual direction is inseparable from contemplative prayer. The bulk of the direction given by the Eastern Orthodox monks from the fourth century onwards was concerned with the attainment of *hesychia*, the condition of interior and perpetual prayerfulness, while in the West, St John of the Cross is largely concerned in his writing on direction with the movement of the soul towards deeper contemplation. Contemplation involves moving away from dependence on props and structures, being set free from idols and false images of God. And here too the work of spiritual direction is akin to that of the prophet, for the prophet sees idolatry as more threatening to true religion than atheism is. Indeed both the prophetic faith of the Jews, and the contemplative tradition of 'dark prayer', have at times been seen as atheistic by those for whom God is a super-object attainable by direct mental knowledge. The spiritual director, however, is concerned to help people grow away from such a limited view of God towards the deeper wrestling with the God of cloud and darkness, the hidden God of the prophets and the mystics. So in the work of contemplative prayer, the stress is on silence, on listening, on the 'way of ignorance' (*agnosia*), and on the transcendence of thought and concept.

Thirdly, spiritual direction, like prophecy, seeks to perceive reality correctly and clearly. And this reality encompasses the structures of the world as well as of the soul. Thus, Thomas Merton's insight into the forces shaping the United States in its social and political turmoil gave spiritual nourishment and direction to many of the activists of the 1960s. Merton saw that contemplation and the critique of social and political institutions were closely related, and that the ascetical disciplines of solitude and reflection should lead one to a deeper insight into and solidarity with the anguish of the world. Radical action begins with radical contemplation. So the spiritual director cannot ignore this essential task of helping people who are deeply involved with social and political action to see more clearly the realities behind the stereotypes with which their world is littered. Merton saw this task as an 'unmasking of illusion'. It is an aspect of spirituality which is never popular with the dominant power, for it speaks truth to power and uncovers the bogus and the sham.

Fourthly, spiritual direction is concerned to interpret, and to help others to interpret, the significance of events both within them and without. The director stands within the tradition of Christian insight and Christian critique within a changing world, entrusted with the theological task of seeing the events of the day *sub specie aeternitatis*, in the context of eternity. This task of interpretation involves drawing upon the personal history of the individual in his or her social context as well as upon the theological insights gained through brooding upon the Scriptures and the wisdom of the Christian tradition.

What, fifthly, of the crazy bizarre element? Spiritual directors do not, as a whole, seem to fit this description! Yet we should not be too quick to dismiss this dimension. John Saward's study *Perfect Fools* has traced the concept of folly for Christ's sake from St Paul through to the present day. He shows how important was the figure of the 'holy fool' in both Eastern and Western monasticism, the very movements within which spiritual direction developed. Essentially the fool is a sign of contradiction, of refusal to conform to the dubious sanity of conventional society and its accompanying conventional religion. The fool symbolises the dimension of scandal, of surprise, of unreasonableness, in the Gospel and the demands of discipleship. So in the work of spiritual direction there is an inescapable element of conflict, of spiritual warfare, of resistance. The director seeks to help nourish the inner resources needed in the struggle with principalities and powers, a struggle where often only the fool will enter the battleground.

Finally, the spiritual director, like the prophet, is concerned with humanity and with human progress. Spirituality which makes one less human, albeit more religious, is less than Christian, and is at odds with the incarnational basis of spiritual theology. Like the prophet, the spiritual director must look beyond the 'religious' world towards the fulfilment and transfiguring of human personality and of human society. As the prophet calls men and women back from the captivity of ritual and law to the human demands for justice and mercy, so the director must seek to guide people away from false spiritual paths which hinder maturity and inhibit progress. St John of the Cross is particularly hard in his attacks on those directors who actually encourage the prolongation of religious adolescence and immaturity. The purpose of the Dark Night is the attainment of a deeper integration of religion and life, of mind and heart. Its goal is the unified personality.

What may happen to spirituality from which the prophetic dimension has been lost? Such spirituality may well deteriorate into the quest for inner peace and comfort. Non-prophetic spirituality, spirituality without struggle, spirituality without justice, is notoriously popular in times of turmoil and upheaval. Ruysbroeck had much to say of its manifestations. Spirituality can so quickly and so easily lose its contemplative, visionary dimension, and become a quest for salvation by technique, a matter of finding the right mantra or formula for instant enlightenment. Without the prophetic demand for sharpened perception, the prophetic negative against all that would reduce the divine, spirituality can become a drug, a form of illusion, of clouding of consciousness, 'another resource of the culture instead of a resource against the culture'. It is all too easy and too common for non-prophetic, privatised spirituality to become mere convention, as well as to lose its humanity and become nothing more than religiosity. True spiritual direction is concerned to discriminate and to avoid false paths, to create a healthy ecology of the spirit.

9
Worship Before Doctrine

The faith is about worship before it is about doctrine. Liturgy is the primary theological act. It follows that liturgy and worship are key elements of contextual theology.[1]

Baptism as prayer[2]

Christian prayer is the manifestation of Christian Baptism, and it is in the liturgy of the Baptism that we see the life of prayer in microcosm. Baptism is a once-for-all event: *ephapax* (Rom. 6:10) is the New Testament word. Yet there is a sense in which we live a Baptismal life, a life of daily renunciation, of daily drowning, of daily dying and rising. The Baptismal liturgy embodies the spiritual life in miniature. In the early church *baptisma* means far more than the term 'Baptism' signifies. It described the entire rite of Christian initiation, incorporating a series of elements and culminating in the first Holy Communion.

First, there is the renunciation. The candidate strips off her or his clothes, symbolising the stripping off of the old nature with its deeds. As St Cyril describes Baptism at Jerusalem at the end of the fourth century, the candidate faces west in the darkness, repudiates Satan and all his works, and then turns round to the light of the baptistery, then anointed with the oil of exorcisms. So, set free from the tyranny of evil, she or he approaches the waters.

So, secondly, comes the drowning, the going through the waters, the symbol of Christ's dying and rising (Rom. 6:4; Col. 2:12). The Fathers are full of the symbolism of drowning. The dragon Behemoth lived in the waters, says St Cyril of Jerusalem, and Jesus, by his descent, destroyed the dragon's power. So with the new Christian. Many of the early Fathers speak of the drowning of the demons in the waters. So in Baptism Christians put behind them the seas of eternal death and destruction. But the most powerful expression of the death and resurrection symbolism of water comes in the Holy Saturday liturgy of the Blessing of the Font. The Paschal Candle is plunged into the font as a sign of fertilisation, while the celebrant, in the old rite, breathed over the waters, a clear reference to creation as well as to Christ's rising, linking them both in the baptismal process of renewal. The font, wrote Theodore of Mopsuestia (350–428), is 'the womb of the sacramental birth'.

Then, thirdly, the candidate is clothed in the baptismal robe and puts on Christ (Gal. 3:27). Fourthly, the newly baptised is signed with the Cross, for it is in Christ crucified that we find 'the Spirit and power' (1 Cor. 1:4). The Fathers speak of the signing as the *sphragis*, a term used originally of the wax seal which was used to indicate possession of cattle. The Christian is thus sealed with the sign of Christ, bearing on their body the marks of Christ (cf. Gal. 6:17).

The fifth act is the baptismal anointing. The symbolic oil of Chrism stresses our participation in Christ. We are *Christ-ened*. The earliest account of Christian Baptism, that of Justin Martyr (100–165), says that 'we come up from the washing and are anointed with the blessed unction'. In 215 the Apostolic Tradition of Hippolytus refers to the anointing with consecrated oil, while St Cyril of Jerusalem (315–86) says, 'Having become worthy of the holy chrism, you are called Christians'. The newly baptised, according to St Cyprian, the Bishop of Carthage (died 258), are to be made perfect by the seal of the Lord. St Ambrose (339–97) tells us that 'after the font, the fulfilment is still to be accomplished', and he links together the 'water bath in the Spirit' and the 'seal of the Spirit', calling the whole process 'Illumination'.

Sixthly, the candidate is given a candle, the sign of Christ's resurrection light, and, the rite of initiation completed, receives Holy Communion. The baptismal process reaches its climax in communion. There is a progression from darkness to nakedness, from confession of the creed to drowning, from dying with Christ to the putting on of the new person and receiving of the Spirit, and finally to union. The classic 'Three Ways' of the life of prayer are thus present in microcosm in the baptismal rite. First the Way of Purgation (renunciation, confession, and drowning). Secondly, the Way of Illumination (clothing and anointing – baptism is actually called 'Illumination' by some of the Fathers). Thirdly, the Way of Union (communion). The baptismal sacrifice, like the eucharistic sacrifice, is complete and yet also goes on. For our lives are lived within the baptismal mystery.

The dying and rising in Christ which is dramatically enacted in the liturgy of Baptism has to be renewed and experienced in prayer. All Christian prayer is baptismal. So in all prayer there is renunciation of false paths, confession of sin, and turning to the light. There is the need for deliverance from evil. Again, in prayer there is a daily drowning, a renewal of the experience of the font. We die daily (1 Cor. 15:31).

Liturgical renewal[3]

Firstly, the renewal of the Eucharist. The Eucharist needs to become not only the centre of our prayer and action, but also the sign of a renewed world. Father Adderley once called the Sunday Mass 'the weekly meeting of rebels against a Mammon-worshipping world order.' And yet it is still possible to believe in 'the magic of the Mass' without really accepting the sacramental understanding of the world. It is possible to believe in the Sacraments, with a capital 'S' without being a sacramentalist at all. The Sacraments become freak events in a world which runs on quite different rules. And so the transformation occurs *only* in the liturgy and not in the world, and there bread and wine remain hoarded, but not offered, concentrated and not broken, maldistributed and not shared. The Eucharist becomes a freak, a contradiction of social reality, instead of a pointer to how reality should be reshaped. If we then go back to read the early Christian Fathers we find how far we have come from their understanding. St John Chrysostom draws the closest connection between the real presence of Christ in the Blessed Sacrament and his real presence in the poor and oppressed. We need to recover this connection between the Sacraments and the structures of the world, and to take seriously the social and political consequences of being one body in Christ.

Secondly, the renewal of the Office. I believe that it is of the most desperate importance for the future of Anglican Catholicism and indeed for the future of Catholic spirituality throughout the world that we find a form of Office which can both be a vehicle of adoration and also provide us with adequate nourishment, and our present miserable little offices do neither. In my view there is a distinct shortage of glory and unless there is improvement there will undoubt-edly be an abundance of dust for they will cease to be used. The Office needs to awaken in us wonder and the sense of splendour, the glory of God. It also needs to fortify us for the spiritual warfare and it seems to me that the renewal of the Office in the Church is absolutely essential to any Catholic Renewal.

Thirdly we need to rediscover the Sacrament of Reconciliation as a means of repentance and healing. Having written a book on this subject I don't want to have say much more about it here, but again there must be renewal and not resuscitation. Sacramental Confession can be as distorted and as misused as anything else. It can simply become a way of ritually avoiding coming to terms with our true sinfulness, with our true self, a way of preserving immaturity through the avoidance of human contact. There must be a real radical renewal of the Sacrament of Penance and so the 1974 Ordo, in faithfulness to the Catholic spiritual tradition, stresses the essential link between confession and spiritual guidance. That is very much within the mainstream Catholic tradition, but it won't half surprise a lot of priests at the present time. We need desperately to recover the tradition of spiritual guidance, and I believe that we often flounder about in the spiritual life because as individuals we fail to trust ourselves to the exercise of humbly opening up our souls to a spiritual friend, to a guide, to one who will bear us within his soul, or her soul; because there is nothing peculiarly male about spiritual direction, nor is there anything peculiarly priestly about it.

It is precisely because of the lack of adequate spiritual guidance within the Church that many people have sought help from non-Christian teachers because they find in them, if they find nothing else, two features: a spirituality which works and which manifests itself in direct experience, and a methodology and techniques in the life of meditation and prayer. But of course this raises the disturbing and very worrying question of the spiritual renewal of the priesthood and the laity. Are we in fact, in theological colleges and elsewhere, preparing young priests to celebrate the Ministry of Reconciliation? I don't believe we are. Are we preparing them to understand the movements of the spirit in individuals? Are we taking seriously the distribution of spiritual gifts among the *Laos* – people of God – or have we too come to the blasphemous use of the term 'Lay' as meaning second-rate or untrained? Spiritual guidance has never in the Catholic tradition, West or East, been restricted to the priesthood or to the confessional. But spiritual guides cannot be produced by pastoral training courses, important as they are. They will only manifest themselves to the extent that there is a renewal in the life of prayer and in concern for personal holiness.

More importantly it seems to me that we need to rediscover the essential unity of prayer and social action, of contemplation and resistance. They are not alternative modes of discipleship. They are essential and inseparable elements in a whole spirituality. And it is vital, absolutely vital, that we recover the tradition of contemplative prayer. For we are starved of the wisdom of the great spiritual guides. Spiritual progress is not chronological. We may find that not only do we learn more from John Chrysostom and Julian of Norwich and John of the Cross than many of our contemporary writers, but we might also find that they speak more closely to our condition. But let me refer you to at least one modern writer, who for me more than anyone else has wrestled with the unity of contemplation and action, and that of course is Thomas Merton. By the irony of history he died on the same day as Karl Barth, and I celebrated a requiem for the two of them in the Convent at Fairacres. I am quite sure that Barth would not have approved, but maybe Merton would!

Barth, through his experience of Nazism, was led to a consciousness, a theological consciousness, of the resistance to evil, in some ways in spite of his theology. Merton's theology is essentially contemplative and political, at the same time. It is through his solitude and inner ascesis, that he became more, rather than less, sensitive to the nature of the Vietnam war, to the struggles of the Black people, to the necessity for a spiritual rejection of capitalism as an ungodly and anti-Christian system. And it was Daniel Berrigan, steeped in the spirituality of Merton, who said that the time will shortly come when the pursuit of contemplation in the West becomes a strictly subversive activity. And that is why the contemplative, the true contemplative, is always more threatening to unjust social systems than the social activist can ever be.

Baptism and monasticism[4]

Now at the heart of Christian spirituality is the sense of spiritual warfare, of wrestling against principalities and powers, and it was precisely as a witness against the structure of the fallen world that the monastic vows were developed. And I want to suggest that monasticism has a permanent place in the church, not simply because religious communities are a good thing, but because monastic vows are simply a specific form of baptismal bows, and all Christians share in the commitment to protest and conflict which marks the vocation of the monk and the nun. 'The problem for monasticism', Thomas Merton warned us, 'is not survival but prophecy', and that too seems to be true of the Catholic movement in the Church of England and of Christianity as a whole. Spirituality is inseparable from conflict. 'Think not that I come to bring peace upon earth. I have not come to bring peace, I have come to bring a sword, I have come to set fire to the earth.' There are frequent references today to the church as an agent of reconciliation and unity, to the church as a harmoniser, a smoother over of conflicts, and we forget that the New Testament reconciliation comes only through struggle and conflict and the cross. The New Testament presents a picture in which faithfulness to the Gospel brings division, isolation and pain. The only people who seem to have been reconciled by the preaching of Jesus were Herod and Pilate.

This inescapable element of conflict is brought out forcibly in a most important little book which I would strongly recommend to you by the American evangelical Jim Wallis called *Agenda for Biblical People*. 'What matters most today', he says is 'whether one is a supporter of establishment Christianity or a practitioners of biblical faith. Establishment Christianity has made its peace with the established order. It no longer feels itself to be in conflict with the pretensions of the state, with the designs of economic and political power, or with the values and style of life enshrined in the national culture. Establishment Christianity is a religion of accommodation and conformity, which values realism and success more than faithfulness and obedience. It is heavily invested in the political order, the social consensus and the ideology of the economic system. Its leaders are more comfortable as chaplains than as prophets, its proclamation has been rendered harmless and inoffensive to the wealthy and powerful; and its churchly life has become a mere ecclesiastical reproduction of the values and assumptions of the surrounding environment.' But Wallis insists, 'The biblical witness does not support the notion that God's people are meant to be allies of the world's power; rather they are to be a new and different gathering of people whose presence is to play a decisive role in God's action in history. Biblical faith then is quite uncivil. That God is on the side of the poor and that the Scriptures are uncompromising in their demand for economic and social justice is much more clear biblically than most of the issues over which churches have divided. The Scriptures claim that to know God is to do justice and to plead the cause of the oppressed. Yet this central biblical imperative is one of the first to be purged from a church that has conformed and made accommodations to the established order.'

Now this sense of conflict and renunciation is built into the framework of the Christian life at Baptism. And in a sense the whole of Christian spirituality is a manifestation, a revealing, of Baptism. 'Prayer', said St Gregory of Sinai, 'is the manifestation of Baptism', and the first act in the Liturgy of Baptism is the renunciation. To reject Satan and all his works and all his pomps, to repudiate the world, the flesh and the devil is an essential element of all Baptismal Liturgies from the earliest days. There is a renunciation of the world, of the fallen, unredeemed, world order and the commitment to the new world of God's kingdom. And so Christian Spirituality calls us to a rejection of this dying order and a commitment to struggle for a new heaven and a new earth. For it is through much tribulation that we enter the Kingdom of God. It is precisely this vision of the Kingdom coming which ought to prevent our being conformed to this present age and its false systems. The renunciation of the world in the Baptismal Liturgy is a call not to an escapist pietism, but to spiritual resistance. It demands that we take very seriously our attitude to material structures and their redemption and within that framework to our life-style as children of the New Age.

Again the flesh is renounced; the sinful lusts of fallen humanity. Spirituality is not compatible with the treatment of human beings as raw material for the satisfying of my lusts, whether they be sexual, financial or economic. But equally spirituality is not compatible with immaturity or pseudo-innocence. 'Unless you become as little children,' is a call to authentic innocence – a preservation of childlike attitudes into maturity without sacrificing the reality of one's conception of evil. Spirituality is necessarily linked with human emotional fulfilment, and so the rejection of the flesh, in the Pauline sense, must be completed by the sanctifying and embracing of the flesh in the

Johannine sense, for, as Tertullian said, 'The flesh is the hinge of salvation.' And again there is a renunciation of the devil, of all false spiritual paths and a commitment to the living God.

And so Christian Spirituality demands that we place at the centre of our faith and prayer, the contemplative gazing at the God who is ineffable and beyond description. So the Liturgy of Baptism expresses the centrality of conflict and struggle in the spiritual life. The demand of the Baptismal life is a revolutionary demand. It is nothing less than death and resurrection.

Christian Spirituality is therefore a state of life within the conflict which Baptism both expresses and initiates. And a spirituality which is not concerned with wrestling with the structures of evil in the world is not Christian. The 14th-century mystic Ruysbroek attacked those quietists who pursued peace and tranquillity but ignored the demands of fraternal love and justice. 'They are', he says, 'the most evil and most harmful men that live.' And yet so much so-called Catholic spirituality is of this pietistic nature, and we need to reject it in the name of Catholic Renewal.

Priesthood and sacraments[5]

The priests who minister in the drug scene will experience a terrible sense of sacramental aloneness as they articulate the prayers of those who cannot pray and feed on the body of Christ for those who cannot share it with them. They will lean very heavily on the group of fellow-Christians whom they have gathered around them. But a very large part of their ministry will be spent with those for whom the inner reality of his life in grace will mean nothing. Yet their ministry is set within the sacramental life of the Body of Christ.

The sacramental world exists at the heart of the drug scene as it does anywhere else. Here, in the mystery of Baptism, the Christian soul turns his back on the powers of darkness and is plunged into the waters of liberation and cleansing. Here, in the Sacrifice of the Mass, the soul loses itself in the cosmic offering of the Son of Man and shares in his life. This is the heart of the Christian experience of life in God, and it may be the priest's joy to guide some souls out of slavery into the liberation of the children of God, to initiate them into the mystery of Christ's dying and rising. But in reality, whenever the sacrifice is shared, those who share Christ's suffering in the world also share his life and are drawn into his Body.

Priests too act as confessors and spiritual directors. They will certainly find that they hear more 'informal confessions' in the bars of pubs, clubs, and coffee bars, in prison cells, court waiting-rooms, and streets than in the confessional. It is difficult to know in such cases where the seal of the confessional should be upheld. It seems best to treat any conversation which is explicitly of a confidential nature as if it were under the seal, even though technically this is not so. The priest's responsibility here is very great, for from the moment that he or she reveals any fact which has been told in confidence their ministry ceases to be trustworthy and secure. Young people in particular will not feel that they can rely on them. In principle it is wise, even before speaking to doctors, psychiatrists, and probation officers, to ask the person's permission first. It hardly needs to be emphasised that anything told in the confessional must never be revealed, however grave or terrible it may be.

Two types of problem which will face priests in their role of confessors must be referred to briefly. The first is that, in the drug field as in the whole field of mental illness, the priest will find themselves in contact with people for whom 'sin' and 'guilt' are often confused, and where it is hard to draw a meaningful distinction between voluntary and involuntary behaviour. Priests, as confessors, are concerned solely with the absolution of *actual* sins consciously committed. They are not there to diagnose the movements of the unconscious, nor trained to do so. It is probably best, in cases where actual sin is uncertain, to err on the side of leniency, but there are some souls who need fairly strict guidance and direction if they are to make any progress at all.

The second problem concerns the moral status of drug-taking. There is no sin about drug-taking as such. The ingestion of a chemical substance into the body, itself a series of chemical substances, is in itself neither good nor bad. The Christian must be very careful not to fall into the Manichean heresy of regarding the body as evil and looking with disapproval on the physical components of the world. Nothing which goes into the body can defile (Mat. 15:11ff): this is a basic biblical principle. The taking of drugs under strict medical control does not concern the priest. The point at which moral questions arise lies in the field of non-therapeutic drug use. What attitude should the priest take here?

First, if the person concerned is an addict, whatever the cause of their addiction might be, they must be treated as a sick person. Whatever may be the rights and wrongs of his becoming an addict, at this moment in time their dependence on drugs is a physiological and psychological fact and must be accepted. Secondly, the priest must try to lead the person to view their drug-taking responsibly. He or she needs therefore to point to the Christian teaching that the body is the temple of the Holy Spirit (1 Cor. 6:19) and is formed in the image of God. If the person has come to the point of confession, one can assume a degree of Christian commitment. The priest has no authority or right to direct a non-Christian, although he or she may advise one if advice is sought: but the commission is to feed the flock of Christ within his Body. Christian drug-takers will need very careful spiritual guidance. It should not be difficult, in principle, to advise those whose drug use has reached the point of chronic abuse with harmful effects. The difficulties may arise, generally in the case of cannabis, where the young Christian genuinely sees nothing sinful in the use of the drug for pleasure. In such cases, the priest may *advise*, as a personal opinion, that it is unwise to continue, and may feel the need to avert a forthcoming casualty: he or she has no right, as a priest, to treat such drug use as *per se* sinful. If the person sincerely, after prayer and reflection, is convinced that they are right, they must not be refused absolution any more than the drinker, the cigarette-smoker, or the taker of snuff.

There remain two aspects of sacramental activity which should be mentioned. First, the laying-on-of-hands and anointing. This sacrament is applicable to drug dependence as to any other illness and the caution and judgement applied elsewhere should be used in this sphere also. The danger of 'mechanical' or even 'magical' concepts must be avoided. But clearly there is an important place for the use of anointing within the framework of a healing ministry. The addict who is a Christian will, of course, be guided through prayer and sacrament, and anointing will take place in this context. The addict who is not a Christian but who expresses faith in God of some kind can also be anointed, and this may indeed have a profound spiritual impact upon them.

Secondly, the ministry of exorcism or the binding of evil powers. This ministry needs to be studied very carefully indeed before any action is taken, and there is clear danger of irresponsible use of these spiritual powers. Briefly, the theology of exorcism is based on the New Testament teaching about the existence of non-human evil forces and the triumph of Christ over them. It is important to remember the exorcism of persons was a normal routine action for all candidates for baptism and has been an element in baptismal rites since the time of Hippolytus. The emphasis is on the liberation of creation and individuals within it from disorder and distortion. The act of exorcism consists of the recital of a formula, accompanied by some action such as the sprinkling of holy water, the sign of the cross, or (as in the Paschal blessing of the font) a deep directed breath. The more specific exorcism applied to a case of demonic possession can only be performed by a priest under the express authority of the bishop, and it should not take place except after long medical and psychological investigation. The short exorcism, however, which is of 'every unclean spirit', could certainly be used in cases where the influence of uncertain evil forces was perceived. It is dangerous to assume that addicted persons or any other sick individuals are necessarily 'possessed': it is evident, on the other hand, that, like the rest of us, they share the consequences of evil in the world, and it would seem right to accompany prayer and sacramental acts with a prayer for their liberation from the influence of any adverse power.

The priest in the drug scene acts as one mediator of the life of Christ in his Body the Church. The priest is present both to heal and, by prayer and sacrament, to draw the scene within the love of Christ. It is a scene characterised at many points by loneliness and desolation, but so is the spiritual way itself. The priest's privilege is to guide the children of God until they 'expire into the eternal namelessness, where we are lost … in a pathless unknown darkness'.

Christmas meaning[6]

The saving power of the Christmas celebration depends upon the truth that Christ is risen from the dead. It is the presence of the risen Christ in the eucharistic mystery which transforms a nostalgic memorial into a source of life and glory. The powerful symbolism of light shining out of the winter darkness must inspire the Christian who worships at this time to cry out: 'Christ is Risen!'

It is the joy of the resurrection, of the Christ who is present through his conquest of death and decay which enters our hearts at Christmas.

This recognition that it can only be the risen Christ whom we encounter seems strange and wrongly timed, yet the atmosphere of the liturgy drives us to make the connection. For this above all else is the day of light.

The collects for the Midnight Mass of Christmas and for the Easter Vigil have a close, almost uncanny resemblance. 'You have made this night holy with the splendour of Jesus Christ our Light.' 'You have brightened this night with the radiance of the Risen Christ.' Both nights are referred to as 'holy night' and the readings of each liturgy focus on light and glory.

The celebration of what we now call Christmas was not in origin concerned with the birth of Christ at all but his Baptism. In his descent into the waters and his rising up, was seen both his manifestation, his *epiphaneia*, and also the prefiguring of his resurrection, and ours. While the conventional focus on 25 December has, since Constantine, weakened the original emphasis on light and resurrection, the Christmas season still reaches its climax on the Feast of the Baptism.

To see the centrality of the symbol of light as common to both incarnation and resurrection is to see how inseparable are the Christmas and Easter mysteries. Together they constitute the basic framework of God's activity in and beyond history and time, as they form the heart of Christian faith and hope. Without Easter, Christmas has no point: without Christmas, Easter has no meaning. Both incarnation and resurrection have significance because in these events God is glorified in the flesh. The flesh becomes the source of light, the raw material of glory.

So at midnight on the feast of the incarnation we celebrate Christ as God of God, Light of Light. But the Christ whom we greet is the adult, mature Christ, the rabbi, the friend of Galilean and Jerusalem outcasts, the leader of the attack on the Temple, the rebel hanged in the outer darkness. He does not stay an infant but shines with his mature and transformed humanity.

The light of Christ is a persistent light. It shines through the most powerfully oppressive darkness, shines in the midst of devastation, disaster and upheaval, yet without explaining them, justifying them, or making sense of them. The gospel of incarnation and resurrection is not the answer to a set of questions. It is a persistent and defiant light. And its persistence is paradoxical. For the truth of the gospel of incarnation and resurrection stands in contradiction to, and seems to be contradicted by, the realities of a world in which there is still no room, and where the dead bodies pile up, inexplicably, meaninglessly, in Somalia, Bosnia, Ireland.

Is the light of Christ then no more than an illusory comfort, a false reassurance that all is well when in fact all is clearly unwell in the 'demented inn' of the world? Certainly religious light is often of this illusory kind. But the gospel of incarnation and resurrection cannot be preached in an authentic and truthful way unless it faces the terrible reality of homelessness and meaningless death.

It is these two realities which provide the only possible material context for the light of Christ. For it is as the homeless unwanted Christ of Bethlehem and as the naked condemned Christ of Golgotha that the light shines with its strange persistence and its baffling power to draw people to its shining, enabling them to become dynamic agents in the historical process, lights in the world.

The light of this holy night is not a light of explanation. Yet it is a simple light, a light which penetrates to the heart of humanity and of creation. And it is only as it penetrates, simultaneously drawing and repelling, illuminating and blinding, that we come to understand the power of that light. It is a transforming light. As Paul says, we are being changed into the likeness of the Lord whose glory we have seen.

The Western Rite[7]

For over 150 years many Anglican Catholics have taken the view that the Church of England forms two provinces of the Western Church which were severed from the main body of that church in the 16th century, and, consequently, have used the Western Rite of the Mass in its Tridentine and later in its post-Vatican 2 form. While strictly illegal, the use of the Western Rite has been common in the Church of England, particularly in London, and has gone hand in hand with dedicated pastoral care, theological conviction, and a rich devotional life and spirituality. This has been in marked contrast to some other forms of Anglican existence.

It seems now that, in some dioceses, the hierarchy may be attempting to bring the use of the Roman Missal – none of the hierarchy ever refers to the Breviary, either because they have never heard of it, or because it is of no concern to them – to an end by insisting that new incumbents promise not to use it. It is difficult to be clear on this since, to my knowledge, no public statement has been made. As on so many other matters, bishops tend to nail their colours to the fence, and direct and unambiguous utterances are at a premium. (It does often seem that, once a person is consecrated bishop, ability to speak clearly and openly on many matters acquires the status of moral sin!) However, even if only to invite refutation, some reflections may be helpful.

1. Whatever the rights and wrongs of the use of the Missal, it seems both extremely bad psychology and appalling political strategy to overturn a liturgical practice which in some cases has been in place for a hundred years without first building up the trust and confidence of the people. This does not omen well for the future of the church in inner-city areas where many 'Missal parishes' are located.

2. In the present state of Anglican theology, in which a mushy middle-class liberalism with little clear belief or theological depth is widespread, bishops and archdeacons need to realise that to throw out the liturgical bathwater may also be to lose the baby of Catholic theology and spirituality which is inseparable from it, and may further erode what is left of the Catholic consciousness within Anglicanism, struggling to survive in its fragile state. Many of those parishes which use the Missal belong to the very strands – working class, poor, left wing, deviant, marginal, unbourgeois – which have helped to undermine the Anglican alliance with the ruling class and its hangers on. The attack on the Missal will serve to encourage this process, and to promote the spread and dominance of a genteel, moderate, bourgeois, safe, acceptable form of 'Catholic' life.

3. At a time when other parts of the Anglican Communion (e.g. US, Canada) have deliberately framed their eucharistic liturgies in close cooperation with Roman Catholics, to seek to outlaw the Western rite becomes incoherent and anachronistic as well as foolish. In most Anglican liturgies, England being typically backward, the Roman and Anglican rites, including the lectionary and some eucharistic prayers, are virtually identical. It is a far more sensible policy to incorporate the Roman texts into Anglican rites – a practice which has been going on informally for some considerable time – than to cause unnecessary confusion and distress to congregations by outlawing the use of the Western Rite.

The Charismatic Movement[8]

In the New Testament, the symbol of the demonic is used of warped institutions in the ordering of society. In the New Testament it is both a theological and political concept. It is very probable that the demonology which is assumed by the New Testament writers derives from the widespread astral beliefs of the period, and there is a central theme of cosmic warfare, involving heaven as well as earth, and involving a great army of invisible beings.

The coming of the Kingdom of God and the liberation of humanity is seen, both in the Gospel exorcisms and in the thinking of Galatians and Colossians in particular, as being manifested in the freeing from slavery to the demonic powers. The exorcisms in the Gospels are 'signs of the coming of the Kingdom', Christ, according to the New Testament, has conquered the powers, and Paul in Romans looks forward to the liberation of the entire created order, perhaps including the demonic powers themselves, from oppression and slavery.

It seems clear then that the liberation from slavery to the demons is not something which is peripheral to the New Testament, but is rather 'an altogether central article of faith'. It is, however, equally clear that the cases cited in the Synoptic writers were cases of disease for which we today would offer a different kind of explanation and description: mental disturbances, epilepsy, convulsions, dumbness, and blindness. What is crucial, therefore, is that in all cases, physical and mental healing was accompanied by the setting free of the person from oppression, from those forces which stunted and distorted his humanity. It is this liberation, this achievement of the freedom, to be fully human, which is the central purpose of the Christian Gospel. The contemporary demonology expressed the oppression in terms of evil spirits, but the reality of oppression is still present, and it is this which is portrayed in the demonic symbol.

There seems now to be two current misconceptions about exorcism, and they are reflected in most recent writing. One is the view that exorcism is inseparable from, or limited to, the concept of possession. In fact, in the traditional practice of the western church, as well as in psychiatric experience, possession is rare, though the possession syndrome is well known. Yet the solemn exorcism of the possessed has always in practice represented a small range of cases, and the idea of exorcism is a much wider one. It is certainly not of medieval origin, as has been claimed, and indeed it was an integral element of the Baptismal liturgy from the earliest times. Many of the Fathers refer to the drowning of the demons in the waters.

As early as Hippolytus, there is a pre-Baptismal exorcism. The rejection of the dominion of Satan is a crucial element in the Baptismal teaching of St Cyril of Jerusalem and St Gregory of Nyssa. The watering-down of this element in modern Anglicanism has serious repercussions in the acceptance of so much in the realm of darkness, and in the avoidance of any real conflict with the Devil over the fallen world-order. In the modern Roman Baptismal rite, the Prayer of Exorcism is a prayer that God who sent his only Son into the world to cast out the power of Satan, the spirit of evil, to rescue people from the kingdom of darkness and to bring them into the splendour of his Kingdom of Grace, would set the candidate free from original sin, make them a temple of God's glory, and send them the Holy Spirit. Thus exorcism is one element in a total liturgy of deliverance and healing, in which the realm of evil is rejected, and humanity restored to the Divine realm.

The second error is to isolate the demonic from its origins in political theology. So the demonic ceases to be a powerful symbol of deeply rooted evil in the created order, and becomes a literal description of entities within people. In the process of pseudo-spiritualisation, the real demons in the world are missed. It is striking that Black Theology, a theology rooted in the experience of human racial oppression, has rediscovered the true sense of the demonic.

Today the 'Charismatic Movement' or, to use a less emotive and less loaded term, Neo-Pentecostalism, seems to lend itself to the distortion of the demonic symbol, and to an unbalanced and harmful pre-occupation with demonology. There are a number of reasons why this is so. First, Biblical literalism of an extremely unintelligent kind is very common, if not the norm, among Pentecostals, and it can lead to irrational and often absurd interpretations of Biblical concepts. Of course, it is frequently argued today that Biblical literalism is not essential in those who share the 'charismatic experience', but in actual practice the group expression and interpretations of that experience seems to go hand in hand with traditional Pentecostal use of the Bible.

Secondly, the absence of a sacramental life seems to lead to an unbalanced stress on such forms as exorcism or speaking in tongues which may come to assume the status of pseudo-sacraments. The routine sacramental means of deliverance and healing are under-valued, and emphasis is placed on the unusual and the sensational. To some extent, the spread of Neo-Pentecostalism is a reaction against the dreary anti-sacramental types of Protestantism which have marked so much of western Christianity for so long, and a desperate search for ways of expressing the inarticulate element in worship which the non-sacramental, over-cerebral style has obscured or ignored. Significantly the 'Charismatic Movement' in the Roman Church has avoided many of these dangers. Thirdly, the individualis-tic theology which lies behind most forms of Pentecostalism leads to a view of evil and the demonic which is theologically unsound, pastor-ally dangerous, and socio-politically reactionary. Theologically, one can point to the doctrine of total depravity, the absence of a real theology of grace and nature, a wrong view of humanity's relationship to the created world, and a sectarian and elitist vision of the working of God's Spirit. Pastorally, such views can lead to serious mis-handling of people, and there are now many cases of disturbed individuals who have fallen into the hands of enthusiastic exorcists and healers with Pentecostal views, and whose condition has subsequently become much worse. Sadly, but not altogether surprisingly, it seems that a high proportion of ministers and others who become pre-occupied with exorcism soon become obsessed with it, and may themselves become psychologically unbalanced as well as theologically heretical. A recent Roman Catholic theological memorandum about the charis-matic movement warned that 'excessive preoccupation with the demonic and an indiscriminate exercise of deliverance ministries is based upon distortion of the biblical evidence and is pastorally harmful'.

In terms of social and political thought and action, there is a real danger that the false demonology of the Pentecostal tradition will lead in practice to a blindness to, and therefore indirectly a support of, the really demonic forces in the world. It has been claimed that the 'charismatic renewal has the potential for developing a far more solid, long-term, radical commitment to social justice at all levels than any other movement in the church'. One cannot simply write off such views, but the evidence from Britain seems to be heavily against them. If anything, the spread of the Pentecostal movement in Britain seems to have aided the general shift to the political Right, the suspicion of working-class movements, and the spiritual defence of a dying capitalist order.

Worst of all, there seems to be a fundamental irrationality and lack of theological and intellectual seriousness which prevents any real assessment of these dangers and trends with the movement. The Pentecostal experience often seems to produce a sentimentality and immaturity in human relations, and an abdication of hard theological analysis in favour of pietism. In a society so complex as ours, the retreat into pietistic forms of religion was predictable, and there are strong indications that the charismatic movement is only one way of evading problems in the real world which are too difficult to handle. In terms of social ethics, the movement is virtually barren. In its social and political witness, it is either very trivial or positively reactionary, identifying as demonic the very forces which are working for change and for justice in society. In general, there is a loss of the wholeness of Christian truth in the movement to such an extent that the description 'heretical' might not be too strong. The heretical demonology is certainly merely one facet of a wider breakdown.

The Eucharist[9]

Within the community of his followers, Jesus is remembered – in the most literal sense, re-membered. Week by week, day by day, in the eucharistic offering, in the exposition of the word, and in other ways, there is a ritual re-enactment, an *anamnesis*, of the dying and rising of Jesus. It is the Eucharist or Mass – that regular act in which Christians claim to 'eat the flesh' and 'drink the blood' of Christ – which most dramatically manifests and makes present the mystery of the cross and resurrection. This ritual or liturgy is central to Christian consciousness and to the nurturing and sustaining of Christian identity. 'Do this in remembrance of me' stands at the heart of Christian worship. Yet it is a strange act and seems to the outsider to be a foolish one. For here Christians not only retell the ancient stories, they claim to re-enact the Last Supper, relive the sacrifice of Calvary and of heaven, and remember their own broken body through solidarity with the broken and glorious body of Jesus Christ. This 'unbloody sacrifice' of the Mass is strange, mysterious, fascinating and impenetrable, and, for all the attempts to dispense with its mystery and reduce it to a crude one-dimensional meal, the complexity of the mystery keeps returning. In the mystery of the Mass we are, as it were, present at Calvary and at the resurrection. It is a strange event rooted in a strange memory.

While most Anglican eucharistic prayers use 'remembrance', the English versions of the Roman Mass use the weaker word 'memory'. However, while memory is often seen as a looking back to past and finished events, in recent years there has been a renewed emphasis on corporate memory, the memory which recovers lost traditions and suppressed histories, the memory which nourishes and strengthens movements and struggles. Memory is of the greatest importance in the lives of Christians. Without memory there can be no forgiveness, no healing of the hurts and pain of the past. And forgiveness and healing are central to Christian existence. The trouble is that our memory is often blocked. Past hurts and sufferings are too painful to remember, so we blot them out of consciousness. We often justify this organised amnesia by saying that we 'live for the present'. But living for the present can easily be an evasion of the reality of our past. It is this evasion which must be undermined, lovingly yet deliberately, by the Christian community. For to live within a community of faith is to live within a community of memory, and the Christian community is shaped by what J. B. Metz calls 'the dangerous memory of the passion of Christ'. It is a community with a history. T. S. Eliot in 'Little Gidding' tells us that a people without history is not redeemed from time, and, in Christian thought, redemption takes place both within time and from the captivity of time.

However, the word 'remember' brings out the present dynamic in the past events. To re-member is to put together again. And this is what happens among the disciples of Jesus. Week by week, day by day, the Christian community celebrates the mystery of his dying, breaking bread in his memory, and in that fragmentation, that brokenness, celebrates its own unity as 'one body in Christ'. The term 'body of Christ' is used in Paul to mean both the Eucharist and the people. This continual memorial or *anamnesis* is more than an act of nostalgia. It is a putting together again of the body of Christ which was broken and given for the life of the world. There is something immensely powerful and energising about this movement, and yet we must admit that it is very odd, very strange – indeed, on the surface, utterly absurd. For one would have thought that the event of Calvary would have marked the end of what we call 'Christology', thinking about Jesus as the Christ, the Messiah: it would seem to mark the disastrous failure of a project. Yet this seems not to be so. Christ was broken and crushed, and it is when we are broken and crushed that we know him. Christ was a failure and it is in the midst of our failure that we know him, not as another failure but as a source of life and power.

Part Five

The Pilgrim
Journey

10
Nearer to Holiness

*In reflecting on one's own priestly ministry and
life, it is immensely valuable and deeply moving
to identify those key influences on one's life which
enabled some progress to occur; people who were
put in one's path at the right time, and who
enabled one to move a little nearer to holiness.*[1]

Stewart Headlam[2]

We have recently celebrated the fiftieth anniversary of the
death of Stewart Headlam, the founder of the Guild of St Matthew
and one of the heroes of the second stage of Christian Socialism, when
the theology of F. D. Maurice and others became fused with the
pastoral work of priests in the slum districts of East London.

Writing about Headlam in 1926, two years after his death, one of
his successors in the movement wrote that for him 'the Mass was the
weekly meeting of rebels against a Mammon-worshipping world
order'. In fact, as long ago as 1877, he viewed the Church as a true
counter-culture, a zone of freedom. The Eucharist was 'the feast of
national emancipation', 'the Great Emancipator's supper', 'the service
which tells of brotherhood, solidarity, cooperation'. 'It is to this idea
of international brotherhood that the word Mass specially bears
witness', he wrote in 1905. Headlam's socialism derived from this
sacramental view of reality: the Eucharist was 'powerful for working ... social and secular salvation'.

Some of Headlam's insights are even more relevant now than in his
own day, for he was a prophet who in many respects was ahead of his
time. For instance, in 1872 he was referring to the Church as a 'secular
society' and to Jesus as 'the Servant of humanity', language which
became fashionable 80 years later through the writings of Bishop John
Robinson.

Headlam was appalled by the Church's obsession with liturgical
minutiae. 'I dread the turning away of people's attention from real

disorders, the social and industrial disorders, to mere irregularities in worship', he wrote. He would not have been impressed with the current preoccupation of so many church people with liturgical change to the neglect of social change. For him, liturgy was the symbol of and stimulus to change in the world, not a substitute for it.

But Headlam was no modernist, revisionist or reductionist, and he rejected all talk of 'new theology'. 'There is no need for a new theology, no need for a new church', he claimed in 1907. The urgent need was to liberate orthodoxy from its interpretations and distortions. He knew the importance of dogma, and he anticipated the collapse of the liberal Christian left with its lack of clear theological thought. Orthodoxy, right worship and right belief, was for Headlam the essential prerequisite of radical theology. He would have viewed much of the current pseudo-radicalism in the Church as 'revisionist' and pathological, that is, based on an unhealthy theology.

As a vigorous defender of music halls and the ballet, Headlam came into conflict with the hierarchy, which saw such placed as centres of moral pollution. Bishop Jackson described them as places where many young people 'lost the blush of shame, and took the first downward step towards vice and misery'. His successor as Bishop of London, Frederick Temple, refused to license Headlam unless he denounced the ballet as sinful, and the ban was not lifted until 1898.

Headlam's reply to the Bishop's attack expresses a profound theology of the Incarnation. Christ, he insisted, had sanctified human passion, mirth and beauty, and this included the area of public amusement. He was aware of evil influences at work in society, but when in 1885 the *Pall Mall Gazette* published a series of revelations of sexual vice, Headlam, in contrast to the popular reaction of moralisers in the church, pointed to the need for the liberation of women, sex education, and 'the ending of the tyranny of wealth over poverty'. Eighty years later, we still see church-based campaigns on the narrow sexual front, and we read Sir Keith Joseph's call for 'remoralisation' but Headlam's perspective still abides. It is idle to call for moral change unless we are prepared to question the underlying morality of the social order.

So for Headlam the critique of capitalism was at heart theological. Eighty years before Anthony Wedgwood Benn, he saw the ownership of land as the crucial *moral* issue. God was the only Landlord, and the restoring of the land to the common people was a primary concern of

Christian theology. For him, the process of 'remoralisation' began at the very basis of the organisation of society, for human society was to reflect the sharing and unity within the Holy Trinity.

God was a social God, salvation was for the entire created order, and within that creation, humans were to live in an environment of sharing. There was no 'social gospel' for the Gospel itself was social, as God was social. Headlam rejected the inadequate view of salvation which stressed only the individual and ignored the restoration of the creation to peace and wholeness. He rejected equally the 'social gospel' of those who 'went about doing good', but ignored the preaching of the Kingdom and the vision of God's glory. Today, as we gaze across the wastes of individualistic pietism and social service religion, are we not led to admit that Headlam was right?

Father Gresham Kirkby[3]

Father Gresham Kirkby, who has died a few hours before his 90th birthday, was the longest-serving parish priest in the east end of London in recent years. An anarchist socialist, early supporter of the Campaign for Nuclear Disarmament and a member of the Committee of 100, he pioneered liturgical renewal in the Church of England and was a dedicated parish priest.

Born in Cornwall, he was influenced by Methodist hymnody (his mother and an aunt were Methodists), though he moved early towards Anglo-Catholicism, inspired by Fr Bernard Walke, a socialist priest at St Hilary. His musical abilities were memorable, and he was known to play the organ at services in his own church while another priest officiated at the altar.

After Leeds University in the early 1940s, Kirkby studied at the College of the Resurrection, Mirfield, west Yorkshire, during the time that (the later Archbishop) Trevor Huddleston was a novice. He regarded Huddleston, at the time, as rather conservative. Ordained deacon in 1942 and priest in 1943, Kirkby served his first curacy at the church of Our Lady and St Thomas in Gorton, Manchester. After three further curacies in Middlesborough, Becontree and North Kensington, he became vicar of St Paul, Bow Common, in 1951 where he remained until 1994.

The church had been destroyed in the second world war. One of Kirkby's achievements was the building of the new church, consecrated in 1960, and described at the time by the *Architectural Review* as the most important church built in the 20th century. He chose the architects and they asked the question: 'What will Christian worship be like in the year 2000, and how can we build a church to reflect this?'

The liturgy at Bow Common followed the Roman rite, but anticipated the reforms of the Second Vatican Council by at least 10 years. For many years the Divine Office was sung daily to Gregorian chant. 'Rome will catch up with us eventually', said Kirkby, and to some extent this was the case.

As an anarchist socialist – he usually said 'anarchist communist' before 1956 – he was influenced by Kropotkin and by Dorothy Day, founder of the Catholic Worker movement in the United States. The Bishop of London visited him in hospital two days before his death and reported that Kirkby had 'proclaimed his undying faith in anarchy'. He was one of the first priests to march to and from Aldermaston, and probably the first priest to go to prison for anti-nuclear activities, in 1961. He certainly livened up the worship in Brixton prison chapel during his time there.

He was the last surviving member of the League of the Kingdom of God (founded in 1922), and chaired the Socialist Christian League until its dissolution in 1960. He had no sympathy with reformist socialism, especially the Blairite version of it.

Kirkby's abiding vision was of the Kingdom of God as a hope for the transformation of this world. His essay, 'Kingdom Come: the Catholic Faith and Millennial Hopes', in *Essays Catholic and Radical*, edited by Rowan Williams and myself in 1983, accurately represents his thinking.

He influenced thousands of people, was the best known priest in his area of east London, but remained a visionary thinker, always dissatisfied with his own thought, always restless and struggling, always moving on. Up to a few days before he died, he was expressing concern about the state of the world, the state of the Church of England, and the needs of individuals. He was at heart a local, grass-roots parish priest, greatly loved, and incredibly inspiring and influential.

Three East London priests[4]

Brother Neville Palmer was a shy Franciscan priest, born in Prince Edward Island, who had, in 1944, been sent by his community to begin a work of prayer and service in the Cable Street district. Taking over one of the many brothels, the Franciscans converted it into a 'house of hospitality' on Catholic Worker lines. Neville was a major influence on my life. More than anyone else he taught me to pray, by example, rather than method, and to see the integral unity of prayer and action, contemplation and social struggle. From him I began to understand the earthliness of doctrine, and of the doctrine of incarnation in particular; to see that doctrine was tested and tried, purified and realised, in concrete witness, life, and conflict. Neville lived out the incarnational theology, the truth of the Word made flesh, in the concrete reality of Cable Street. From him I began to learn that the servant church must be a prayerful church; that the pursuit of justice must go hand in hand with the deepening of love and humility; that the struggle for racial equality had to begin with the creation of more just and equal relations at the local level; and that the church, located at the heart of a situation of conflict, must be a silent, listening community before it becomes a community of discourse.

A hundred yards away from the Franciscan house was the flamboyant, charismatic figure of Father Joe Williamson, who campaigned for the demolition of the slum property and pioneered pastoral ministry with prostitutes all over Britain. Father Joe was the last of the ritualist slum priests of the Dolling tradition. He pushed that tradition – clerical, paternalist, and individualist – to its farthermost limits, and, in so doing, inadvertently helped to prepare the way for a new model of priesthood. He was first and foremost a pastor, and his life was devoted to the care and defence of the neglected and downtrodden. An old-fashioned Anglo-Catholic, with a preaching style more akin to the Salvation Army, he believed that it was the world – and specifically the streets and homes of Whitechapel – which was the context of the church's ministry. He saw the church not as a sanctuary to be protected against contamination, but as a resource centre from which he and others were sent forth into the mess and danger of the battle.

The third of these radical East End priests who helped to shape my theology and ministry was Stanley Evans. Of the three, he was the most disturbing, the most prophetic, and the most visionary. Evans was a pioneer of the parish communion movement as long ago as the mid-1950s, and he saw the church, not as an end in itself, but as a herald of God's Kingdom. He believed that the church's social and political witness began with the raising of consciences and consciousness of the local Christian community, and therefore saw theology as a vital component of the church in the back street. In the 1950s Evans was emphasizing that the most fundamental division between Christians was not a division running along denominational or confessional lines: it was, he argued, a division between those Christians in all churches who believed, in some sense, in the coming of God's Kingdom on earth, and those who did not. In his little parish in the back streets of East London, Evans anticipated much that was later to appear as liberation theology, though that term was not used until three years after his death.

Ruth Glass[5]

Ruth Glass (1912–90) belonged to Weimar Germany, where she was born into a family of rich rabbinical traditions. She herself was an atheist and an unfaltering Marxist, though the fiery humanism of the Jewish prophetic tradition was in her blood. She began her literary career as a teenage journalist on a radical weekly in Berlin, and one of her earliest essays, recently reprinted, describes the condition of unemployed youth in the year before Hitler came to power. The account, as disturbing in its passion as in its precision, could well be mistaken for an account of the position of the urban 'underclass' in American or British cities in the 1990s.

After escaping from Berlin, she came to London (via Prague and Geneva) and began her career as a social scientist. Though she spent several years during the Second World War as a research officer with the Bureau of Applied Social Research at Colombia University in New York, most of her academic life was spent in London, with periodic visits to India and other developing countries. She was the pioneer of urban sociology in Britain, and through her Centre for Urban Studies which she established at University College, London, in 1954, passed most of the future urban planners of the Third World. A principal area of her expertise was social statistics, and she was the first academic in Britain to make use of the sophisticated data of the 1961 census to combat popular myths about black minorities and housing. Her academic work was meticulous, thorough, and, at times, devastating in its attack on established assumptions. She was a constant critic of the planning dogma that, since the 1940s, had led to the decline of the urban economy and to social and racial segregation in the inner city. She was one of the first to call attention to the problem of land exploitation as a result of the denationalising of land development rights and values through the Town and Country Planning Act of 1959. It was this Act that led to the massive spiral in profiteering, symbolised in central London by the commercial building called Centrepoint – 'this insolent building' as she described it in 1973. Empty since 1964, the building had been receiving supplies of heating oil throughout the oil financial crisis of the mid-1970s.

Ruth Glass was no ordinary academic. Her entire life and work was dominated by a passionate concern for the downtrodden and the oppressed. From 1960, when she published *Newcomers*, the first detailed study of the West Indian immigrants in London, much of her work was concerned with the position of minorities in the urban areas. She saw that racism still generated vast destructive forces, and she believed that one of the most destructive of current beliefs was the assumption that 'racial prejudice is immutable'. She was a leading critic of what she termed 'the number theory of prejudice', the view that prejudice increased in direct proportion to the numbers of black people in a society. It was this view that was to form the basis of British immigration control policy. She saw, and warned of, the increase in scapegoating of minority groups in Britain in the early 1960s. She was totally opposed to immigration controls based on colour, describing the theory behind the controls as 'a new doctrine of original sin combined with a new faulty political arithmetic'. But she was equally critical of apparently liberal devices that, in the current climate, could be misused. Thus she denounced the question about parents' country of birth in the 1971 census and the 'inflated highly elastic pseudo-statistics' that it produced, leading to the reinforcement of stereotypes.

Much of Ruth Glass's work was concerned with the contradiction between labour needs and social provision. She pointed out that while immigrants were recruited from the Caribbean to service the labour market, there was no housing provision for them and considerable discrimination in the private rented sector. 'The very people who are wanted on the labour market are regarded as expendable on the housing market.' More and more she saw racist stereotypes reproduced and used as the basis of policy. In a letter to *The Times* that was not published – itself an indication of the changed political climate, for almost all Ruth Glass's letters to that paper had been published from the 1940s until the early 1980s – she responded to an American professor who had 'roamed the streets of Brixton' in search of Britain's race problem. Why had he insisted on the emotive word 'roamed', and not simply walked, asked Ruth Glass, and she went on to describe the four principal ingredients of a racialist stew, all contained in his article. First, you create racial stereotypes, writing about groups in the unisex singular – the black, the Jew – while we (plural), white people, relate to this phenomenon in a We–It relationship. Second, the stereotype is then reinforced by depicting 'it' as alien, the carrier of problems. Third, the stereotype is aided by the use of verbal fog and an obtuse lingo. Finally, it is heated up by the use of the language of violence and terror, the portrayal of racial minorities as a threatening presence.

Ruth Glass was one of the first researchers to examine the 'twilight zones' of London and to warn of the deterioration of conditions in areas such as North Kensington, scene of the race riots of 1958 and of the housing racketeering associated with Perec Rachman that came to public attention during the Profumo scandal of 1963. She was there during the years of Rachman, the most notorious slum landlord for the black community, and she stressed that he was only the best-known representative of a whole system of profiteering. But in the hysteria and horror around the Rachman revelations, the underlying issues were not dealt with. She saw the danger that the divisions between the wealthy and the poor districts of London would become increasingly sharp, that the poor districts would become more con-centrated districts of 'marginal people', and that they might become more divided from the wealthier districts along racial as well as class lines. All her warnings have proved valid during the 1980s. She coined the term *gentrification* during the early 1960s, warning that the poor would be squeezed out of the inner areas by the very wealthy, leading to 'upper-class ghettos': in this too, what she predicted has come to pass.

Though she was a distinguished researcher, Ruth Glass was strongly opposed to research for its own sake, particularly where the political will and the commitment to change were lacking. She attacked the international Habitat conference of 1976 as 'a costly pretentious exercise in obfuscation' and suggested that the planners should abandon their conferences and use the money to supply water taps in Third World cities. She was scathing about those who called for more research when the data was already available, seeing such calls as excuses for further inaction. North Kensington's housing problems, she pointed out, had been known and documented well before the Milner Holland report (a government report of 1965) was published. Her words are still applicable: urgent needs are still 'met' by calls for more research, almost always as a way of delaying or avoiding effective action.

Of all the influences on my ministry, my friendship with Ruth Glass is perhaps the most extraordinary. As far as I know, I was her only close Christian friend. As a parish priest in the East End of London and in Soho, I constantly drew on the resources of this atheist and used her in seminars and training sessions with clergy, youth, and community workers, and others concerned with urban problems. She helped us all to place our work in the context of accurate knowledge. She helped us to see that our pastoral ministry and our political action needed to have this solid basis in sound research and unassailable factual information. Moreover, she strongly believed, as a social researcher, that research and struggle must be closely related, and from her home, close to Notting Hill Gate, she kept a very close eye on events in North Kensington and other districts of potential crisis, offering support to deprived and struggling communities. She anticipated the urban uprisings in British cities long before they occurred. In an essay of 1964 she predicted that 'there will be turmoil in and around many cities of the world even before 1984'; two years later, she warned that 'aloofness from conflicts ... does not lead to their comprehension'.

Two important people[6]

Wilf Allen was an important presence around St Botolph's through most of the 1990s until his death in 2002. He worked in the crypt kitchen and was of great support and help to other homeless people. He was an alcoholic who had been greatly helped by Barbara Townley of St Botolph's Project. He had phases of sobriety and rented accommodation, and phases of binge drinking. One of these binges, he arrived at Mass one Sunday when a Church Army trainee was preaching his first sermon. He was an excellent pastoral worker but his sermon was painful. He was very nervous, read from a text without looking at the congregation, and the delivery was without expression. The congregation lost interest within minutes. After about five minutes, Wilf, very drunk and sitting in the second pew, said, in a voice which could be heard throughout the church, 'What a load of fuckin' crap!' The whole congregation, including the preacher, collapsed in hysterics. The preacher tore up his text and preached a brilliant extempore sermon. He said later that this moment had taught him how to preach. Wilf had no memory of the occasion, but it had a prophetic character.

David Brandon, who died on 26th November 2001, was probably the only British academic to be continuously involved with the study of homelessness for over forty years. It began because he was homeless himself, having run away from a violent father, and slept in doorways near St Botolph's. We met in 1964, by which time he was working with a project for homeless people in central London. David was a deeply spiritual person, with an equally deep distrust of 'spirituality', and he moved from the Society of Friends to Zen Buddhism. As I reflect on our long friendship, four areas seem important: the dignity of all persons, the inevitability of darkness and depression, the necessity of struggle, and the vision of the future. He combined a fierce confrontational public style with a profound respect and care for individuals, and a deep sense of his own inadequacy. David's passionate commitment to truth, and refusal to play political games, was vital to the work against homelessness. I miss him enormously. Like the ancient prophets, he was a destabilising presence in any group, and could divide a room faster than anyone I knew. In a field populated by smooth-talking functionaries, his unreasonableness and uncompromising stance were desperately important. He testified to a homelessness of soul which cannot be met by a fallacious doctrine of 'family' or 'homeland', and which all of us must face it we are to be truly human.

Mother Mary Clare SLG[7]

Mother Mary Clare of the Sisters of the Love of God was one of the great spiritual guides of the post-war period. Originally a sister in an 'active' order, it was her experience of wartime care in Cardiff, and her insight into the mystery of evil in the world, which led her to the contemplative community, based at Fairacres in Oxford, where she was to spend the rest of her life.

Her move from active to contemplative was no quest for escape: rather, as she once put it, it was in order to enter more fully into the heart of the spiritual conflict. She entered the Sisters of the Love of God in 1941, and was Mother General of the community from 1954 to 1973.

During her years as Mother, she guided the community into a new vision of the contemplative vocation, of the interdependence of contemplation and action, and of the crucial role of the enclosed community in the ministry of spiritual guidance.

In her work she was greatly helped and deeply influenced by the then warden of the community, Father Gilbert Shaw. The relationship between Mother Mary Clare and Father Gilbert was one of the most remarkable spiritual partnerships of recent Christian history. Shaw, coming from a background of urban ministry in the East End of London and at St Anne's, Soho, was drawn to the life of contemplative prayer and spiritual direction. Together they helped to shape an understanding and practice of contemplative living in the midst of a world of action.

Under the guidance of Mary Clare and Gilbert Shaw, the community underwent a major renewal during the 1960s. It was a time of liberation for a community rooted in the Carmelite tradition of St John of the Cross and St Teresa of Avila, now enriched and deepened by the influence of Thomas Merton and other modern visionaries.

One aspect of the renewal was the emergence of the SLG Press and the growth of a whole industry of teaching through Fairacres Pamphlets. From the press poured forth a vast range of basic literature in response to the growing thirst for knowledge of the Christian mystical tradition. Many people, Christian and non-Christian, have been introduced to the works of the Desert Fathers, the Jesus Prayer, Julian of Norwich and *The Cloud of Unknowing*, through the medium of Fairacres Publications.

Mother Mary Clare's own writings on guidance in prayer are among the most popular. A few years ago they were bound together as *Encountering the Depths* (Darton, Longman and Todd, 1981), a book which contains the essence of her spiritual teaching.

Mary Clare was a powerful resource as the Church of England sought, with some uncertainty and puzzlement, to recover its ministry of spiritual direction. In July 1974 Sydney Evans, then Dean of King's College, London, called together a small group of people at Glenmazaran, near Aviemore, to consider the future shape of this ministry with particular attention to the training of priests and pastors.

Among those present was Mother Mary Clare. Her paper, which was never published, was prophetic and wise. She emphasised four needs for the contemporary church. First, the ability to 'live with eternity', calling for deep inner resources of wisdom, spiritual discernment and vision. Service to the world and commitment to the demands of justice could never survive the loss of transcendence or the abandonment of traditional wisdom.

Second, the gift to know and interpret what God is doing in the present crisis of the world, and in the dying and rising of the Christian church. She spoke of this as a 'corporate dark night'. Christians must enter and encounter the darkness, not seek to evade it by regression to false certainties.

Thirdly, the commitment to the healing and wholeness of the human person and the human community, a commitment which was at the same time personal and social. Like Thomas Merton, with whom she felt a great affinity, Mary Clare acted as a director to many of those who were active in social and political struggles: that too was an overflow from, and authentic expression of, her contemplative exploration. Finally, the recognition of the role of the praying community as the spearhead of the conflict with the powers of darkness.

These were her preoccupations throughout her life.

Revd Dr David Nicholls[8]

David Nicholls, who died suddenly on 13 June, was one of the most distinguished priest-scholars in the Church of England's recent history. He had been parish priest of Littlemore, Oxford, since 1978.

After obtaining a first in economics at the London School of Economics, he went on to do a PhD in history at King's College, Cambridge, and a Master's in theology at Yale. He was ordained in 1962 and became chaplain of the London School of Economics. He was part of that dynamic movement of London student chaplaincy which gathered round the charismatic figure of Gordon Phillips and the Church of Christ the King. He was lecturer in politics at the University of the West Indies (Trinidad campus) from 1966 to 1973. On returning to England, he became fellow and chaplain of Exeter College, Oxford, and during this time helped to move the Oxford theology syllabus beyond the fourth century with a series on liberation theology.

Nicholls was a political scientist of outstanding ability, and influenced many other political thinkers, including Bernard Crick and Paul Hirst. He was strongly committed to 'socialism from below', deeply suspicious of Fabian statism, and of what he called the 'grandmotherly state'. His political interests were wide. He was one of the leading world authorities on the history and politics of Haiti, and of the Caribbean as a whole, being for several years president of the Society for Caribbean Studies. He chaired the Christendom Trust, set up by the late Maurice Reckitt for the promotion of Christian social thought.

His major published works were *The Pluralist State* (1975, revised 1994); his two books on Haiti, *From Dessalines to Duvalier* (1979) and *Haiti in Caribbean Context* (1985); and his Hulsean lectures at Cambridge, *Deity and Domination* (1989) and *God and Government* (1995). The third volume, on the 17th century, remains unfinished. These lectures dealt with the political dimensions of images of God, an area which took up much of his time in the last few years. They are among the most important recent British works in political theology.

But it was as a polemicist and pamphleteer that Nicholls was best known to many in the Church. His pamphlets and discussion papers for the Jubilee Group, of which he was a founder member, included an account of the political theory of E. R. Norman; a brilliant attack on the Lichfield report, *Marriage and the Church's Task* (1978), and a critical assessment of the Terry Waite affair. His open letter to the Bishop of Oxford, *Of Bishops and Biscuits, or How the Cookie Crumbles* (1993), was provoked by the Bishop's pamphlet, written jointly with the life president of United Biscuits, on business ethics. His most recent Jubilee discussion paper, *Visions at Regular Intervals*, written under the name of William Paley (see below), was a critique of the Turnbull report.

An essential aspect of Nicholl's personality, which endeared him to many but produced anger and outrage in others, was his humour, wit and capacity for practical jokes. His comic poems on ecclesiastical topics resembled those of Eric Mascall. In his wit an astute perceptiveness combined with gentle ridicule. There was not a trace of malice, but an almost childlike innocence and incredulity that anyone should think there might be.

Nicholls owned a beautiful parrot named Archdeacon William Paley, which he had acquired in Trinidad and which died recently at the age of 28. He used the parrot's name as a nom de plume, and letters from William Paley, Archdeacon Emeritus, often appeared in the national press. Paley, under whose name Nicholls covered the Haiti elections for the *Daily Telegraph* some years ago, is listed in the Oxford diocesan directory as a non-stipendiary curate of Littlemore, and received an obituary in *The Tablet*. Occasionally the Paley cult rebounded on Nicholls with comic effect: the summer 1995 issue of the *Anglican Theological Review* contained an article by Nicholls on Thomas Malthus, below which the unsuspecting editor placed an article on William Paley.

David Nicholls will be greatly missed, not only in Oxford but among the vast community of friends, students and people to whom he was, often without knowing it, a wise guide and mentor. He and his wife Gill provided a loving and informal home-base for many visitors to Oxford. The Church of England had no idea what to do with him, yet he was one of the most scholarly, most politically aware, most theologically alert, most prayerful, most gentle and loving, and most perceptive priests of his generation.

Martin Luther King[9]

The sky is red and threatening.

MATTHEW 16:3

The sky is red and threatening. Red is the colour both of fire and of freedom, and on the eve of May Day our minds are on the unity of the human race. Red, in theological well as in political mythology, is the colour of unity, of the blood which unites humankind in solidarity.

For red, too, is the colour of the blood of the martyrs which unites the freedom fighters in a red stream of sacrifice, and we have come together to remember one such martyr. Martin Luther King died, as he lived, for the unity and freedom of the children of God. His blood flowing in death symbolises his life's witness to the gospel that God 'has made of one blood all nations'. We celebrate his living and dying with gratitude and joy, and yet with a sense of apprehension.

Apprehension because the sky is red and threatening. We know only too well that red symbolises also the blood shed in race riots, which do not unite but divide humanity. The fire which set the church alight is not the fire of justice but the fire of hell, the red agony of the racial nightmare of which James Baldwin speaks in the frightening last paragraph of *The Fire Next Time*. And, in England, too, the murder of Martin Luther King should scream at us that the sky is red and threatening.

There was a cynical irony in the fact that so soon after the American freedom fighters marched with Martin Luther King, a section of British dockers marched for Enoch Powell with placards saying 'Back Britain Not Black Britain'. The march to freedom is followed by the march to hatred and slavery. It was horribly significant that so soon after the death of Martin Luther King, we should see in Britain the kindling of the fires of racial hatred. To us, then, the central message of his death is that the sky is red and threatening.

First, because Martin Luther King lived and died for a non-racial society. He fought for the liberation of an oppressed minority from the slavery of the ghetto. We applaud him, and the establishments and governments of the West applaud him now. But if ghettoes are wrong in the US, they cannot be right here. Racism is indivisible. You cannot fight segregation and discrimination abroad and condone it here. Equally, you cannot accept discrimination at the doors of Britain and pretend to oppose it within Britain. Once the principle of racism is incorporated into legislation – as it now has been incorporated in this country – we have created a situation where all talk of conciliation and Race Relations Acts will seem suspiciously like window dressing.

For this country has in recent years witnessed a growing movement of racism under the name of realism. Sentiments which were regarded as fanatical and the fruits of prejudice in 1958 are now expressed by the pillars of liberal opinion. The Commonwealth Immigrants Act, the 1965 White Paper, the Kenyan Asian episode, Enoch Powell – these are only facets of a pervasive disease. Black people, it is now argued, are undesirable *per se*. A few years ago even the 'extremists' were at pains to stress that 'this is not a question of colour': now nobody bothers to deny the fact. So now we have what Ruth Glass has called 'a new doctrine of original sin combined with a faulty political arithmetic'. For racism is a vicious doctrine which cuts at the heart of the gospel and of catholic Christianity. The true opposite of catholic is not Protestant but racist, for catholicism proclaims the unity of humankind while racism divides people and returns us to a fallen world, the dominion of the demons.

Second, Martin Luther King lived and died for nonviolence. Racial hatred breeds violence and thrives upon it. The sentiments expressed in this past week are in essence no different from those which led to the shootings at Sharpeville and the tragedies revealed at the Eichmann trial. To counteract violence by more violence generates still more of the same; but to compromise by making more and more concessions to prejudice and hatred under the name of liberal opinion sets us on the typically British slide to respectable racism. Nonviolent resistance, Martin Luther King argued, is not just the only practicable alternative to race war, it *is* the Christian gospel of love and justice expressed in terms of conflict with evil and injustice.

Third, Martin Luther King lived and died for social justice. He did not see race relations as a special sphere isolated from the social structure. As long as there is poverty and squalor, there will be scapegoats. As long as there are twilight zones, acres of desperation, stagnant decaying districts without hope of renewal, as long as these remain, people will continue to blame the new minorities for the long-standing evils of the social order. Martin Luther King saw that racial goodwill could not be separated from housing exploitation, poverty and capital, or from the Vietnam war where black conscripts are sent to defend a liberty which they do not enjoy at home.

The sky is red and threatening. No amount of compromise and no amount of reformist tinkering with the status quo will avert a racial holocaust. Only the rise of a new generation dedicated to freedom and justice will cut through the vicious reality of racism which threatens to engulf the cosmos in a baptism of blood. Martin Luther King saw that a new world order based on love and justice and the rejection of war, poverty and inequality was a possibility, and he was wild enough to see the Church as the vanguard of this new world.

But not the Church as it stands, a ritual re-enactment of the old order, riddled through and through with racial and class divisions, tamed and compromised by the establishment. The old decaying structures must be burnt down in the furnace of God's love and justice. While the sky is red and threatening, the Sun of Justice must arise in the Church like fire in the heavens, for the liberation of humankind for which Martin Luther King lived and fought and still prays.

Saul Alinsky[10]

'Radical is teaching ministers tactics of social revolution', announced *The New York Times* on 2 August 1965. A few weeks later, on 13 September 1965, *Newsweek* described this same radical as the 'gadfly of the poverty war'. Saul Alinsky (1909–72) was at various times accused of being a communist, a Trotskyist, and an agent of the Vatican. The best-known community organiser in the United States, he brought together insights and methods of work from the Roman Catholic Church, the Al Capone gang, the department of sociology at the University of Chicago, and union organising. As a sociology student in Chicago under E. W. Burgess and R. E. Park, the founders of the 'Chicago School' of urban sociology, Alinsky devoted his postgraduate work to the Al Capone gang, and it was from these early experiences of urban conflict that his community work began.

Alinsky was never in the strict sense a revolutionary, rather an American radical (as he called himself) in the tradition of Thomas Jefferson and James Madison rather than Marx or Engels. There is no hint of Marxist influence anywhere in his work. His only two books, *Reveille for Radicals* (1945) and *Rules for Radicals* (1972), became best-sellers and continue to influence urban activists all over the world. His name became legendary, and he was feared by the powerful. 'Wherever I go,' he once remarked, 'there is trouble'. Beginning with the 'Back of the Yards' community in Chicago's meat-packing district, Alinsky moved on to found the Organization for a South West Community, the North West Community Organization, and the Woodlawn Organization on the South Side, the first major black neighbourhood movement in Chicago. He was described by *The Economist* in 1967 as 'the only radical who has succeeded in organizing the Negro communities'.

Alinsky was one of the first people in the modern period of urban life to recognise the organisational potential of the churches, especially of the Roman Catholic church, with its solid working-class and immigrant base. Although he was a Jewish agnostic, much of his work was with churches. Yet it was from the churches that much of the opposition to him came. In 1959 the Lutheran theologian Dr Walter Kloetzli attacked him, accusing him of a 'hidden purpose' and hinting at racism and subversion. The *Christian Century*, the influential liberal Christian journal, pursued a vendetta against him from 1959 to 1964. Editorials in the *Century* accused him of 'exploiting urban decay' and of 'Marxist class war'. 'Alinksy denounces reconciliation', announced another editorial. In one issue, on 3 August 1963, he was described as part of a Roman Catholic conspiracy, though the editor, Harold Fey, saw him as a Marxist. In fact it was Fey who 'pinned a Marxist label on Alinsky', a label that remains to this day among the ignorant and ill-informed sections of the media.

Certainly there was much support for Alinsky from the Roman Catholic community. In the 1950s Monsignor Jack Egan, himself a legendary figure in Chicago community action, introduced Alinsky to Cardinal Stritch, and he was very close both to Stritch and to his successors, Cardinals Meyer and Cody. It was during the 1950s also that the French philosopher Jacques Maritain asked Alinsky to meet with Cardinal Montini (later Pope Paul VI) to advise him on trade union work in Milan. Maritain was one of Alinsky's greatest admirers. He saw him as one of the few really gifted persons of the twentieth century and described *Reveille for Radicals* as 'epoch making'. Alinsky in his turn saw Maritain as his 'spiritual father' and often quoted one of his sayings: 'The fear of soiling ourselves by entering the context of history is not virtue but a way of escaping virtue.'

Though I have some serious doubts about the way Alinksy's methods have been developed by his successors, the figure of Saul Alinsky himself has been a constant source of strength to me and continues to influence my work. Though he himself was not a Christian, many of his insights offer important contributions to Christian social action at the neighbourhood and community level. An obvious example is his emphasis on the need for effective organising. He was first and foremost an organiser. 'To hell with charity', he wrote. 'The only thing you get is what you are strong enough to get. So you had better organize.' On the other hand, he was a great believer in keeping his opponents in the dark about his plans and his power base. He held the view that 'power is not only what you have but what the enemy thinks you have', and many of his most effective tactics were based on threats. The occupation of the urinals at O'Hare Airport in 1964 has become part of Chicago mythology, even though it never actually took place. The threat was enough.

Another characteristic of Alinsky that attracted me to him was his tremendous sense of humour. Not for him the serious, unrelaxed intensity of so many activists. He was a brilliant practitioner of ridicule and an exponent of the social power of fun. 'The establishment', he wrote, 'can accept being screwed, but not being laughed at. What bugs them about me is that, unlike humourless radicals, I have a hell of a time doing what I'm doing.' He saw ridicule as his most potent weapon and believed that a good tactic was one that people actually enjoyed. And this was part of a much deeper aspect of Alinsky's faith: his deep trust in the ability of ordinary people to think and to act. He saw how vital it was that radical organisers should not lose touch with the sense and the style of the common people. 'Never go outside the experience of your people', he advised, adding that one should, 'whenever possible, go outside the experience of the enemy'. Alinksy was a great listener, and his stress on listening to the people has been a major influence on my ministry in East London. He was committed to help and support, not paternalism.

Most of all, Alinsky saw that real change could not take place without conflict, and it was this conviction that brought him into dispute with the liberal wing of the churches, which sought change without conflict. The Roman Catholic church accepted his methods more easily than did Protestant groups; it would be valuable to explore the reasons for this.

William Stringfellow[11]

Stringfellow was an important influence on me, and was involved with the same pastoral, theological and political concerns. A lawyer in East Harlem, his quarrel with the parish led him to leave it after only eighteen months. The East Harlem Protestant Parish (EHPP) was a flagship for inner-city ministry in the US, and its work was popularised in Britain by Bruce Kenrick's inspiring book *Come Out the Wilderness* which influenced me and many others to work in the inner city.

The EHPP had an important effect in London on ministry where Kenrick himself worked. After the inter-racial conflicts of 1958,

Donald Soper, then president of the Methodist Conference, encouraged the formation of a ministry in the Lancaster Road area of Notting Hill based on the ministry in East Harlem. The three ministers who began that ministry had all worked in the EHPP with Stringfellow, who had come to East Harlem when he was 28. But he was troubled by its focus on care and neglect of the challenge of the gospel. Kenrick referred to Stringfellow's belief that there was a radical failure to take the Bible and Christ seriously.

In one sense this was a classic conflict between prophet and pastor, or, perhaps, between the prophetic Church and the servant Church. Stringfellow was playing the role of prophet, the role which Brueggemann once described as a destabilising presence in any community, a trouble-maker, one who upsets the apple cart. But was it fair? Did he actually take seriously what the East Harlem workers were trying to do? One-and-a-half years is not very long to give a parish a chance. And in fact it is interesting that much of the critique that Stringfellow made was subsequently incorporated into the parish programme.

What was it about Stringfellow which led him into dispute with this important experiment in urban ministry? I think there are a number of things which give us a clue. He was not a fundamentalist, but he was steeped in the scriptures. He wished to develop what Jim Wallis, very much a disciple of his, later called an 'agenda for biblical people', a kind of biblical consciousness. He felt that there was a neglect of the Bible's challenge to the contemporary scene, and that the EHPP was deeply conformed to the world. It is a dilemma that we have all shared, and one with which I lived at St Botolph's all the time. I suppose that one of the differences between Stringfellow and me is that he found that the conflict was an impossible one to negotiate and left after a year and a half, and I stayed.

The neglect of the challenge of scripture was fundamental to Stringfellow's critique. He believed that the parish was playing down, and at times ignoring, the prophetic, confrontational dimension of the Christian message, substituting the servant Church for the prophetic Church. Martin Luther King Jr, in one of his sermons, said that the role of the Church is not to be the servant of the state, but always its conscience. It was that which Stringfellow found missing.

The apocalyptic strand in Stringfellow led him into dissent with East Harlem. He felt that they were picking up the pieces, doing good to broken people, but not challenging Babylon. He was essentially a dissenter, often speaking of resistance as the only way to live humanly under a totalitarian regime. He must have been one of the first American writers in the modern period to talk of the need for a 'Confessing Church', a term from the Nazi period. Part of me says that Stringfellow was very impatient and arrogant. There are other dimensions to pastoral ministry than constant polemic and confrontation. There are dimensions of gentleness, care, silence, listening, staying with the suffering. There doesn't seem to be a lot in Stringfellow's writings about that. And it may well be that the EHPP had quite a lot to teach him about those dimensions, and he didn't stay long enough to learn.

I never met Stringfellow, and all I know about him is what I have picked up from the books, the odd tapes, and discussions with people who knew him. But the story is a very familiar one. It is the story of the destabilising presence in a community. It is the story of the clash between the prophetic and the pastoral, the story of what Richard Holloway has called the 'antithetical preacher' who 'throws kerygmatic parcel bombs through the windows of those who are at ease in Zion'. It is an old conflict which is going on still. I am not sure how much of this was to do with incompatible theologies, different views of the relationship of Church and world, different views indeed of what the Church is, or how much of it was to do with personality.

I am always worried about people like Stringfellow, Thomas Merton, Dorothy Day and Conrad Noel, and all those people who were trouble-makers. (I realise that, in worrying about these comrades, I am worrying about myself.) When I look honestly at some of Stringfellow's work, I sense a certain impetuousness, impatience and inability to understand the position of those less charismatic people who simply get on with the boring work and are still in East Harlem now. I see a kind of modern monastic with a strong commitment to poverty; a single-minded chaste vision, and a strong sense of obedience (which, of course, led to disobedience of, and resistance to, the principalities). But what seems to be missing, but which was clearly present in some of the people he fell out with, was the Benedictine tradition of stability: of staying there and not moving, and saying 'God has put me here, and as far as I know hasn't told me to go, so here I stay'. So when I realise that the EHPP is now over fifty years old (it's not called that any more but the storefront churches are still there), I look back at Stringfellow's critique and I have to ask: is he really being fair to these people who are still there forty to fifty years on?

The experience of Stringfellow and East Harlem is uncomfortably close to us in all but the geographical sense. The questions I ask about Stringfellow I have to ask about myself. My impression has been that the churches in East London have always had a strong social conscience. However, local crises may put it to the test. There were times when I felt that some Christians were retreating from social involvement into piety and a defensive kind of 'churchiness'. For some Christian groups, there had been no significant tradition of thought or analysis of events and trends in the social, political and economic fields. What was evident, as in East Harlem, was social *action*. Yet action without thought, without theology, can be at best superficial and at worst harmful.

Dorothy Day[12]

Dorothy Day (1897–1981) is best known as the founder of the *Catholic Worker*, both a newspaper and a movement. Since her death, campaigns for her canonisation have been supported by both radical and conservative sections of the Catholic community, though it is interesting that much 'mainstream' church literature about her has ignored, or played down, the anarchism that was so central to her life and work. Dorothy Day was both a traditional Catholic, and a revolutionary anarchist. She took the papal encyclicals with great seriousness and continually embarrassed the American hierarchy with her nonviolent civil disobedience campaigns, always supported by quotations from sources of impeccable orthodoxy. Her style, it has been said, was mystical, liturgical, sacramental, and orthodox.

The *Catholic Worker* newspaper began on 1 May 1933. Its original audience was the people of the streets of New York. For many years it was impossible to obtain it in 'respectable' Catholic circles. In London at the end of the 1950s, when the Catholic bookshops refused to stock it on the grounds that it was 'communist', and the anarchist bookshops because it was Christian, the only source was the Anglo-Catholic anarchist Laurens Otter, who used to sell it at Speakers' Corner in Hyde Park every Sunday. Today, still selling at one cent, the paper is read all over the Christian world and is a source of strength and inspiration to thousands of people.

At one level the paper and the movement is deeply conservative, steeped in the papal encyclicals, the liturgy, the lives and sayings of the saints, and the words of Jesus. It has been a radical grass-roots prophetic witness within Catholic orthodoxy, seeking to recall the church to its true vocation and to the roots of its commitment, and it has been interesting – and in some respects disturbing – to note that since Dorothy Day's death the importance of her witness has been recognised by many members of the hierarchy. Not that she was totally without recognition during her life: on her eightieth birthday she was greeted by Pope Paul VI. But since her death a devotional cult has grown up, many of the devotees being people who would have opposed – and, if they understood it, would still oppose – all that the Catholic Worker movement stands for. On the other hand, many individuals, including many non-Christians, owe their social awareness on the issues of poverty and urban deprivation to their experience with the Catholic Worker. One prominent figure who began his study of urban poverty through working as a volunteer in the Worker houses was Michael Harrington, whose book *The Other America* (1962) was the most important single influence on the 'war on poverty' of the mid-1960s.

The Catholic Worker remains a countercultural phenomenon within American religion. From its origins, many years before the appearance of 'postmodernism' and the critique of modernity, it has represented a fundamental rejection of the foundations of the modern world – government, bureaucracy, and industry. In terms of the history of Christian social movements, it combines the traditions of ethical separatism and of prophetic transformation, with its constant insistence on the need for change from below.

In the writings of Dorothy Day, I found a powerful fusion of orthodoxy and daring, of rootedness in the tradition and wildness in the spirit, of solidarity both with the saints and the liturgy and with the poorest of God's creatures. Her storefront Catholicism continues to inspire and shape my ministry.

Thomas Merton[13]

Merton's life was a struggle with illusion, a struggle for humanity. In all his writings he laid great emphasis on the importance of 'accepting ourselves as we are in our confusion, infidelity, disruption, ferment and even desperation'. He had seen many examples of people who were never themselves and who wore out their minds and bodies in trying to have other people's experiences. Merton was concerned with the attainment of solitude, of interior harmony and peace. His writings were taken up with such themes as the desert, conflict, and contemplation in the midst of action. In his view, contemplation was not a way of escape, an avoidance of action; it was an advance into the reality of solitude and the desert, into the confrontation with poverty and the void. Only through this process could any wholeness be achieved.

I discovered Merton in the midst of a very active ministry in Soho. He was a wise guide to me in a number of ways. He saw the danger of 'do-gooders' who rushed into the work of helping others but did not deepen their own self-understanding and integrity. They could only communicate to others the contagion of their own obsessions, delusions, and prejudices. Merton was a prophetic sign and warning to me as I slogged away at the problems of Soho, but he was also an illuminating symbol, a light for my path, for he spoke to me of the work of the solitary explorer, the monk who searched the existential depths of faith. The monk in Merton's vision was a marginal, restless person. The monk withdrew from 'the world' in order to 'deepen fundamental human experience'. The monk confronted humanity at the point of darkness and despair. I came to see that what Merton said about the monk was actually true of all Christians in the modern world. 'The monk is essentially someone who takes up a critical attitude toward the contemporary world and its structures.' But Merton went further than this: he held that the marginal position of the monk brought him into a solidarity with other marginal people and groups.

Merton embodied in himself the trends, crises, spiritual currents, and polarisations of his age in a unique way. Though his early writing was addressed to the world of pre-Vatican II Roman Catholicism, his later work reflected, and helped to develop, a new age: the age of the counterculture, of Vatican II, of the East–West dialogue, of the struggle for racial justice, of the recovery of the contemplative spirit, of resistance to nuclear weapons, of post-Constantinian Christianity. His writings from 1963 until his death in 1968 were the most important and most influential of his life. In these writings there was the concern to unite contemplation and action, the mystical and the prophetic, the revolution of the spirit and political revolution. These are among the key issues that will determine the shape of the Christianity of the future. They were the key issues of Merton's' spiritual quest.

More than any other single individual, it was Merton who shaped my understanding of priesthood.

Michael Ramsey[14]

It is said that, when Michael Ramsey arrived in Rome to visit Pope Paul VI, there was a gasp of amazement from the waiting crowd, many of whom instinctively dropped to their knees. Such was the impact of Ramsey's presence.

Yet this awe-inspiring figure was also a humble and caring pastor, never more himself than when exercising pastoral ministry. It is not surprising that reflections on his years as Archbishop of Canterbury keep on appearing.

Part One of the book is, according to the publishers, 'an edited collection of the best of his work'. This takes up 135 of the book's 260 pages. The selection is related to the liturgical year, based on the themes of the Word of God, the cross, the Lord of Glory, and the Body of Christ. It is a good selection, and I was pleased that it includes extracts from Ramsey's Seabury Lectures *From Gore to Temple*, and also his small book on F. D. Maurice.

Nevertheless, I counted only seven extracts from these works on social theology, of which one reference seems to be a misprint. Most of the selection relates to his writing on Christian doctrine and spirituality; and the social context, which was important to Ramsey's thought, is not very evident.

This is an unusual book in that it is written by four people of whom one is an archbishop, and one a former archbishop. Parts Two and Three consist of nine essays by the four authors on aspects of Ramsey's thought. Four of these are by Rowan Williams, three by Douglas Dales, and one each by the other authors.

Each is valuable, but I was particularly struck by Geoffrey Rowell's essay on transfiguration in connection with Ramsey's relation to Eastern Orthodoxy. The neglect of the transfiguration in Western Christianity is depressing, and Ramsey's book on this theme is important in helping to restore the emphasis on the glory of God in the face of Jesus.

John Habgood's essay is a moving and warm personal account of Ramsey as a person of God.

The book stresses the centrality of glory in Ramsey's theology, but it also brings out three other aspects of his life and work: his sense of the Body of Christ in its brokenness, and yet its solidarity with the crucified and risen Christ; his strong biblical roots and biblical consciousness; and the integration of prayer, theology, and pastoral care which was so central to his being.

There is a story, which I think I have confirmed as authentic, that, when it was reported in the press that Ramsey would probably succeed Geoffrey Fisher as Archbishop of Canterbury, the Prime Minister, Harold Macmillan, received an urgent phone call from Fisher. Macmillan and Fisher met. Ramsey, said Fisher, would be a most unsuitable successor since he was a theologian, a mystic, and a person of prayer. This book helps us to give thanks for, and rejoice in, the fact that this was the case.

Rowan Williams[15]

Two evangelical organisations, the Church Society and Reform, are very opposed to Rowan Williams and want him to withdraw from becoming Archbishop of Canterbury. The grounds of their objection seem to be his attitude to homosexuality and to the interpretation of the Bible.

The four evangelical theologians who have rightly sprung to Rowan Williams's defence in the columns of the *Guardian* (8th October) may not be correct in their claim that 'disputes among Christians should be settled in private'. Positions which are stated publicly need to be critiqued and challenged publicly. I suspect Rowan would agree with this. The idea of settling disputes in private smacks more of the Oxbridge old-boy network than of the gospel which speaks of things hidden being revealed. In the Church of England, the refusal (and eventual inability) to deal with issues in the public arena, and the preference for cosy fireside chats over sherry, has done immense damage. However, there is an equally serious issue. Terms such as 'orthodox', traditional and 'liberal' are being used meaninglessly.

No Christian theologian is more rooted in Catholic orthodoxy, more traditional in his faith, and more critical of theological and political liberalism than Rowan Williams. It is clear from all his writings. The inability of some 'evangelicals' (I use inverted commas deliberately) not to see this is itself a cause for concern. But so is their claim to orthodoxy and their obsession with a small range of sexual issues.

Orthodoxy is about balance, coherence and the 'proportion of faith' in contrast to heresy which is unbalanced, often literalist and partial. It is bizarre that the issue of homosexuality, on which the scriptures say little and Jesus said nothing at all, should be exalted to central position by these groups. Such lack of balance seems more heretical than orthodox, and suggests a kind of theological pathology. It is, of course, important to realise that these groups are not typical of evangelicals in the Church of England, and many of my evangelical friends are embarrassed to be thought to be associated with them. Nevertheless these groups do reflect a mood in current western Christianity, greatly under the influence of North American fundamentalists, and of the consumerist dimension of capitalism. The groups who stand within this mood will find Rowan baffling and threatening.

I first heard of Rowan Williams in 1974. A group of left-wing Anglican priests had met in Bethnal Green, where I was rector, and started a support group. It became the Jubilee Group, a loose network of socialist Christians, mainly within the Anglican catholic tradition. One of our founder members, John Saward, offered to write a manifesto with 'my friend Rowan Williams', then a graduate student at Oxford, whom none of us knew. It was a fascinating document, but rather triumphalist, and we rejected it. But it contained some important material which helps us to understand Rowan's theology and spirituality.

It began with a quotation from the Russian theologian Nikolay Fyodorov, one of the people who had figured in Rowan's doctoral thesis on modern Russian theology: 'Our social programme is the dogma of the Holy Trinity'. It was emphatic that work for justice was rooted in theology. I would not want to commit Rowan to the language of that 1974 document, and I have problems with some of it, but it does really show the heart of the theological focus of the man. And this has not changed.

Some years later, Rowan and I met, and he became a member of the Jubilee Literature Committee. He co-edited, with me, the Jubilee symposium *Essays Catholic and Radical* in 1983. Jubilee people see him as a humble, kind, gentle and holy person, one who has not changed since becoming a bishop, in that he remains first and foremost a human being and Christian, and treats every person with the utmost reverence and respect. Margaret Ronchetti, who organised our pilgrimage to Milan some years ago, expressed her amazement and delight that Rowan, though now a bishop, was 'just the same' in his friendship and concern for people.

In 1988, the crisis over the Lesbian and Gay Christian Movement's presence at St Botolph's, Aldgate, came to a head. The Jubilee Group published *Speaking Love's Name*, and Rowan's words in the introduction are worth recalling.

> It is becoming harder all the time for a gay person to be honest in the Church. We have helped to build a climate in which concealment is rewarded – while at the same time conniving with the hysteria of the gutter press and effectively giving into their hands as victims those who do not manage successful concealment.

His intervention in the legal action against LGCM was important. He denounced the Diocese of London for operating a deliberate policy to humiliate, and for going to law with other Christians in clear defiance of New Testament teaching. In *Speaking Love's Name*, he called the Diocese's action a 'vendetta' and saw it as 'the lowest point' of the church's anti-gay polemic.

Rowan is first and foremost a man of prayer. Rowan stands very much in the Ramsey tradition. His prayer is the root and source of his theology and is inseparable form his passion for justice. Prayer, theology and justice are all of a piece in his mind and heart. When he becomes Archbishop, he will be the first one for many years who can hold his own in debates with secular intellectuals. (Only William Temple and Michael Ramsey are comparable, and Rowan's intellectual range is way beyond theirs.)

To be Archbishop of Canterbury is not a position that we should wish on anyone, especially one we love. It is vital that we surround and embrace him with prayer, love and support. As we have already seen, the spiritual struggle with principalities and powers will become very focussed and hard. I believe that Rowan's obvious honesty, prayerfulness and holiness of life will be a great threat to many religious people, and may well bring many of the worst aspects of religion to the surface – ironically something he warned about in *Writing in the Dust* after his own personal experience of September 11th 2001 in New York. But also one of the worst things that could happen, and Rowan would not welcome it, would be that radical Christians would simply rejoice and applaud him, resisting the attacks from the evangelical right. That would not help. Rowan is committed to debate and critique, and would not want people to view him uncritically. But those who debate with him must be prepared for a level of thinking and spiritual struggle which they may never have encountered before.

I believe the future is exciting and potentially glorious, but we do need to surround Rowan with our prayer.

Theology and Place

*Physical location is a critical element in
theological work.*[1]

North American journeys[2]

For over twenty-five years I have spent between three and six
weeks each year in American cities. This began when I was a parish
priest in Bethnal Green in the 1970s. In 1978 I spoke at the Catholic
Renewal Conference in Loughborough on the renewal of the Anglo-
Catholic social conscience. In the bar, later that evening, an American
priest said to me, 'You should come and say that in Chicago.' There
followed a curious conversation, at the end of which I was no wiser
than at the beginning as to who he was, or why he wanted me to go.
However, he seemed an interesting person who clearly did something
in Chicago. Several months later the phone rang at midnight. 'Hi,
Dick Young. When are you coming?' said the voice. After pointing
out that I could not come the following Tuesday, as he proposed, we
negotiated what turned out to be an attempt to see what two inner-
city areas, the East End of London and the South Side of Chicago,
could learn from, and give to, one another. That kind of relationship,
though now involving many other places, is still a primary focus of
my time in the USA.

The early years with Dick Young were very interesting. Chicago is
one of the most racially segregated cities in the world. The South Side
of Chicago is divided by various main roads, one of which is 47th
Street. North of 47th Street, at the junction with Ellis Avenue, is a vast
ghetto occupied by a large black proletariat. South of 47th Street and
north of 63rd Street is the University of Chicago, a district known as
Hyde Park. Beyond 63rd Street, one moves back into a ghetto area of
great deprivation. Between 47th Street and the University area is a
neighbourhood known as Oakland-Kenwood, which is a mixed,
multi-racial neighbourhood, including white and black, some academics, young families, and members of the black bourgeoisie as well

as poor black and white people. Some of the cafes and restaurants are significant meeting places for diverse, and otherwise divided, groups. One of these, where I spent a good deal of time, was Valois's Cafeteria in 53rd Street, which became widely known as a result of Mitchell Duneier's book *Slim's Table*. Breakfast at Valois's with local people helped me to correct some of the stereotypes of polarisation and racial separatism which recur in the writing and discourse about Chicago.

In the early years in Chicago, I encountered churches which, while they were physically present on the South Side, and elsewhere, hardly touched the people of the neighbourhood, and indeed didn't seem interested in doing so. They were – and often still are – gathered churches of people drawn by a particular style or form of worship or by a particular pastor or preacher, or for historical reasons, but their involvement with the local residents or local issues is minimal or non-existent. This 'gathered' type of church, in which 'parish' effectively means 'congregation', and in which the local community is simply the backcloth to the work of the church, seems particularly common among Anglicans. I also encountered storefront churches, often Pentecostal or Baptist churches, which were integral to black organisation in their neighbourhood. Two churches stand out in my memories of the late 1970s. One was the African Orthodox Church which has its only Chicago base on the South Side. This small church, a breakaway from Anglicanism over racism in the 1920s, really did seem to be ministering with the very poor and oppressed people of that area. Indeed, in the late 1970s, its membership was more representative of the neighbourhood than the local Anglican parish a few hundred yards away.

More dramatic, colourful and triumphant was the huge Apostolic Church of God in 63rd Street, part of the Pentecostal Assemblies of the World. With a congregation of several thousand, the church has played a key role in community life for many hears, and its pastor, Bishop Arthur Brazier, is something of a legend in Chicago. Here I found contextual theology being done, theology being rediscovered as the people's work, within a framework of gospel singing and vigorous social involvement.

It was in Chicago in the late 1970s also that I first encountered the work of Claude Marie Barbour, founder of the Shalom Ministries. This remarkable woman, a French Protestant minister teaching in a Roman Catholic seminary, has made an impact throughout the world through her stress on listening to, and learning with, marginalised communities.

Since 1988 my work in the USA has been co-ordinated by Sam Portaro, the Anglican chaplain at the University of Chicago. His enormous range of contacts all over the country has meant that my experience of urban (and to a lesser extent rural) church life has extended way beyond Chicago to include Washington, DC, New York, Oklahoma, Arkansas, Northern Michigan, Idaho, Los Angeles and San Diego, and many other parts of the US, and beyond the US to include Toronto, Vancouver and Nova Scotia.

Throughout almost all my writing, there is a dynamic engagement with the question of space and place. I see space as a scientifically measurable location, while place involves the encounter between space and human interpretation of its significance. The idea of a place involves emotional bonds, identity, and so on. Place is the result of human beings working with and giving character to space. But space itself is never a neutral background to action. Space in East London is seen throughout its history as the site of social struggles, and it is in the course of such struggles that it becomes place, contested territory, home. Like the bread of the eucharistic offertory, place is something 'which earth has given and human hands have made.' For me, whether I am in Nova Scotia or in Whitechapel Road in East London, the local context, the place, even the physical space, is of critical importance to theological work. If the combination of air travel and computer technology has brought about 'the death of distance', it has also brought home to us on a global scale how central is place to human life and human flourishing.

North American itinerary 1998[3]

This trip was one of those which happens every few years in which there is no geographical coherence, and all kinds of places which have requested me to come get put together in one month. I began on 13th October in Halifax, Nova Scotia, the most extreme NE point in the continent, and finished on 9th November in San Diego, the most extreme SW point – a distance, I guess, of 4000 miles. In Halifax, from Wednesday 14th to Friday 16th October I gave the MacKinnon Lectures at the Atlantic School of Theology on 'The Hospitable Kingdom: pastoral care, spiritual formation and the Kingdom of God'. I left there on Friday 16th and went to the Page Centre in the upper peninsula of Northern Michigan where I led a retreat and study day and preached at Holy Innocents parish.

It took me longer to get from Halifax to Northern Michigan than it did to get from London to Halifax. Northern Michigan is a vast and poor area, one of the biggest dioceses in terms of size and one of the smallest in terms of churches. I was very impressed with the way in which the churches had developed a real sense of solidarity and common purpose.

On Monday 19th I flew to Chicago where I was based with my old friends Jackie Schmitt and Tim Hall in Evanston. I spoke at Northwestern University, Seabury Western Theological Seminary, and various parishes. I spent one day on the South Side where I preached at the weekly Mass for students at the University of Chicago and spoke at a seminar with a local community organiser.

On the weekend of 23rd–25th October I spoke and preached at St Giles Church, Northbrook, Chicago, and in the evening of the 25th I preached to Northwestern University students.

From Tuesday 27th to Friday 30th I was at the Episcopal Seminary of the South West at Austin, Texas. It was good to meet John Downing, curate of St Dunstan's Stepney in the early 60s, who is now Professor of Media and Communication at the University of Texas. I spoke also at three parishes in Austin.

On Monday 30th I flew to Tulsa, Oklahoma, and from then onwards was based at St Bernard of Clairvaux Parish and the Monos Community. I spoke at various conferences – at St Bernard's, and at Our Lady of Sorrows Convent in Broken Arrow. On All Saints Day I preached at Holy Trinity Church, Tulsa, and on that evening spoke at the Osage Monastery, where the Benedictine Sisters of Perpetual Adoration live in an ashram on Bede Griffiths lines. It was nice to have the Bhagavad Gita read at Evening Prayer, though the very conservative Bishop, a former colleague of Cardinal Cody, would not think so. On Monday 2nd I spoke at a conference on Spiritual Direction at Our Lady of Sorrows Convent.

On Tuesday 3rd I flew to Los Angeles area where I was based at All Saints Church in Pasadena. On Wednesday 4th I preached at the Mass and met with the large staff, many of whom are involved with homelessness. Union Station, the biggest centre for homeless people in the LA area, is an offshoot of All Saints. In the evening I lectured at

All Saints on spirituality and justice. I spent Thursday 5th in the Los Angeles area, preaching at the Cathedral centre, and meeting with the diocesan clergy. I visited various projects including one in the main El Salvadorean district, and then met with Alice Callaghan, founder of Union Station, now running a day centre in the Skid Row district. She spent six months at St Botolph's in 1980.

On Friday 6th we drove to San Diego, where I was based at St Paul's Cathedral. On Saturday 7th I spoke at a conference at St Bartholomew's Church, Poway. In the evening I went to a performance of T. S. Eliot's *Murder in the Cathedral*. One of the actors was born in Vallance Road and knew Bill Fishman.

On Sunday 8th I preached twice and spoke three times at St Paul's Cathedral, San Diego, and on Monday 9th, after a visit to the original Spanish mission, left for the airport. The flight to the UK took over 12 hours, but was helped by a 100 mile per hour wind in Arizona. I arrived back on Tuesday 10th in the late afternoon.

Hoxton life[4]

I was ordained as a deacon in May 1964 and went to the Church of the Most Holy Trinity, Hoxton, on the northern tip of the East End. Some years later I wrote a small book called *The Social God*, based on my experience in the area. I took the title from two great Anglican pastors, Conrad Noel and Stanley Evans, who used this phrase often in their teaching and writing. They held that the whole gospel and the whole of Christian theology was social, rooted in the dogma of the Trinity, the expression of the social character of God. To speak of 'the social implications of the gospel' or of 'the social gospel' as if there were some other gospel would be confusing, for the entire Christian reality was social from beginning to end. It is this truth that lies at the heart of my experience of the Christian community in East London.

In the East End, neighbourhoods, and their history and culture, are of crucial importance. Cable Street was perceived as a strange and alien zone by many in the mainly white neighbourhoods. It was to one of these white working-class neighbourhoods, Hoxton, that I moved in 1964. The three years that I spent there as deacon and priest had a profound impact on my understanding of the corporate character of Christian discipleship and my understanding of the place of the

Eucharist and of daily prayer in the life of the parish community. It also raised for me some disturbing questions about the nature of community itself, and about the danger of communities that become closed in on themselves.

Hoxton, part of the district called Shoreditch, is an old working-class neighbourhood of London, an urban village. It was the setting for *Oliver Twist*, Marie Lloyd, and the Eagle from 'Pop Goes the Weasel'. The district had the lowest rate of population movement in Greater London; it was a tightly knit complex of families interrelated since the time of Dickens. In my time there it was almost entirely white. The district had known extreme poverty and deprivation, and some of that had survived into the 1960s. Crime rates were high, and the underworld of criminal syndicates was powerful. The pubs were the centre of community life. Here was much of the traditional culture of East London – jellied eels and whelk stalls, pearly kings and queens, music halls, street markets in Club Row and Brick Lane. There was an abundance of street life still in the 1960s, but new influences were appearing – Mods and Rockers, the drug culture, the music of the Who and the Beatles – and the young people were moving away from the pubs to the discotheques and coffee bars.

The Church of the Most Holy Trinity stood at the centre of the neighbourhood. It was in the very strict sense a neighbourhood church. Nobody worshipped there who could not walk to the church in ten minutes. The church, not surprisingly, reflected, and in some ways, reinforced, the positive and negative aspects of the local community: its amazing sense of mutual care and support, its networks of information and help, its sense of being an extended family, its tremendous sense of fun; but also its wariness of, and hostility to, strangers, its racism, and its inward-looking character.

The whole life of the parish centred upon the Parish Mass. Holy Trinity, and most of the adjoining parishes, had been built as part of the sacramental and liturgical revival associated with the 'Romanising' wing of the Oxford Movement of the nineteenth century. Here in the 1840s, 1850s, and 1860s, were built back-street baroque churches with massive altars and multitudes of lamps, lights, and statues for eucharistic worship. Historically the recovery of the centrality of the Eucharist in the Church of England coincided with the recovery of the parish unit; the Mass became the central act in these new churches of the poor. And all the pastoral and social outreach to the neighbourhood was seen as flowing from, and back into, the sacramental action, for beneath the sacramental action was a sacramental view of reality: not only bread and wine but all material things, all created life, were vehicles of the divine.

I learned more than I can express both from the neighbourhood life of Hoxton and from the eucharistic life of the parish there. While I was there, the Second Vatican Council was meeting. Liturgical changes were prefiguring and symbolising fundamental theological and social changes whose full impact is only now being felt. As a young priest I felt that the new sacramental atmosphere was being created not only externally in the church but in me personally. I was being forged, often painfully and paradoxically, into a sacramental person, in Austin Farrer's phrase, a 'walking sacrament'. The old language about carrying Christ mystically present within me, about the extension of the incarnation, was important and held deep meaning for me. I had come to see all Christian action as an extension of the incarnation and the Eucharist. The situation in Hoxton in some respects was almost medieval: church and sacrament, pub and street market, an urban village. And yet there was something that worried me very deeply about it; it was the sense that what the church was doing was baptising and ritually reenacting the old order, strengthening the sense of local community and solidarity, in a way that had potential for real danger. By the late 1960s the dangers became evident as Hoxton began to mobilise against the influx of black people from districts to the south and north. In 1965 one of our parliamentary candidates was Sir Oswald Mosley, whose British Union of Fascists had gained considerable support in the area in the 1930s. In 1967 the National Front, the first significant postwar fascist party, was formed, with one of its leading London strongholds in the streets around the church.

This sense of unease led me to focus on the sacraments, and particularly on the Eucharist, as embodying a fundamental question. Is the church the shrine of an old, stable order, or the sign of a new world, struggling towards transformation? Does the Eucharist sanctify the past or anticipate the future? Are there perhaps two different theologies, possibly even two different gods, one a static, cultic, settled god of the status quo – the pagan harvest festival kind of religion – one the liberating God of the Exodus who leads the community of disciples out of false securities into freedom? I had become interested in Stewart Headlam, that early precursor of liberation theology, who in the late nineteenth century saw the Eucharist as a feast of human liberation, the foretaste of a new age. Headlam's view of the Eucharist in relation to the life of the community horrified the more pietistic church people in East London in his day. For him and for me, the Eucharist and the church itself only made sense as pointers toward the Kingdom of God, the new age of God's justice. I came to see the church as a pilgrim community. Yet the Eucharist as celebrated in many churches, by its stress on correctness, order, restraint, and formality, seemed merely to recreate and sanctify the past, freezing it, protecting it against the changes and upheavals, not to point toward the new.

I began to see the real danger of a creation-centred, incarnational, sacramental religion that had no room for judgment, prophecy, redemption, or struggle. It was precisely such a religion that provided the spiritual soil for Mussolini, Franco, and Salazar, and for other oppressive regimes today. Sacramentalism is not enough. And yet the doctrine of the Body of Christ is a powerful weapon in the church's struggle against injustice. It is more than a vague sense of fellowship; it is the doctrine of a new creation, a new humanity in which there is neither Jew nor Greek, male nor female, bond nor free. In terms of modern racism, of the nation-state, of patriarchal and sexist society, this is highly explosive and seditious teaching. It was a truth that came home to me powerfully in the church, and in the streets, of Hoxton in the middle years of the 1960s, though I did not grasp many of its implications until years later. It has become more powerful as the years have progressed.

Bethnal Green[5]

Bethnal Green has a good claim to have been the original home of 'community studies', since Michael Young founded the Institute of Community Studies (ICS) there in 1952. After Young and Willmott produced their classic *Family and Kinship in East London* in 1957, there was a succession of related studies. This new volume is both the last of the ICS reports and the first from the new Young Foundation (Michael died in 2002). Here, the authors revisit the areas studied in the 1950s, and some that were not studied in the earlier work.

Although no direct attention is paid to the part played by churches, this book, and similar sociological studies, can be of enormous help in understanding the character of an area, and therefore in clarifying the nature of local ministry.

I arrived in the East End soon after the publication of the pioneering work of 1957, and lived in Bethnal Green and Whitechapel for most of my 46 years in London. Having known all three authors, and worked closely at various points with two of them, I am reluctant to be too critical of this book, but it really is unsatisfactory at several crucial points.

First, the research is seriously out of date, much of it having taken place a decade or more ago.

Second, like earlier publications from the Michael Young 'school', it tends to blur the distinction between 'East London', 'the East End', and 'Bethnal Green' (where most of the research took place), a confusion to which I drew attention as long ago as 1966 in a review of Willmott's *Adolescent Boys of East London*.

Bethnal Green differed from other East End districts in important ways, not least in the fact that it was, for many years, an urban village with low rates of migration, both from within the UK and beyond. Yet this book speaks of the East End as a 'point of entry to British society' (which was certainly true of Whitechapel), while, three pages later, claiming that immigration was not a significant issue in the 1950s. In fact, Cheshire Street in Bethnal Green was a well-known site for anti-immigration polemic in this period, and immigration had been a significant factor in many districts of the East End for more than 100 years.

Third, I was concerned that the account of the appeal of racist and Nazi groups to some sections of the white working class tended to blur the boundary between faithful reporting and the expression of sympathy. I am sure that none of the authors is in any way supportive of such groups, but a clearer statement of their opposition to racism would have been helpful, and might have prevented a favourable review of this book on the British National Party website.

Although religion figures in the index – 21 page references – most of the references are to Islam and Bangladesh. The 2001 census data indicates that 36.4 per cent of the local people identified themselves as Muslim, and 38.6 per cent as Christian, though my experience is that the practising Christian population is very much lower. Yet there is a significant history of what has been called 'diffused Christianity', particularly in Bethnal Green, as work by Hugh McLeod and his students has shown. No attention is given in this study to the presence or impact of the Christian churches, apart from the claim that Roman Catholic schools represent white enclaves in multiracial neighbourhoods.

Nevertheless, wider lessons for urban (and rural) churches emerge from the book. First, it is essential to know our communities, and to keep up to date with local developments and feelings. (This must include not relying on research data from more than a decade ago.) Second, we need to remember that the Church's task is not to reflect local (or national or international) feeling, but to challenge it. I was disappointed that, in the case of both these needs, this book failed us.

Oldham and London[6]

I was born in Ashton-under-Lyne, next door to Oldham, in 1939, and have lived and worked in the East End of London for most of the time since 1958. I live on the corner where Brick Lane meets Whitechapel Road, the heart of the largest Bengali community in Britain, and a district which was once over 95 per cent Jewish. Reading the accounts of the recent disturbances in Oldham raises questions about similar events which took place in this area of East London in the 1930s and 1970s. While it would be arrogant and wrong for someone living 180 miles from Oldham to presume to 'explain' the factors behind its recent troubles, there are some parallels and disturbing similarities as well as some important lessons that might be learned.

The importance of the presence of fascist and Nazi groups had been recognised by everyone who has written on the Oldham events, and was confirmed by the vote for the British National Party (BNP) in the General Election. Similar groups had been present at many such outbreaks in the 20th century. In the 1930s Sir Oswald Mosley and the British Union of Fascists created a reign of terror in East London. Their target was the Jewish community, originating in Eastern Europe, and they gained considerable support in areas adjacent to the Jewish quarter of Whitechapel, particularly in Stepney, Bethnal Green and Shoreditch. It is important to note that the fascists always campaigned in these adjacent, mainly white areas, and particularly in districts where there was low mobility, strong kinship patterns, high levels of deprivation, and suspicion of 'aliens'.

In the second half of the 1970s the National Front, formed in 1966–67 as the first significant post-war fascist movement, gained considerable support in almost exactly the same districts of East London. Their target was the Bengali community, at that time heavily concentrated in the Brick Lane district. The term 'Paki-bashing' had first been used on the nearby Collingwood Estate in Bethnal Green in 1968, to be followed within months by the first use of the word 'skinhead'. In 1978, when both the fascist organising and the resistance to it reached its peak, there was a massive increase in racially motivated violence. Of course not all of this was the direct result of fascist activity, but they had given the green light to it and created an atmosphere in which it was tolerable. I have told the story of this period in my book *Brick Lane 1978: the events and their significance* (Stepney Books, 1994).

A major turning point in the East End experience occurred when the Bengali community refused to accept the label of 'helpless victim', and became an organised political force. The Bengali youth in particular 'came of age' politically in those terrible years of organised fascism. It was their radicalisation and mobilisation, combined with the work of the (mainly white) Anti-Nazi League, which drove the fascists out of the area, and made their presence and their rhetoric disreputable.

The National Front, for a variety of reasons, disintegrated, though it was to regroup later, and the BNP emerged as the main fascist group in East London. After the events of 1978 they concentrated their energies further east, in the Isle of Dogs (where one of their candidates was briefly elected in 1993), Beckton, Canning Town, and elsewhere. A major alliance of churches, Bengali groups, trade unions and others led to the defeat of the BNP councillor in 1994, and their candidates have done badly in Millwall, Blackwall and Poplar areas in subsequent elections. Again, the mobilisation and raising of consciousness among the people, in this case mainly white people, of the area was a key factor.

The raising of consciousness among the police was the result of a long struggle and is still uneven. It took a very long time to convince the police in East London both that racial violence was serious and also that the fascist groups were a threat to the common good. (Many police in the 1970s refused to accept that racial attacks existed at all, and a British Movement slogan remained on the wall of Bethnal Green Police Station for many weeks, the police claiming that they did not know what it was!) Police responses have never improved automatically as a result of good will or education among the police alone, but only as a result of pressure from outside.

The link between fascist groups and racial violence is well documented from the 1930s onwards in East London. It has always been denied by the groups themselves who usually claim that they are simply articulating and expressing public resentment, and that they have not encouraged violence. But this is simple mystification. The language and the violence associated with these groups without exception leads to an increase in unrest and violence within the areas.

However, to lay the blame on these groups alone, ignoring the structural racism within the country as a whole, is never wise or correct. Oldham may be experiencing and repeating a pattern of events which other areas went through a long time ago. Some sharing of insights could be very helpful in preventing over-reaction, complacency or false panics. More important, it could encourage a more effective national mobilisation against both the fascist groups and structural racism within British society.

London churches [7]

Michael Yelton, who has already written a fascinating study of Anglican papalism, has produced this valuable study of important churches in London, all Anglo-Catholic in a broad sense, that have now disappeared. Some, though not all, were papalist. They include some well-known churches such as St Francis's, Dalgarno Way, North Kensington, whose first vicar was Bernard Markham, later Vicar of St Benedict's, Ardwick, in Manchester (also now closed), and then Bishop of Nassau. Later priests included Edwyn Young and Gresham Kirkby.

The demise of some of these churches, and of the tradition, pastoral dedication, and sacramental ethos they reflected, is very sad. Yet any attempt now to recapture the 'glory days' is doomed. The story of St Columba's, Haggerston, is particularly depressing. By 1964 it had a congregation of about six, of whom several seemed to live in the vicarage. There is no mention of the nearby St Augustine's,

Haggerston, famous for the *Haggerston Catechism*, which closed in the late 1960s and had declined in a similar way.

What went wrong? Why did these great shrines, in the end, fail miserably? There has still been no serious study of this tragic history.

The magnificent shrine of St Michael's, Shoreditch, which appears on the cover, is also discussed. In March 1964, I was asked by Robert Stopford, Bishop of London, to accept a curacy there, and had to point out that the church had been closed, by the Bishop himself, on 31 January.

It is a little surprising to find St Paul's, Whitechapel, included, with inevitable references to my old friend and colleague Fr Joe Williamson. Joe was not really an Anglo-Catholic in the 'party' sense, although he was inspired in childhood by Fr Dolling. He had no interest in the niceties of ceremony, nor in attitudes to the Church of South India. He was an intensely prayerful priest, committed to the daily mass, and the care of the people; but the neighbouring Anglo-Catholics did not know what to make of him, for their concerns and connections were different.

Also included is the saga of St Andrew's, Carshalton, and the part played by Mervyn Stockwood, then a new Bishop of Southwark. Yelton concedes that Stockwood's behaviour in this episode was 'certainly tactless' (he is, after all, a lawyer). Some of us might have used stronger language. It was a pity that he did not include the poem of the late S. J. Forrest about the Carshalton affair, which ended:

> So call the bobbies, bar the door,
> Raise high the churchyard wall,
> For those who won't be C of E
> Shan't worship God at all.

I hope that we may have learned something from these years, and from the sad story of the 'empty tabernacles', but I am not sure that we have. All the same, we should be deeply grateful for this study.

St Clement's[8]

St Clement's is an old Tractarian parish located in a poor district of London, adjacent to some very posh districts. In an earlier period the parish provided the inspiration for Ernest Raymond's novel *The Chalice and the Sword*. During the years of David Randall's ministry, he led the most colourful and inspiring worship of any church in West London. The highlights of the year were Holy Week and Easter (with the Easter vigil at 5 a.m.), the Notting Hill Carnival Mass with steel band and fantastic costumes, and the Feast of Christ the King in November. In the preface for that feast, the Kingdom of God is described as 'a kingdom of truth and life, a kingdom of holiness and grace, a kingdom of justice, love and peace.' David was a 'kingdom priest', more interested in the struggle for the Kingdom of God than he was in the 'success' of the church. The parish was in the literal sense 'eccentric' – off-centre as far as the conventional structures were concerned, but truly centred on God and God's Kingdom of justice. David had an intense devotion to the Virgin Mary, and St Clement's was probably the only church in the world to have a shrine for racial justice focused on a statue of Our Lady of Fatima, beneath which was printed the Litany of Our Lady of the Freedom Fighters (written by some Catholic Worker activists in jail in Alabama). The liturgy at St Clement's combined the best of Anglo-Catholic splendour with a warmth and a crazy informality rarely seen in Anglicanism. But beneath the flamboyance and eccentricity, there was that same sense of celebration and festivity which we saw in an earlier period in Noel and Groser.

Every August, Notting Hill (Notting Dale being the district beneath the hill) is the centre for an enormous Caribbean carnival, the biggest street festival in Europe. David was a key figure in bringing church and Carnival together, and in making the church open to the community on the Lancaster West and Edward Woods estates. Unlike most churches, St Clement's church door was always open – indeed, at one point nobody had a key, and it could not be locked. In a neighbourhood marked by high crime, it was rarely vandalised because the community, Christian and non-Christian, saw it as their home. St Clement's combined warmth with the spirit of liberation, joy, and prayerfulness, from which flowed pastoral zeal and commitment to social justice. It was not respectable, it defied the establishment, it was a genuinely back-street church, rooted in adoration of God and commitment to the people.

These are the kind of churches which have nourished me and kept me in (albeit on the edge of) the Church of England. But I fear that such places may be diminishing, as 'middle Anglicanism' – the religion of the dull, nondescript, middle-class, boring, safe, clerical elites – takes over. I hope desperately that I am wrong. But I am sure that Anglicans need to lose most of the respectability, restraint and control which mark their worship and culture if they are to make a genuine contribution to the worship of the coming Church.

St Francis House⁹

The 1950s and the early 1960s were key periods in my life. It was in those years that I came to Christian faith, began to pray, became a socialist, and was inspired by a number of movements and individuals. I hope that I have learned, and am still learning, from movements of thought and from people who have called many of my earlier assumptions into question, yet these years were formative.

A number of places stand out historically. One, which was demolished over thirty years ago, was the basement chapel of 84 Cable Street, in East London, which, from 1944 to 1963, was a Franciscan 'house of hospitality'. It was called St Francis House and was located at the heart of the 'cafe quarter' of the London Docks. This was a slum area with massive social deprivation, and it was the main centre for juvenile prostitution in London. Living there at the end of the 1950s, and learning to pray in that chapel, was a formative period in my life and approach to prayer and ministry. Since then, other places have been important, both at critical moments and in an ongoing way. I recall with great affection the apartment of the Little Sisters of Jesus in Roxbury, Massachusetts to which I was taken at a particularly desolate time in my life at the end of the 1970s and where I felt a powerful sense of the presence of Christ in an hour of adoration before the Reserved Sacrament. Then, and ongoing, Bede House, a centre for spiritual life in Kent, England, run by the Sisters of the Love of God, remains an important resource and source of strength for me. Houses of this kind are of critical importance.

My early experience in the Franciscan house in Cable Street was crucial. Its integration of prayer and service, contemplation and action, hospitality and commitment to justice, made an abiding impression on my whole spiritual, theological and pastoral praxis. More than any other place, this tumbledown slum house helped me to pray, to listen, to learn, and, only then to try to minister within this troubled and turbulent, yet, in many respects, caring and loving neighbourhood.

It represented in a very powerful, yet humble and largely hidden, way the hidden importance of prayerful contemplative presence developed by Charles de Foucauld and the Little Sisters and Brothers of Jesus. Without attempting directly to evangelise, the Franciscans in Cable Street, by their stability and consistent commitment over two decades, helped to make Christianity respected, and helped to prepare the way for other forms of Christian presence in the East End of London.

I originally thought the title 'house of hospitality' was an unfortunate one, since most of the houses at that end of Cable Street were brothels, houses of hospitality of another kind! I had not realised how important the influence of Dorothy Day was on the pastoral approach. This is not surprising for I had never heard of Dorothy Day or of the Catholic Worker movement. I believe that Cardinal Griffin had banned *The Catholic Worker* from all Catholic bookshops in London on the grounds that it was 'communist'. (Had he realised that it was not communist at all, but anarchist, he would probably have had apoplexy!) But the anarchist bookshop wouldn't stock it either because it was religious. It was left to an Anglo-Catholic anarchist, Laurens Otter, to import it and sell it every Sunday at Speakers' Corner, Hyde Park.

The Catholic Worker model for a house of hospitality was simple yet profound: prayer, hospitality, and waiting. My guess is that this is important for the new St Francis House too. Prayer is central, and without a disciplined life of corporate prayer, the whole enterprise will fall. Hospitality is vital for we are disciples of One who put the sharing of food and fellowship at the heart of his ministry. But waiting matters too. It is essential; to be patient, to listen, to learn from people, from the neighbourhood in which God has set us, before we start to utter. We need to earn the right to be heard, we need to be credible. Inner-city neighbourhoods in particular are used to people and groups who appear, stay for a while, and then move on. Word and action must grow out of stability and silence.

It is a great joy to me, having lived in, and, to a large extent, been formed by, St Francis House in East London in the mid-20th century, to find myself involved in a new St Francis House for the beginning of the 21st century.

12
Forging Connections

It seems better always to write from the situation one knows best, and it is often when one speaks most personally and concretely that one finds connections being forged with people from very different backgrounds.[1]

The limits of patriotism[2]

Loyalty to ideals has been the glory of civilised humanity; loyalty to State has been its curse. But first let us define loyalty. Generally speaking, the word as we have received it can be one of two things: loyalty to the Sovereign, or loyalty to one's country.

Loyalty to the reigning Sovereign is a dangerous affair as the victims of Hitlerism discovered. It can soon develop into the worship of a demi-god. The Roman doctrine of Caesaral infallibility was the terminus of many conscience-stricken men and women.

Loyalty to one's native land is a nobler ideal, for with it is embodied the loyalty to the Sovereign when he or she is worthy of it. Mark Twain's 'amor patriae' was loyalty to the land of his birth and not to a 'bundle of rags'. We must beware, however, of the attitude of 'My country right or wrong'.

This fanatical form of Jingoism springs from wrong thinking, the supposed superiority of nation over nation, and the desire to see in the State, the object of worship. Compare, for example, the patriotism of St Paul with the supposed loyalty of blind leaders and even more blind disciples in the modern amusement calling itself politics. Nobody could deny the title of patriot to St Paul when he said, 'I am a man which am a Jew of Tarsus, a city of Silicia, a citizen of no mean city' but the same Paul rose up in protest at all signs of bad leaven there.

The Romans had other ideas, as a glance at a fourth-form Latin reader will show, where patriotism is the great 'esse' of Roman 'philosophy'. In contrast with this view the Socialist revival, as might be expected, brought along with it the statement of Mr H. G. Wells that 'Patriotism has become the enemy of civilisation.'

But let us look at the fruits before we judge. On the one side patriotism has been the inspiration of some of our best hymns, folk songs, paintings and literature. It has been the cement of the British Commonwealth. But we cannot ignore the fact that if it were not for the fanatical patriots we should have no wars. After petty quarrels, people have rallied and said, 'My country, right or wrong', and fought to the death so that no blot might shew on their escutcheons, ignoring the fact that, in so doing, they were not only blotting their escutcheons but upsetting the whole inkpot, and the ink takes a long time to remove.

The colour bar has come as a result of the illusion that one race is of a higher social standing than another, and although the idea that all are equal is utter rubbish, for they are, as Dr Joad said, still less equal in intellect than in bodily strength – yet all can achieve the highest dignity by serving society faithfully. An even more ridiculous fallacy is the refusal of certain Anglicans to receive Mass from a coloured priest, ignoring the essential 'communism' of the Mass.

It was blind leaders and blind disciples who led Holy Russia into the mess of today. And as the result of modern corruption of the word, the perfect 'Koinonia' which might have been the Rock of the Catholic Church is now a hated word to be torn to shreds by witch-hunters and bigots.

We must stop boasting of our battles and murders and sudden deaths, and strive for a higher ideal (and a much more complicated one) putting not our trust in princes. Perhaps after much bloodshed we shall find that there is no help in them. Magna est veritas et prevalebit.

Early poetry[3]

Renunciation

The twelve stones,
And one a devil, came
Into a garden,
Blood drop upon moist soil

United but in posture,
Dreaming and crumbling
In a garden of dust.
The three called
To a mountain of sand
In a lonely garden,
Piercing, tearing, dying,
United but not in love,
Passionate but for thrones
In a heaven of rust.
One remains
Comforted by an angel
In a garden,
Blood, stifled cry and cock-crow,
Hell gaping but for death
Living but to die
For die one must.
O agony!
The veil is rent;
In a garden of weeds
A primrose leaps fiercely;
In an abyss of thunderings
Dying but to love,
For life is trust.

[1957]

Becoming a socialist⁺

I became a Christian and a socialist at the same time and, in my innocence, for a while as a teenager, assumed that all Christians were bound to be socialists! I have remained both socialist and Christian in spite of regular discontent with the failings, betrayals and corruption of both the church and the left.

I was born into a working-class family in the 'cotton towns' – Ashton-under-Lyne, Stalybridge and Dukinfield – in Greater Manchester. Voting Labour was taken for granted, but was compatible with many reactionary positions. My father, an engineer, had, as a teenager, heard Ben Tillett speak on Ashton Market, and this seemed to have been a 'conversion' experience for him. He spoke of it in more or less religious terms. He was also very insistent that he was a Methodist, though what he meant by that was that he didn't go to church, and it was the Methodist Church that he didn't go to. There was a vague sense that somehow Methodism was more sympathetic to working-class issues than were the other churches. (Though I never heard the 'more to Methodism than to Marxism' quip until many years later.)

Yet I was aware, at the age of eight, that, while my dad was strongly committed to the trade union movement, he hated the Polish immigrants who had settled in the area under the Polish Resettlement Scheme. 'They're no good to man nor beast, Poles', I heard him say, and it set my little brain worrying. The two ideas – socialism and 'racism' – a word which I did not know and which was not even in the dictionaries at that time – didn't quite seem to fit. It set me thinking hard.

Neither of my parents were at all religious, and they saw the church as the enemy of working-class people – though my father had great regard for a priest called Cummings who was known as the 'red vicar' in Ashton-under-Lyne in the 1920s. (He was one of a number of socialist clergy in this period, the most famous being Conrad Noel, vicar of Thaxted in Essex from 1910 to 1942. One of the reasons given by the CP for the expulsion of the early Trotskyists was the association of some of the key figures with Noel's movement.)

The year 1956 was critical for me. It was a turning point in the history of socialism and of radical movements across Europe and elsewhere. It was a critical year for anyone with a social conscience. The Civil Rights movement was well under way in the United States. Trevor Huddleston had returned from South Africa and was addressing massive audiences around Britain. The impact of Huddleston's denunciation of apartheid in the Free Trade Hall in Manchester remains with me to this day. At an emotional level he was a key influence on my taking Christian faith seriously. If this faith could drive this man to oppose racism with such passion perhaps it could drive me too.

The resistance to nuclear weapons was also building up. The Russian invasion of Hungary and the 20th Congress of the CPSU had thrown the Stalinist left into confusion and led to mass exoduses from the Communist Parties and to the growth of the 'New Left'. I used to visit the Left Wing Coffee Bar in Manchester, run by the Socialist

Labour League, but I never joined it. I did join the Direct Action Committee Against Nuclear War which became CND, and had close links with the Committee of 100, first in the north west and then in London. All these were formative influences in shaping my socialism.

But it was coming to the East End of London in 1958, as a student, which was the real turning point. I arrived at the time of the 'Notting Hill riots' and came to live at 84 Cable Street. The East End seemed full of left-wing Christians – Stanley Evans, John Groser and others – and co-operation between Christians and Marxists was common. I got to know some the old Communist councillors – Solly Kaye, Phil Piratin, Max Levitas – all of them atheists, but all of them having a long history of cooperation with socialist Christians with whom they had a lot in common. The East End has shaped me more than any place. Much of my time here, since 1958, has been involved with fighting fascism, working for decent housing, trying to create communities of resistance and solidarity.

In all this, my Christian faith and my socialism have been equally central. If I stopped being a Christian I would still be a socialist. I am not sure that if I stopped being a socialist I would, could, still be a Christian. I suppose this means that my commitment to equality, justice, human dignity and common ownership is fundamental, and that the fact that I am a human being – and therefore a socialist, because that flows from being human – comes first. That does not mean that my Christian faith is secondary or less important, but that it flows from, and builds on, who I am and where I stand.

And, by the way, I think that 'socialism or barbarism' is still the issue.

Casting out demons[5]

Exorcism has been a topic of conversation ever since they made William Blatty's dreary novel into a film, but more especially since the terrible murder case in Yorkshire.

What do we make of it all? I think there are a lot of mistakes being made about the whole business in the press. It is all getting mixed up with ghosts and haunted houses. Exorcism doesn't have to do with ghosts; if there are such things, they are departed people who have 'got stuck'. It is more likely that they are memories deeply buried in the unconscious mind. Exorcism has to do, not with ghosts, but with the casting out of evil spirits. Now the trouble here is that in the New Testament, a lot of illnesses which the people at the time didn't understand, like epilepsy and mental illness of various kinds, were attributed to evil spirits and demons. It was their way of explaining what seemed to them pretty frightening things: and casting out the demons meant setting the person free and healing. Today we know more about the causes of illness, which isn't surprising if we believe that the Holy Spirit really does lead us into truth. We shouldn't cling to earlier crude beliefs when the Holy Spirit has led us into a fuller understanding. Sadly this is what a lot of people are doing, and some extremely stupid and dangerous clergy are using demons and exorcism in a highly irresponsible way. It does seem as if people who get over-involved with this subject go off the rails sooner or later, and can do great harm.

But we shouldn't throw out the baby with the bathwater. Many people who think they need exorcising in fact need listening, caring, help in their lives. Some of them need vitamin B tablets rather than exorcism. In almost all the cases, the right spiritual approach to the troubled soul is not to assume that he is full of evil spirits but to see him as a sinner like you and me who needs grace, forgiveness and communion with God. That is what prayer, confession and communion are all for. But that does *not* mean that we throw out the important truth which the Bible teaching about the demons is getting at, any more than it means that because we no longer believe that the earth is flat that we don't believe in heaven. What then does it mean?

The demons are a way of saying that the evil in the world is much greater and goes much deeper than personal wrong-doing by us. There is something in the fallen world which distorts it, which messes it up. The world is fallen, it needs deliverance. That is what exorcism is: the proclamation that Christ has conquered the demons, the forces of evil in the world. Picture them as monsters with horns if you want to, but they are all around us: war, injustice, racial hatred, poverty, lack of care for people, slavery to money. These are the real demons. The Christian Gospel is not only about the healing of the individual, but also about the deliverance of peoples from slavery to the principalities and powers, the corrupt and evil systems which crush and kill. That deliverance is the real point of exorcism.

Franciscan poverty[6]

The growth of Franciscan movements within the Anglican Communion has been one of the most remarkable features of the revival of religious life in that Communion since the 19th century, and it is good that Peta Dunstan has given us this detailed work on the history of the European Province of the Society of St Francis, the largest of these movements. The emergence of the Society involved a fusion of two elements, one inspired by the Anglo-Catholicism of the Oxford Movement, the other by an evangelical zeal for the care of the unemployed. The world of chronic unemployment, homelessness and the casual wards is the essential social background to the emergence of the Society, and the Vagrancy Reform Society was actually founded at the Home of St Francis in 1928.

Dr Dunstan describes the development of the Society from its early years in Oxford, and the move to Flowers Farm, near Cerne Abbas, Dorset, originally as an 'Industrial Home for Vagrants', and still the mother house of the Society. It was the arrival of Brother Giles at Flowers Farm in 1921 which began the modern movement. She gives us the background of the earlier groups – the Brotherhood of St Francis, the Christa Seva Sangha, and the Brotherhood of the Holy Cross. She tells us of the benefactor Colonel Lloyd, a puritanical evangelical who was so outraged by the Cerne Abbas giant – an ancient fertility symbol on the hill – that he took some wayfarers and tried to remove its genitalia (p. 22)! The book is full of fascinating detail about the history of the Society, yet here is a problem. It is so thorough that it is, at one level, almost unreviewable, since the author has drawn on sources such as minutes of chapters and meetings, and the notes, comments and memories of the friars. Since the author is probably the only person in the world to have drawn on these sources, there is probably nobody who knows if her account is correct or not. Criticism of fact and interpretation must therefore be restricted to those areas of which a particular reviewer has close knowledge.

The work is in fact so detailed that I felt that some key issues, developments and areas of actual or potential conflict tended to get lost in the detail, and I want therefore to identify some of these which seem rather important.

First, there was clearly a tension, going back to the early years, between the tramp preachers – the late Brother Kenneth was the last survivor of this stream and the more 'refined' group personified by Father Algy who, according to the author, had 'the air of Oxbridge' (p. 88) about him. The dedication of some brothers to work in the 'public' schools is mentioned as an important area of activity (p. 112), but there seems not to have been any sense of conflict between the values, even the existence, of the 'public' schools and the demands of a radical Franciscan tradition. It would have been helpful to have been told more of this. Has anything survived of the early tramp preachers' vision?

Secondly, and linked with the first point, there seem to have been two parallel streams in the Society from the start, a working-class, earthy, non-academic, lay stream, and a cultured, clerical, sometimes rather precious, and more 'churchy' one. The early disapproval by the latter group of some brothers' practice of smoking and playing cards is passed over rather quickly (p. 81) and I suspect it may be more important in shaping the culture of the Society than the author realises.

Thirdly, the tension between the evangelicalism of Brother Douglas and the rigid Anglo-Catholicism of some others receives only slight treatment. How important, for example, was the conflict over the Church of South India, mentioned but also passed over (p. 95)? Father Algy is said to have been CSI's 'most searching and persistent critic' (cited p. 110). What effect did it have on the Society?

Fourthly, there seems to have been a period in the 1960s when the Society grew in numerical terms somewhat irresponsibly and with a high turnover rate of novices. Some of the new members seem to have been attracted more by the mystique of St Francis, but to have had a rather vague grasp of Christian theology, and some were certainly psychologically unstable. The problems of a romantic devotion to the Franciscan ethos, without ascetical discipline and theological rigour, are only vaguely hinted at. These were the years when Brother Michael, described by another of the brothers as being 'most awfully attractive to everybody' (cited p. 129), was the Minister. How important was Michael's charismatic personality in attracting members? Were there other factors, such as the impact of the late 60s counterculture and other cultural shifts? And how did the Society recover its stability? All we are told is that 'a larger novitiate was not necessarily a sign of long term growth or stability' (p. 216).

I restrict my criticisms of factual inaccuracy to one area, that of the

Franciscan house at 84 Cable Street, East London, where I lived for much of the period from 1958 until its evacuation in 1963. Dunstan is wrong on a number of details here. The house was not at the east end of the street (p. 138) but at the extreme west end, close to Leman Street. She refers to the important work of Daphne Jones, a tertiary, but ignores that of her colleague Nora Neal (pp. 138ff). The omission of all reference to Nora Neal, also a tertiary, who does not even appear in the index, and whose work with Father John Groser was partly responsible for the Society coming to the East End at all, is extraordinary and rather serious. The claim that 'Cable Street was expected to be demolished by 1962' (p. 142) is incorrect. The Graces Alley Compulsory Purchase Order of 1963 related to a small part of the west part of the street, and major demolition did not occur until 1967. Two-thirds of the street was not affected. Kathleen Wrsama, a key black resident of the area and neighbour of the SSF, and her husband Solomon, are called 'keen Christians' (p. 139). In fact, Solomon was Muslim, and Kathleen always said that she was not a Christian, and insisted that there was no religious service at her funeral. The London Hospital psychiatrist Desmond Pond is wrongly called Donald (p. 210).

The mistakes seem to be restricted to the account of the East London work in which it is sad that the remarkable figure of Father Neville Palmer is given such brief attention. But none of this detracts from the immense value of this book which will be a major resource for students of religious life in the 20th century.

The drugs scene [7]

It is important to say something about my own background within, and perspective on, the drug scene. I first became aware of illicit drug use while living in the Cable Street district of East London at the end of the 1950s when local prostitutes were using Drinamyl as a 'wake-amine', and where Frances Tucker, known in the East End as 'the Queen of Indian Hemp', was operating a well-organised dealing network in cannabis. She was murdered a few doors from me on 11 January 1960. But it was as a curate in Hoxton in 1964 that I first got heavily involved with addiction as a result of discovering that the two sons of my churchwarden were heroin users. Through working with them I soon found myself involved with all the heroin addicts in

East London. At the same time, the use of amphetamines and cannabis was increasing among the younger kids in Shoreditch and Bethnal Green, many of whom were frequenting the fairly new discotheques which had sprung up in Soho.

By 1966, work with young drug users was taking up a good deal of my time. Because of this, in 1967, I was asked to go to work at St Anne's, Soho, with a brief to develop work with drug users in the clubs and bars, and with homeless young people. In Soho I was one of the founders of the Soho Drugs Group, perhaps the first interdisciplinary local group of its kind, in 1967, and of Centrepoint, the all-night shelter for homeless young people, in 1969. I have been involved with drug problems ever since, particularly since returning to the East End of London in 1974. Today I chair the Maze Project, based in Bethnal Green, which works on drug education and prevention in the East End of London, and out of which has grown the Marigold Project, working with young commercial sex workers in Whitechapel.

The Jubilee Group[8]

One of the problems about growing even to the age of 10 is that increasing numbers of one's comrades know nothing about how we came to be. In fact, Jubilee was an accident. What happened was that towards the end of 1974, soon after I had been appointed Rector of St Matthew's, Bethnal Green, I sent a letter round to a small group of priests in the Catholic tradition suggesting that there might be some point in forming a support group for each other. I think what I had in mind was some sort of support group and stimulus group for broadly like-minded priests, mainly in the East End. And for a while that is what we were. It was when we started to realise that we were not so unusual or freakish as we thought, and that we were an increasing number of Catholic socialist clergy getting in touch, that the group as an entity took shape. But still it was a clerical, Anglo-Catholic and mainly socialist grouping, though it became less exclusively an East End group quite soon.

I don't recall that there was any conscious wish to restrict the group to priests: more the fact that, having started like that, it was priests who linked up with us, and we did not at the time have the will, or the consciousness of a need, to take 'affirmative action' to laicise it. That came later. We were criticised by some clergy for being too Anglo-

Catholic. I think most of us felt then that there was a specific task to be done in relation to the Anglo-Catholic movement, or what was left of it, and that this task did require a narrow base if it was to work: I think we would have called that task something like 'recalling the movement to its lost traditions'. And we were in fact all socialists of one kind or another, though the initial group included some Slant-type Catholic Marxists, two anarchists, one ex-WRP, and various LP and unattached socialists. Later we began to gather people who were not socialists but were in some sort of sympathy with us, the beginning perhaps of the 'SDP at the Parish Eucharist' syndrome.

In the early days of moving towards becoming some sort of group, we did toy with the idea of a very conscious 'revival' of one of the names of the past, in order to establish our continuity with the tradition (e.g. Guild of St Matthew, Catholic Crusade, etc.). I don't think anybody regrets that we didn't do that. The name 'Jubilee' was suggested by Gresham Kirkby on the grounds, if I recall, that it would mean a lot to people familiar with the history of Catholic socialism (shades of Stewart Headlam's comments on the jubilee of Queen Victoria in 1886!) and yet it would not make the fringe people switch off. (They would possibly connect it with the Pope. It was typical of our naivety about monarchy that none of us cottoned on to the fact that the Queen was going to have a jubilee in a few years time, and that we might get confused with that – as indeed we did for a while!)

During 1975–78 there were a number of important developments. The first was that we 'went public'. Two occasions brought this 'coming out' about. The first was that September 1975 was the 10th anniversary of the death of Canon Stanley Evans. Stanley had been an important influence on a number of us, and we felt it would be valuable to commemorate his death. So we held a Mass at St Paul's Bow Common, and I wrote a piece in *The Times* on the significance of Stanley for the Christian Left. The second was the 'Call to the Nation' of Archbishop Coggan. I wrote a piece for *The Times* again called 'Some thoughts on hearing the voice of non-prophecy'. These two articles, combined with published pieces by others, attracted some publicity for the group.

The second development was the beginnings of the movement called 'Catholic Renewal in the Church of England'. I got involved in this at an early stage and in fact wrote the statement which formed the basis of the movement. This movement, which some Jubilee people got involved with, led to the Loughborough Conference of 1978 when we picked up a bit of support. Some of this caused us a fair amount of anxiety, and there was talk of 'gentrification' and becoming respectable, losing our socialist purity, etc. Certainly we picked up some hangers on who didn't really understand what we were on about.

Thirdly, 1977 was the centenary of Stewart Headlam's founding of the Guild of St Matthew, and we held a celebration in Bethnal Green, including a week's conference on 'The Catholic social movement today' at which Michael Ramsey, John Orens, Reg Groves, and others spoke.

By 1978 we were clearly a 'movement' of some kind, though we had always resisted any formal organisational structure. There was a mailing list of sympathisers (plus some others: some early bits of discussion papers got onto the right-wing circuit in a confused form and are still quoted occasionally). In fact, most of the work and material remained East End based. Although local groups had appeared in various places, the public face of Jubilee remained an East End face. But some significant changes were occurring. We were drawing more lay people, and a lay group (the Stepney group) began in 1978. We were also attracting the interest of Christians from other traditions (e.g. Pax Christi, Mennonite, Shaftesbury Project, types) who had come to a similar kind of political position by a different route, and of non-Christians who felt they could relate to us in a way that they could not with the church as a whole. A series of May Day parties, at Bethnal Green and at the 'Still and Star' in Aldgate, gathered people from a wide range of Christian movements, as well as the CP, SWP, IMG, and stations beyond. We had also got into the publishing area on a bigger scale. All our early stuff was duplicated in a hurry, and not very attractive. By 1978 we had produced a fair number of pamphlets and were beginning a series of Lent Lecturers, the first of them sparked off by Edward Norman's Reith Lectures of that year.

My impression is that since 1958 the gap between Jubilee and the formal Anglo-Catholic structures (Catholic Renewal, Church Union et alia) has got wider and wider. When, in 1983, we got together those London Jubilee people who had been at the Loughborough Conference to consider our response to the next one, there was a clear division about whether there should be any involvement. In the event, five Jubilee people produced *Can Dry Bones Live?*, a series of critical issues on Catholic Renewal, and the bigger collection *Essays Catholic and Radical* came out the same year. A glance at our publications over the last few years (on common ownership, on liberation theology, on Marxism, on urban issues, etc.) shows how different are our concerns with those which seem to consume the energies of 'the Catholic movement'. So an obvious question arises: how does Jubilee relate to ACism as a whole?

In 1983 also I think we became aware of the danger that we were becoming very vague and that our identity as a Catholic socialist grouping needed to be restated. This was not because we wished to exclude people, but rather so that people who wished to be included knew what it was that they were linking with. A draft statement of what the Jubilee Group is was accepted at the Manchester gathering in 1983.

I feel – and these are purely personal views – that we have managed to steer a path between excessive party line organisational structure, and total shapelessness, but that there is still quite a bit of clarification and tidying up to be done. We seemed, at Manchester, to be happy with the existence of Jubilee as a 'tendency', a network of thought, solidarity and support. But if this is to be effective, the channels of communication need to be improved, and this has always been difficult because most of our people are busy and have little time. It would be excellent to have a more efficient time schedule for the newsletter. It would be excellent if all Jubilee people had access to the mailing list. It would be excellent if we could break the London dominance: we have been saying this for years, and it has happened to some degree. But most of the writing is still done by London people, and people tend to wait for something to happen from London rather than just doing it. I think all these things need more discussion.

Darkness and the East End[9]

Throughout the ministry in Whitechapel the experience of darkness was one which I observed and shared. It was evident at an obvious level, historically and politically. The East End was linked historically with images of the dark, from William Booth's 'darkest England' and Jack London's 'people of the abyss' to the present day. Much of the time, communities, interest groups, subcultures, even

whole populations, are literally 'in the dark' about what the 'principalities and powers' are up to in their schemes of 'regeneration' and
'renewal'. The experience of being on the receiving end of other
people's decisions, linked to the facade of 'consultation', is common,
if not universal, in inner cities. It is combined with a sense, historically
rooted and verified in experience, that there is 'nothing that we can
do', and that those in power – the property developers, central
government, transnational companies, or the local state with its
'hangers-on' – will get their way. There is a sense of impasse, of
paralysis rather than apathy, the fruit, in many cases, of years of
struggle, of banging one's head against a brick wall. Much urban life is
shaped, distorted, and at times crushed, by darkness – the darkness of
physical and mental illness, isolation, perplexity, exhaustion, insecurity and death. Only a theology which has confronted and not
avoided such darkness can be a healing force.

Certainly my years in the East End led me to see the centrality of
darkness in ministry. We do not know it all, we are often in the dark,
and God is not always clear. We live and walk by faith, not by sight,
and often the way ahead is obscure. We live, struggle and work within
'the night sky of the Lord'.

Spiritual discipline[10]

Instead of my usual letter about things external which are
occurring here, I want to focus on some internal matters of spiritual
discipline and prayer which I have been looking at as Lent gets under
way. I am sending this to friends with whom I feel some kind of
spiritual bond. I have recently been in retreat at Bede House and the
following emerges largely from this time. I share it with you so that we
can pray around these issues and in the hope that it may be of some
use in your own life as I have always felt that personal things have a
corporate resonance. And, of course, Lent is a useful time for some
renewal of discipline.

I have been conscious for some time – and have discussed it with
some of you – that the area of my own work and life which is most in
danger of neglect is that of silence, solitude, prayer, reflection and
waiting on God. I am ever so good at telling others how important
this is but not so good at doing it myself. Not an uncommon
syndrome! I realised at Bede House how important the link with a

contemplative community has been to me over the last 30 years, and this while dialectic of the link between centres of contemplative prayer and centres of activity is something that needs developing. More and more good Christians in the urban areas seem to be wearing themselves out, and the establishment of patterns of retreat, maybe involving some kind of rule-based link with a disciplined community would do a good deal to prevent this. Certainly the Sisters of the Love of God have been a tremendous support to me since the early 60s.

I realised yet again in my time at Bede how valuable it is to be able to say the daily office with others from time to time. (I have said the office on my own now for most of the last 15 years.) So don't be surprised if I ask you to share in the daily office with me if you happen to be here at the appropriate time! Interestingly, while many areas of my own spiritual discipline have suffered over the years, I have always remained faithful to the daily office, more or less since I was 18. Interesting too – and no doubt connected! – all of the parishes in which I have served full-time – Holy Trinity, Hoxton, St Anne's Soho, St Matthew's, Bethnal Green, and St Botolph's, Aldgate – have had histories of consistent saying of the office. I discovered recently that a bequest was left in 1624 to ensure that the office was said daily at St Botolph's, Aldgate and that according to a writer in 1898 there had been no interruption in the recitation of the daily office at St Anne's, Soho since its foundation! So I would strongly recommend some form of daily office even if it is an abbreviated form which can be learnt by heart and said anywhere.

My own pattern is that I try to concentrate my serious prayer in the early morning and do all my scriptural and other reflective reading then if I can. It doesn't always work but it usually does and I function better in the very early hours. I have for some time used the extended form of Vigil in the appendix to the *Liturgia Horarum* on Sunday mornings which adds to the office of readings and ends with the gospel of the resurrection. I always try to have said Evening Prayer by 6 p.m. and Compline before midnight. I have found the small pocket office book useful for occasions when I say the office on trains. But, while this pattern of personal prayer seems likely to continue for some time, I must say that I do value being able to say the office with others, and I think within the Jubilee network we ought to do some work on this.

I have also for many years been very much influenced by the

spirituality of Charles de Foucauld and the Little Sisters and Brothers of Jesus with their emphasis on a daily time of adoration before the Blessed Sacrament, and this is something I have tried to do for some time. I find it extremely important to have this time reserved for silent adoration and nothing else, and there is a great spiritual power in praying in the presence of the reserved Sacrament – at least that is my experience, and I would strongly recommend it. Of course that raises the whole problem of locked churches which is also something we need to work on. St Botolph's is open most of the time and so is the German RC church of St Boniface which is almost next door to me on the other side of Altab Ali Park.

I realise constantly how dangerous is the seduction to endless activity and since this is a danger in my own life I assume it is in yours too! Within the last few days my excellent support group has asked me to plan my engagements for the next few months with all this in mind, placing a high priority on times of reflection and then organising things around them. But in the meantime I go to the US on the 15th March and this is always a time both of stimulation and refreshment of spirit. I hope all this rings bells with you, and please keep me in your prayers as I do you.

Further Reading

The following is a sample of books, arranged in chronological order of first publication, designed to introduce readers to the main contours of Kenneth Leech's thought. Some earlier ones are out of print but they can usually be borrowed through libraries, or used copies can be bought through booksellers located via the Internet.

Youthquake: Spirituality and the Growth of a Counter-Culture (Sheldon Press, 1973; Abacus paperback, 1976). An account of a search for meaning in the drugs and youth-culture scene of London and North America.

Soul Friend: Spiritual Direction in the Modern World (Sheldon Press, 1977; various reprints Darton, Longman & Todd, 1997–2000; Morehouse Publishing revised edition paperback, 2001). A classic: originally based on the author's work at St Augustine's College, Canterbury during 1971–74.

True Prayer: An Invitation to Christian Spirituality (HarperSanFrancisco, 1980; Morehouse Publishing paperback, 1995). A footnote-free popular introduction to the nature and styles of prayer; ends with recommended reading.

True God: An Exploration in Spiritual Theology (Sheldon Press, 1985; published in USA as *Experiencing God: Theology as Spirituality*, Harper & Row, 1985 – this US edition is out of print but reprints may be available from Wipf & Stock, Eugene, Oregon, Portland). A biblical *tour de force* drawing upon key symbols that have been used to depict the experience of God.

Struggle in Babylon: Racism in the Cities and Churches of Britain (Sheldon Press/SPCK, 1988). A readable and scholarly approach to issues of race and class in Church and society.

Subversive Orthodoxy: Traditional Faith and Radical Commitment (Anglican Book Centre, Toronto, 1992). A short introduction to Christianity's liberating tradition first given as lectures delivered at Trinity College, Toronto in 1991.

The Eye of the Storm: Living Spiritually in the Real World (HarperCollins, 1992). An eloquent testimony about spirituality and social justice written for a North American readership but drawing on experiences from both sides of the Atlantic.

We Preach Christ Crucified: The Proclamation of the Cross in a Dark Age (Darton, Longman & Todd, 1994; revised edition 2006). A popular set of homilies derived from Good Friday sermons preached over a number of years.

The Sky is Red: Discerning the Signs of the Times (Darton, Longman & Todd, 1997; 2nd edition with new Introduction, 2003). A ruminative journey around political, religious and social themes as they affect the modern world.

Through our Long Exile: Contextual Theology and the Urban Experience (Darton, Longman & Todd, 2001). In two parts – the first historical, the second contemporary – about life and ministry in East London.

Race (SPCK, 2005). A Christian overview of race, racism and the necessity for anti-racist activity that draws on lessons from the United Kingdom and the United States.

Doing Theology in Altab Ali Park (Darton, Longman & Todd, 2006). A semi-autobiographical account of the community theology project, 1990–2004, at St Botolph's Church in London's East End.

Notes

Epigraph

1. *Care and Conflict: Leaves from a Pastoral Notebook* (London, Darton, Longman & Todd, 1990), p. 161.

Foreword

1. *Pastoral Care and the Drug Scene* (London, SPCK, 1970).
2. *True God* (London, Sheldon Press/SPCK, 1985). First published in the United States by Harper & Row as *Experiencing God: Theology as Spirituality*; now out of print but reprints may be available from Wipf & Stock, Eugene, Oregon.

Introduction – from London

1. *The Eye of the Storm: Living Spirituality in the Modern World* (San Francisco, Harper, 1992) p. 238.
2. *Through Our Long Exile: Contextual Theology and the Urban Experience* (London, Darton, Longman & Todd, 2001), p. 1.

Introduction – from New York

1. *Soul Friend: Spiritual Direction in the Modern World* (Harrisburg, Morehouse, 2001).
2. *The Eye of the Storm: Living Spiritually in the Real World* (San Francisco, Harper, 1992).

Chapter 1: The Trinity

1. *True Prayer* (Harrisburg, Morehouse, 1995), p. 8.
2. *True God* (London, Sheldon Press/SPCK, 1985), pp. 56–60.
3. Ibid., pp. 103–7.
4. Ibid., pp. 60–65.
5. Ibid., pp. 379–81.
6. *We Preach Christ Crucified* (London, Darton, Longman & Todd, 2006), pp. 39–45.
7. *True God*, op. cit., pp. 199–207.

Chapter 2: The Political Kingdom

1. *Doing Theology in Altab Ali Park* (London, Darton, Longman & Todd, 2006), p. 213.
2. 'The Christian Left – Then and Now', Jubilee paper given at a Jubilee Group conference at St Paul's Church, Bow Common, East London on the 50th anniversary of the General Strike: 1 May 1976 (Sarum College Library archive).
3. 'Christians and Fascism', an address given at a Public Meeting against Fascism, Toynbee Hall, East London, published as a Jubilee Group paper: 14 April 1977 (Sarum College Library archive).

4.   'The Simplistic Prophets of Community', Jubilee Group Discussion Paper No 110: 1996 (Sarum College Library archive).

5.   *The Eye of the Storm: Living Spiritually in the Real World* (San Francisco, Harper, 1992), pp. 82–9.

6.   Ibid., pp. 58–66.

7.   Ibid., pp. 77–82.

8.   'Transfiguration and Disfiguration' in *Fairacres Chronicle*, Winter 2005 (text of sermon preached at St Ann's Church, Manchester on 7 August 2005 for the Feast of the Transfiguration and the 60th anniversary of the bombing of Hiroshima); in journal published by the Sisters of the Love of God, Fairacres, Oxford, England) (Royal Foundation of St Katharine archive).

9.   'The Theology of Revolt' in *The Anglican Pacifist*, Vol. I, No. 10, October 1962 (monthly newsletter of the Anglican Pacifist Fellowship).

10. *The English Risings: 1381 & 1981* (Walsall, Jubilee Publications, undated; sermon preached on Trinity Sunday, 14 June 1981, at St Peter's, Mile End, East London) (Working Class Movement Library archive).

Chapter 3: Church and Society

1.   *The Sky is Red: Discerning the Signs of the Times* (London, Darton, Longman & Todd, 2003), p. 34.

2.   'Reckitt & Becket: Church & State' in *Christian Today*, 52, Winter 1990–91 (Sarum College Library archive).

3.   'Enough of bondage to Babylon' in the *Guardian*, 9 January 1993.

4.   *Struggle in Babylon: Racism in the Cities and Churches of Britain* (London, Sheldon Press/SPCK, 1988), pp. 14–20.

5.   'Of Methodism, Marxism and the tradition of holy dissatisfaction' in the *Independent*, 4 June 1988.

6.   'Why Churches Cannot Ignore Poverty and Oppression', talk given at St Paul's Church, Robert Adam Street, London to a conference marking the merger of UNLEASH with Housing Justice, 23 May 2006.

7.   *Doing Theology in Altab Ali Park* (London, Darton, Longman & Todd, 2006), pp. 220–23.

8.   *The Sky is Red: Discerning the Signs of the Times*, op. cit., pp. 58–62.

Chapter 4: The Catholic Movement

1.   *The Social God* (Eugene, Oregon, Wipf & Stock, 2003), p. 23.

2.   'Catholic Theology and Social Change', a Jubilee Group Paper, 1976 (Working Class Movement Library archive).

3.   From Ashley Beck and Ros Hunt (eds.), *Speaking Love's Name; Homosexuality: Some Catholic and Socialist Perspectives* (London, Jubilee Group, 1988).

4.   'The Oxford Movement's rebel tradition' in *The Times*, 16 July 1983.

5.   *Conrad Noel and the Catholic Crusade* (Croydon, Jubilee Group, 1993), pp. 44–7.

6.   From Beck and Hunt, *Speaking Love's Name*, op. cit.

7.   *Care and Conflict: Leaves from a Pastoral Notebook* (London, Darton, Longman & Todd, 1990), pp. 159–62.

8.   *True God* (London, Sheldon Press/SPCK, 1985), pp. 365–72.

9.   From Andy Delmege (ed.), *Mary: Mother of Socialism* (Croydon, Jubilee Group, 1995), pp. 16–17.

10. 'Anglican Catholicism in Decay: The Trivializing of a Great Tradition' in *Fellowship Papers* (United States, Catholic Fellowship, 1994).

Chapter 5: Inclusive Ministry

1. *Through our Long Exile: Contextual Theology and the Urban Experience* (London, Darton, Longman & Todd, 2001), p. 168.
2. *Care and Conflict: Leaves from a Pastoral Notebook* (London, Darton, Longman & Todd, 1990), pp. 30–33.
3. *Keep the Faith Baby: A Close-Up of London's Drop-Outs* (London, SPCK, 1973), pp. 89–92.
4. 'The Drug Scene and the Christian Community' in *Community Health*, Vol. 1, No. 2, September/October 1969, pp. 107–8.
5. *Drugs and Pastoral Care* (London, Darton, Longman & Todd, 1998), pp. 99–102.
6. *Keep the Faith Baby*, op. cit., pp. 80–85.
7. 'Ministry, marginality and Mammon: some reflections on the church's "preferential option for the rich" ', text of a final talk to UNLEASH at Vaughan House, Westminster, 7 July 2004.
8. 'Beware the bureaucrats', *Church Times*, 5 August 2005. An expanded version appeared as 'Ministry and the Future: Reflections from and on the Present State of Affairs in the Church of England' in *Sewanee Theological Review*, 51:4 (Michaelmas 2008) (Sewanee School of Theology, University of the South), pp. 435–9.
9. ' "Acts" in Context. Doing Theology in the Community' in *Christian Action Journal*, Spring 1993, pp. 4–5 (Sarum College Library archive).

Chapter 6: Faith and Race

1. *Race* (London, SPCK, 2005), p. 140.
2. *True God* (London, Sheldon Press/SPCK, 1985), pp. 65–71.
3. *We Preach Christ Crucified* (London, Darton, Longman & Todd, 2006), pp. 91–3.
4. *Race*, op. cit., pp. 130–36.
5. Ibid., pp. 136–40.
6. *Through Our Long Exile: Contextual Theology and the Urban Experience* (London, Darton, Longman & Todd, 2001), pp. 149–55.
7. *Race*, op. cit., pp. 98–102.
8. 'Two Cheers and Three Dangers … The Battle Has Only Just Begun' in *Southwark Diocese Race Relations Commission Newsletter*, 2 September 1985, pp. 6–7.
9. 'Anti-Racism & Social Justice' in *New Socialist*, December 1988, pp. 23–4.
10. 'Developing a Spirituality for Anti-Racist Action' in *To Heal the Sin-Sick Soul: Towards a Spirituality of Anti-Racist Ministry*, ed. Emmett Jarrett (New London, Episcopal Urban Caucus, 2003, 3rd printing; first published 1996), pp. 18–22.

Chapter 7: Time and Eternity

1. *True Prayer: An Invitation to Christian Spirituality* (Harrisburg, Morehouse, 1995), p. 9.
2. *The Eye of the Storm: Living Spiritually in the Real World* (San Francisco, HarperCollins, 1992), pp. 167–71.
3. Ibid., pp. 171–3.
4. 'Prayer : Battle for the human heart' in *The Times*, 25 June 1983.
5. *Soul Friend: Spiritual Direction in the Modern World* (Harrisburg, Morehouse, 2001), pp. 163–7.
6. *True Prayer*, op. cit., pp. 130–36.
7. *Soul Friend*, op. cit., pp. 173–5.
8. *True Prayer*, op. cit., pp. 170–72.

Chapter 8: Human Transformation

1. *The Sky is Red: Discerning the Signs of the Times* (London, Darton Longman & Todd, 2003), p. 21.
2. 'Spirituality Today: Address to the Catholic Renewal Conference at Loughborough' (1978), pp. 6–7 (Working Class Movement Library archive).
3. Ibid., pp. 13–15.
4. *Youthquake: Spirituality and the Growth of a Counter-Culture* (London, Abacus, 1976), pp. 107–11.
5. 'Nourishing an urban desert' in *The Times*, 19 March 1983.
6. *Julian Reconsidered* (Oxford, Fairacres Press, 1988), pp. 7–9.
7. 'Is Spiritual Direction Losing Its Bearings?' in *The Tablet*, 22 May 1993.
8. *Soul Friend: Spiritual Direction in the Modern World* (Harrisburg, Morehouse, 2001), pp. 83–5.
9. *The Social God* (Eugene, Oregon, Wipf & Stock, 2003), pp. 77–80 (first published London, Sheldon Press, 1981).
10. Ibid., pp. 50–56.
11. *Spirituality and Pastoral Care* (Eugene, Oregon, Wipf & Stock, 2005), pp. 70–74.

Chapter 9: Worship Before Doctrine

1. *Doing Theology in Altab Ali Park* (London, Darton, Longman & Todd, 2006), p. 55.
2. *True Prayer: An Invitation to Christian Spirituality* (Harrisburg, Morehouse, 1995), pp. 27–30.
3. 'Spirituality Today: Address to the Catholic Renewal Conference at Loughborough' (1978), pp. 11–15 (Working Class Movement Library archive).
4. Ibid., pp. 8–10.
5. *Pastoral Care and the Drug Scene* (London, SPCK, 1970), pp. 124–7.
6. 'A strange, persistent and defiant light' in the *Independent*, 29 December 1992.
7. 'The Attack on the Western Rite', Jubilee Group Discussion Paper 98, August 1995.
8. 'The Charismatic Movement and the Demons', Jubilee Group Paper, 1976.
9. *We Preach Christ Crucified* (London, Darton, Longman & Todd, 2006), pp. 2–4.

Chapter 10: Nearer to Holiness

1. *Spirituality and Pastoral Care* (Eugene, Oregon, Wipf & Stock, 2005), p. 84.
2. 'A Fearless Inquisitor of the Social Order: The Message of Stewart Headlam for the Church Today', paper reprinted with permission from *The Times*, 18 January 1975 (Working Class Movement Library archive).
3. the *Guardian*, 22 August 2006.
4. *Subversive Orthodoxy: Traditional Faith and Radical Commitment* (Toronto, Anglican Book Centre, 1992), pp. 13–15.
5. *The Eye of the Storm: Living Spiritually in the Real World* (San Francisco, HarperCollins, 1992), pp. 195–200.
6. *Doing Theology in Altab Ali Park* (London, Darton, Longman & Todd, 2006), pp. 142–3.
7. the *Independent*, 24 August 1988.
8. *Church Times*, 5 July 1996.
9. *Struggle in Babylon: Racism in the Cities and Churches of Britain* (London, Sheldon Press/SPCK, 1988), pp. 216–19.
10. *The Eye of the Storm*, op. cit., pp. 184–7.
11. *Doing Theology in Altab Ali Park*, op. cit., pp. 93–6.
12. *The Eye of the Storm*, op. cit., pp. 180–84.
13. Ibid., pp. 176–80.

14. Review of *Glory Descending: Michael Ramsey and his writings* by Douglas Dales, John Habgood, Geoffrey Rowell and Rowan Williams (London, Canterbury Press) in *Church Times*, 23 December 2005.
15. Jubilee Group Miscellaneous Paper, October 2002 (Sarum College Library archive).

Chapter 11: Theology and Place

1. *Through Our Long Exile: Contextual Theology and the Urban Experience* (London, Darton, Longman & Todd, 2001), p. 128.
2. Ibid., pp. 5–8.
3. 'Ken Leech in the USA: Fall 1998', November 1998 (Sarum College Library archive).
4. *The Eye of the Storm: Living Spiritually in the Real World* (San Francisco, HarperCollins, 1992), pp. 154–8.
5. Review of *The New East End: Kinship, race and conflict* by Geoff Dench, Kate Gavron & Michael Young (Profile Books), in *Church Times*, 29 September 2006.
6. 'Reflections on Oldham from Brick Lane', Urban Theology Project at St Botolph's Aldgate, June 2001 (Sarum College Library archive).
7. Review of *Empty Tabernacles: twelve lost churches of London* by Michael Yelton (Anglo-Catholic History Society), in *Church Times*, 4 May 2007.
8. *The Sky is Red: Discerning the Signs of the Times* (London, Darton, Longman & Todd, 2003), pp. 177–8.
9. 'From One St Francis House to Another' in *Troubadour: The Newsletter of St Francis House, New London, Connecticut*, Vol. 4, No. 1, Spring 2002.

Chapter 12: Forging Connections

1. *The Eye of the Storm: Living Spiritually in the Real World* (San Francisco, HarperCollins, 1992), p. vii.
2. *Hydonian*, Magazine of Hyde Grammar School, 1954 (Royal Foundation of St Katharine archive).
3. Ibid., 1957.
4. 'Why I Became a Socialist: Socialism, Christianity and East London' in *Workers' Liberty*, September 2000.
5. 'Casting out Demons' in *Dartmouth Dispatch*, 62, July–August 1975 (Royal Foundation of St Katharine archive).
6. Undated typed manuscript (Sarum College Library archive): early text of a review of Peta Dunstan's book *This Poor Sort: A History of the European Province of the Society of St Francis* (London, Darton, Longman & Todd, 1997) published in *The Heythrop Journal*, Vol. 41, Issue 4, October 2000 (London, Heythrop College, University of London).
7. *Drugs and Pastoral Care* (London, Darton, Longman & Todd, 1998), p. 3.
8. 'Ten Years of Jubilee: Some Personal Reflections', 1 November 1984 (Sarum College Library archive).
9. *Doing Theology in Altab Ali Park* (London, Darton, Longman & Todd, 2006), pp. 206–7.
10. Letter from St Botolph's Church to Friends, 6 March 1995 (Sarum College Library archive).

Index